Bernard Bosanquet

Logic

Or, the morphology of knowledge. Vol. 2

Bernard Bosanquet

Logic
Or, the morphology of knowledge. Vol. 2

ISBN/EAN: 9783337219758

Printed in Europe, USA, Canada, Australia, Japan

Cover: Foto ©Thomas Meinert / pixelio.de

More available books at **www.hansebooks.com**

LOGIC

OR

THE MORPHOLOGY OF KNOWLEDGE

BY

BERNARD BOSANQUET, M.A.

FORMERLY FELLOW AND TUTOR OF UNIVERSITY COLLEGE, OXFORD

IN TWO VOLUMES

VOL. II

Oxford

AT THE CLARENDON PRESS

1888

TABLE OF CONTENTS.

VOL. II.

BOOK II. INFERENCE.

CHAPTER I.

THE NATURE OF INFERENCE.

	PAGE
1. The Essence of Inference	1
2. Some Accidents of Inference	4
i. Mental transition in Time	4
ii. Discovery or novelty	8
iii. Omission of relevant matter	9
iv. Selection, and omission of irrelevant matter?	13
v. Three terms?	13
3. The lower limit of Inference	14
i. The reproduction of Ideas	15
ii. General necessity of Judgment	16
iii. Specific necessity of Judgment	18
iv. The true immediate Inferences	20
α. Comparison	21
β. Abstraction	21
γ. Recognition	24
δ. Discrimination, etc.	26
ε. Inferential character of above processes	26
ζ. Comparative Science	27
4. Species of Inference which have been erroneously identified with its principle	29
i. Inference from particulars to particulars	29
ii. Subsumption	30
iii. Calculation and equation	31
α. Calculation proper	32
β. The logical calculus	33
iv. Construction	36
α. Physical	36
β. Imaginative	38
γ. Intellectual, in geometry and mechanics	39
δ. Intellectual, without limitation to geometry and mechanics	40
Scheme of types of Inference	42

CHAPTER II.

ENUMERATIVE INDUCTION AND MATHEMATICAL REASONING.

	PAGE
1. Enumerative Induction	43
α. Syllogism in fig. 3	44
β. Divergent tendencies	45
γ. The Individual Judgment in Induction (Lotze)	46
2. Mathematical Reasoning	48
i. Number and Analogy—Divergence	49
α. Complete Enumeration as false Ideal. Syllogism and Induction	49
β. Enumeration as Arithmetical computation	51
γ. Calculation compared with argument	54
ii. Applications of Calculation	56
α. Substitutive Inference	57
(β. Apprehension of Connections in Space and Time)	59
γ. Calculation applied to Geometrical Reasoning. The Constitutive Equation	63
δ. Calculation applied to disparates. Proportion	68
(1) Homogeneous Terms	68
(2) 'a and a' series	69
ε. Proportion, Analogy, and the Hypothetical Judgment	73
ζ. Consciousness and Conservation of energy	74
iii. The mechanical aspect of Knowledge	77

CHAPTER III.

ANALOGY.

1. Analogy and Enumerative Induction. Examples	83
2. Logical criticism of the Analogical argument	88
i. Fig. 2. Undistributed middle, Import of this defect	88
ii. Real value of Analogical argument	90
iii. No ratio of Identities to Differences	98
iv. Concurrent Analogies. Negative confirmation	103
v. Divergent tendencies in Analogy	105

CHAPTER IV.

SCIENTIFIC INDUCTION BY PERCEPTIVE ANALYSIS.

1. Negative Inference	108
i. Its nature and conditions	108
ii. No conclusion from two negatives	111
iii. The negative instance	115

Table of Contents.

2. Scientific Induction 117
   i. Induction and other Inference 118
   ii. Induction as Perceptive Analysis 122
      α. Symbolic expression of the problem 122
      β. Establishment of ordinary Hypothetical Judgment . . 124
      γ. Establishment of reciprocal Hypothetical Judgment . . 128
      δ. Conversion or Generalisation 130
   iii. Logical character of Perceptive Induction 133
      α. Its essence as Inference 133
      β. Theoretical purpose of representation by symbols . . 135
      γ. Part played by *number* of instances 136
         (1) In Perceptive Analysis proper 136
         (2) In assigning known effects to classes of unknown conditions 137
   iv. Observation and Experiment 143
      α. Natural Experiment 143
      β. Observation with accurate instruments 144
      γ. Experiment expressed in logical symbols 145
      δ. Experiment with the Siren analysed 149

CHAPTER V.

SCIENTIFIC INDUCTION BY HYPOTHESIS. GENERALIZATION.

1. Hypothesis and Postulate 155
   i. Hypothesis falls outside Postulate 155
   ii. But not if Hypothesis alleges *Vera causa* 158
2. Phases of Hypothesis 159
   i. Rudimentary Hypothesis 159
   ii. Mediate Hypothesis 160
      α. Hypothetical nature of Induction 160
      β. Example of fusion between Hypothesis and data . . 161
3. Generalisation 168
   i. 'From many to all' exploded 168
   ii. By mere determination 169
   iii. Material or Analogical Generalisation 170
4. General view of Induction 175
   i. Difference from Jevons 175
   ii. Ultimate nature of Induction 176

CHAPTER VI.

CONCRETE SYSTEMATIC INFERENCE.

1. Philosophical Subsumption 180
   i. Logical content of these Inferences . . . 186
      α. Real system 186
      β. Apodeictic sequence 186
   ii. Their form, Syllogism in fig. 1 . . . 188

2. Disjunctive reasoning
3. The judgment of value
   i. Real Teleology
   ii. Mediation
4. Recapitulation of the main characteristics of Inference
   i. No antecedent scheme of Inference
   ii. Conditions of Inference
   iii. Relation of Syllogism to these conditions
      α. The traditional syllogism
      β. The syllogism as reasoned judgment

CHAPTER VII.

The Relation of Knowledge to its Postulates.

1. The formal postulates of Knowledge
   i. The Law of Identity
   ii. The Law of Contradiction
   iii. The Law of Excluded Middle
   iv. The Law of Sufficient Reason and Law of Causation
2. The material postulates of Knowledge
   i. The maintenance of life
   ii. The reality of human purposes
3. The ultimate nature of Necessity
   i. *A priori* necessity and mediation
      α. Mediate nature of necessity forgotten in controversy
      β. Organised and unorganised experience, with ambiguity test by Conception
   ii. Rehabilitation of formal distinctions in Logic
   iii. Criticism of 'Aesthetic' necessity
      α. Aesthetic necessity as a contradiction in terms
      β. Aesthetic necessity as a mere case of logical necessity

BOOK II.

OF INFERENCE.

CHAPTER I.

THE NATURE OF INFERENCE.

1. INFERENCE shares the essence of Judgment, but, at least *qua* explicit Inference, has in addition a *differentia* of its own. The essence of Judgment is the reference of an ideal content to Reality; the *differentia* of Inference affects the mode of this reference, and consists in Mediation. Inference then is the *mediate* reference of an ideal content to Reality. If I affirm that I spoke to you in the street yesterday simply because I find it in my memory that I did so speak to you, that is, apart from refinements of analysis, simply a judgment. If, as against your denial of the fact, I corroborate my recollection by pointing out that I *must* have spoken to you, because you afterwards acted upon something that I then told you, then I am reasserting the content of my original judgment, but with an addition and modification that turns it into an Inference. I then refer an ideal content to Reality, not as directly given in memory or in perception, but on the strength of a content distinguishable from the former content, bearing a certain relation to it, and itself referred directly to reality.

By speaking of 'mediate' reference to reality we have mentioned the *differentia* of Inference, but have not explained it. Direct affirmation appears to explain itself; but mediate affirmation is even at first sight somewhat mysterious. We are at once met with the old question,

The Essence of Inference.

'How are synthetic judgments *a priori* possible?' The qualification *a priori* adds nothing to the qualification 'true' which is claimed by all judgment as such. The question therefore is in plain English, 'How can one content claim to be true of Reality on the strength of another content distinct from the first?' 'How can any synthetic judgment *qua* synthetic—i.e. going *from* content *to* content and not simply accepting either a mere occurrence or a mere conjunction—how can such a judgment conceivably be justified?' The answer to this difficulty, like all answers in philosophy, is at first sight a mere restatement of it. Whether such a restatement is an explanation depends on its congruity and coherence with reason and with experience. It is possible—so the answer must run—to proceed in knowledge from content to content, because the world as known consists of universals exhibited in differences, and the contents from which and to which we proceed are not shut up within their respective selves, but depend on a pervading identical character or universal of which they are the differences. '*Of which* they are the differences'—for here is the objection which meets us on the threshold. Suppose that I find in a room a hundred different objects—books, guns, china—all marked with the same label, say with the owner's name. Well then, it may be said, here is your 'identical character' or 'universal,' but what can you infer from it beyond itself? It tells you nothing of the object to which it is attached. You may go on for fifty cases affirming that a having the label x is a book, b having the label x is a book and so on, but you cannot tell in the least what the fifty-first object that has the label will be, whether a sporting rifle or a china teapot. There is an identity throughout all the objects, but they are not, or seem not to be, *its* differences. They simply contain it, and are in no way leavened by it. You cannot in any way determine their predicates on the basis furnished by this pervading identity.

The whole of our previous and subsequent discussion

really deals with this radical difficulty. Logic is little more than an account of the forms and modes in which a universal does or does not affect the differences through which it persists. I can only point out that all turns on the distinction between the abstract or powerless and the concrete or dominant universal. To interpret the latter by the former, to reduce all universals to marks, i. e. to the level of the example just mentioned, is a fatal tendency of popular logic. A very elementary example of a relatively concrete universal may be found in the nature of a geometrical figure, say of the circle or the triangle. Given an arc of a circle, we have the radius and centre, and can lay down the whole circumference. The given arc is not simply repeated, it is continued according to a universal nature which controls its parts, and with a result which though involved in the given arc is yet outwardly and as an actual content distinct from it. This is clearer if instead of a circle we take an ellipse, in which the given fragment of the curve cannot in any sense be said to be simply repeated without change in constructing the remainder. There is something in the curve as given which is capable of dictating a continuation and completion of its outline distinguishable from the given arc or fragment itself. Just so with a triangle—given two sides and an angle, we can find the third side and remaining two angles.

And we can now see that in the first example, which seemed so hopeless, the same relation would be traceable *assuming the label to have any meaning at all*. A *mere* mark, which conveys nothing, is not even a mark, for what is it a mark of? But supposing the label to indicate A's ownership of the things, then we could infer all sorts of legal consequences about them from this ownership; and these consequences would not be the same for all the objects, but would be modified by their nature; e. g. it is probable that some of the things would be liable to seizure by a judgment creditor and some would not. Thus here too the universal would be an identity pervading different manifestations.

The universal in its differences is then the basis of mediate judgment or inference. But it is also the basis, as we have amply seen, of judgment as such, i.e. what would usually be called immediate judgment. The above examples, however, furnish the further distinction to which we shall find it convenient on the whole to adhere. Mediate judgment or inference is the indirect reference to reality of differences within a universal by means of the exhibition of this universal in differences directly referred to reality. The differences indirectly referred to reality may fall outside, or include, or even consist exclusively of, the differences directly referred to reality. Immediate judgment, according to its idea, would be the mere reference to reality of differences as united within the identity or universal. It might be more intelligible if we were to substitute 'parts' and 'whole' for 'differences' and 'universal;' but then it would have to be borne in mind that we are not speaking of quantitative parts, i.e. that the kind of whole in question is not necessarily the sum of its parts. Subject to this reservation, I have no objection to defining Inference as the indirect reference to reality of parts within a whole on the strength of the nature of that whole as revealed in parts directly referred to Reality. And the definition of Judgment would bear a corresponding modification. Of course I do not mean that all the forms which have already been discussed under the head of Judgment are *substantially* confined within the definition of Judgment and excluded from that of Inference. But for the present, in order to obtain a clear view *prima facie*, we are considering only explicit Inference and excluding all that takes the outward shape of mere Judgment.

Some Accidents of Inference.

2. The above account of the essence of Inference will be best illustrated by considering some accidents of inference which I have endeavoured to exclude from the definition.

Mental Transition in Time.

i. First among these comes the attribute of mental transition in time, with which that of an advance from known to unknown may in one sense be identified.

The account given above[1] of the Judgment in time applies also to Inference as a mental process in Time. The first and most fatal error as regards both Judgment and Inference is to introduce the idea of an actual and instantaneous transition from content to content. This idea combines the error of denying that inference, as a mental process, has duration in time, with that of denying that as intellectual insight its parts are inward to each other and exempt from temporal succession. The universal itself, or intellectual synthesis of differences, is not a fact in time; and throughout the interval which inference occupies as a psychical process the operation of the universal as a growing insight is traceable in every point of time, but is not shut up within any atomic moment.

But apart from the idea of instantaneous transition, there is an idea of advance in time which has great appearance of truth and which is indeed in one sense true. It is unquestionable that in inference we start from data, from facts thrown down before us, it may be in chaotic disorder and with no suggestion of a result[2]. We go to work upon these facts, and after the labour of hours, of days, or of a lifetime[3], we light upon a conclusion which issues from them and to which they are related as premises; i.e. which exhibits them as differences in a universal. How is it possible to deny that we have here an advance in time from data without conclusion, at any rate to data *plus* conclusion, and, if we go by the old syllogism, to conclusion *minus* a large part of the data? The difficulty which I find in stating the above antithesis is a first indication of its fallaciousness. It was impossible to write simply 'from data without conclusion to conclusion without data.' A

[1] Bk. I. chap. i.
[2] I put the case at its extreme against myself. We must however remember that we can only see in the facts what we are ready to see there, what we bring with us. So however disorderly in fact, the data are really from the beginning theorised upon by our apprehension, because it can only apprehend them on the strength of its own existing content.
[3] See the famous preface to the 'Origin of Species.'

conclusion without data is an obvious contradiction in terms, and if even part of the data are dropped (as the middle term in the syllogism) the conclusion sinks *pro tanto* into a ὅτι rather than a διότι—a fact instead of an inference. No doubt we are apt to pluck off our conclusion like a fruit from a plant and carry it away for consumption. Practical life requires this procedure. But we must remember that from the moment of severance death has begun, and that the intellectual product can bear isolation far less than the material. The idea of an actual transition *from* data *to* result, so far as it is founded on this habit, is in science simply a pernicious blunder. The case in which the result is a systematic insight that includes the premises in a transmuted form does not of course fall under this censure. But this case is not as a rule contemplated by the traditional forms of inference.

And of course it might be correlatively maintained that facts are not data, except by virtue of a result; or if this is not true of data but only of premises, then that inference does not start from data but only from premises[1]. At first sight such a contention seems to blink the difficulty. The conclusion, it seems, may be removed by a week's work from the data or premises; and granting that they are not rightly called data or premises till the week's end when the conclusion is won, still the facts concerned were present and active at the beginning of the week and certainly entered into the advance that has been made.

Two things are here to be distinguished, viz. mere reproduction and inferential reproduction. The universal active in the mind is not apparent as a whole within the mere psychical facts of the transition. Its operation is extended throughout a series of the fugitive psychical facts or ideas, and although in *logical* thinking its operation is conscious, i.e. selects and modifies within the content of these ideas, yet it is not in itself necessarily a conscious activity. It acts in consciousness, but need not be conscious of its own

---

[1] But then it would seem the data must be premises of the premises.

principle of action. In rudimentary reproduction we see a man far off, and a name comes into our mind, apparently as a detached fact, without any reason that we can assign or think of trying to assign. It is only later, when we *clearly* recognise the man, that we become aware either *that* we recognise him, or how and why we recognise him. Logical thinking consists of making this process conscious; but essentially and fundamentally the intellectual tendency which controls reproduction need not be present as a distinct content operating in reproduction. So far the psychical process might in theory begin with data alone and then go on leaving them behind to result alone, *not* carrying throughout the transition any conscious unity or continuity of content.

But in *explicit* inference, at any rate, this is not the case. The essence of inference is to drag into consciousness the operation of the active universal as a pervading unity of content on which inference depends. The conscious operation of the active universal in inference is what we have to distinguish from the mere implicit action of the universal in rudimentary reproduction. Therefore when we speak not of mere reproduction, but of inferential reproduction or passage from data to conclusion, then it is true that you can no more have data or premises without conclusion than conclusion without data or premises. The appearance to the contrary, which I have admitted to exist, arises from our fixing our attention exclusively on the conclusion *par excellence* in which and not before it we happen to rest. This conclusion, though it may close a stage of science or set at rest a longing of our hearts, is in no way different in logical character from the first steps of preparatory activity with which reason penetrates the facts laid before it. We meet the data with a judgment when they are laid before us, and we modify this judgment continuously throughout our inference. Any section taken, so to speak, across the interval of intellectual activity which elapses from first data to ultimate conclusion would lay bare the *whole* structure of an inference, just as a section across the time during which a chord is sounding on the organ would exhibit the *whole* harmonic structure of the compound tone. Of course we may draw partial conclusions, discard their data, and work with these conclusions as with fresh data, and so far we make an advance from content to content, discarding the old in favour of the new. But this process, though necessary in practice, comes under the observation made above upon a conclusion severed from its proof, and is not typical of inference, but of its limitations.

Transition in time from content to content as between data and conclusion in inference is not really possible. But it is true that the process of inference, though continuous and bound together by a conscious unity, is extended in time and includes considerable modifications of the judgments from which it starts. The appearance of a transition arises from discarding data, which is unjustifiable, from transforming data, which is right but is no transition, or from comparing ultimate conclusions and primary data while neglecting the intermediate phases which constitute the continuous and—not *transitional* but—*inclusive* inferential evolution. It is in this character of transition without conscious continuity that rudimentary reproduction differs from explicit Inference.

Thus our definition of Inference did not say that the differences which form the data are *previously* affirmed of reality, although it is only from them as affirmed of reality that the reality of the inferred differences can flow.

Discovery or Novelty. ii. Secondly, it follows from the above considerations that *discovery* is an accident and not an essential of inference. Inference is not essentially passage in time whether instantaneous or extended. Therefore it is not the case that a conclusion ceases to be an inference the moment that it becomes familiar, the moment, that is, that it ceases to be a discovery. On the contrary, discovery without proof is conjecture; an element of proof is needed to constitute inference, and indeed to constitute discovery. The activity of inference cannot be identified with the perception of

CHAP. I.]   *Omission in Inference.*   9

something new. It is quite a normal occurrence that the elements which are indirectly referred to reality should *also* be directly referred to reality. Whenever, indeed, as the ideal of inference requires, the original data themselves are transformed and freshly elucidated, this happens as a matter of course. When the working of a machine is about to be explained we see a wheel or piston to be there as a fact, and we ask what it does. The answer tells us why there must be such a wheel or piston, and this is not superfluous though we knew beforehand that it was there. The part in question then becomes to us an element or difference in the pervading identity or universal which is the working of the machine. And if we live fifty years and see the machine every day, understanding it thoroughly, still the use of any one of its parts, considered as necessitated by the nature of any other actual part or set of parts combined with the working of the whole machine, remains to us an inference and never becomes a mere fact. Thus novelty or discovery is an accident of Inference.

iii. Thirdly, it follows from the above considerations that omission in the conclusion of contents employed in the premises is an accident of inference. Inference is confined neither to what is novel nor to what happens to interest us. The appearance of a necessity of omission arises from various causes. The transformation of data is an ideal which is likely to be misunderstood. It resumes the old data in a new expression. Again, it is usual and in complicated matters unavoidable to confine ourselves in dealing with any universal to some aspect determined by context or by curiosity. And the habitual omission of the middle term in the Aristotelian syllogism is perhaps due in part to the above causes, and in part to the vicious habit of severing the conclusion from the premises which the rhetorical associations of early logic tended to foster[1]. But the entire content of

Omission of relevant matter.

---

[1] Because the rhetorician only wants to prove, not to understand. If he reaches his conclusion, the steps by which he reached it cease to interest him or his audience.

the universal, so far as recognised in the necessity that unites its differences, is the true content of every inference, and there is no logical reason for neglecting to make explicit any portion of truth which our perception of it generates.

A question arises on the margin of this subject of omission with reference to the systematic realities of which we spoke under the head of the hypothetical and disjunctive judgments. If I directly affirm the reality of a complex system, such as a railway, or a government, or a mind, and include in my affirmation a mention of many parts and properties as systematically interrelated, am I in doing so rightly said to be inferring? It rather seems here as if the absence of omission destroyed all semblance of a *conclusion*, and how can there be inference without a conclusion? 'Cannon Street railway station has interlocking points and signals.' To any one who understands the subject it is unnecessary to complete this by the further explanation (which even if inserted may of course be a mere qualification, not a fresh judgment), 'such that opening any one line *ipso facto* needs the signals to be at danger for all the lines that cross it.' In such a judgment, regarding it, as we have every right to do, in the light of a single affirmation, I am obviously embodying matter which has an inferential character. But whether I am actually inferring or not depends—*not*, as one might be tempted to say, on the novelty of the conclusion implied, but—on the degree of insight with which the judgment is made. It is in short either an inference, or the allegation as a fact of relations that must have formed the conclusion of an inference, although the inferential connection *may* now be lost. If however we go into such detail as proves that we have an insight into the why and wherefore of the system, then we have no choice but to say that we are inferring but are stating our inference confusedly. The confusion is in not distinguishing data from conclusion—how much is immediately affirmed of reality, and how much is mediate. The judgment is a mediate judgment simulating an immediate character[1].

An ordinary hypothetical judgment is really an analogous case to the above (which might be represented by a disjunctive judgment). Inferential matter, a relation or nexus, seems to be affirmed of reality; but yet the omission, which would leave as affirmed what seems to be the conclusion, cannot be made. The ground *per se* is not affirmed of Reality, and so the consequent *per se* is not affirmed to be true. The moment that 'If' passes into 'Because' you can omit the ground and affirm the consequent *per se*. But retaining the 'If' we cannot affirm the consequent. We cannot affirm upon mere supposition, nor can we infer without affirming. Yet certainly, as in the last paragraph, we seem to have before us an inferential activity. 'In four-dimensional space (i. e. supposing such space) a knot can be tied in a string whose ends are held.' In this judgment the nexus between four-dimensional space and tying a knot is undoubtedly inferential. The moment we affirm the reality of the ground, we also affirm the real possibility of the consequent. But the hypothetical judgment as such affirms neither the one nor the other. The entire judgment is no doubt itself a consequence of an underlying reality, the affirmation of which it implies, and on the ground of which —a ground asserted to be real—the *whole* complex content of the hypothetical judgment is asserted to be real, subject to its own inherent reservation embodied in its own further ground. But this does not help us to determine the presence or absence of inference within the hypothetical judgment itself.

The fact seems to be that hypothetical affirmation is a contradiction in terms, and so too is hypothetical inference.

[1] The existence of these ambiguous inferences—half inference and half memory or authority—favours in appearance the restriction of inference to what has novelty. When an inference is just made, then, if ever, it has definite data. When an inference is familiar, it is too likely to rest on the ground that it is remembered to have been approved of. Nevertheless, not novelty, but systematic necessity, is the true differentia.

The whole process, apart from any categorical meaning which it may make explicit, which is a matter of degree, is a mere make-believe. You choose to treat as real in one sense what you do not affirm to be really real[1], and you record the groove of necessity which manifests itself when the artificial reality is considered as though forming part of the real reality. Of the differences within the universal which determine the remaining differences (in this case the consequent) part (the hypothetical ground) are only sham reality, and therefore although we seem to exert inferential activity, yet we cannot affirm the conclusion of the inference. Here then we have the two degrees of impropriety in omission. Even when the ground of inference is affirmed, as with ordinary premises, the reality of the conclusion is restricted to the precise sense imposed by that ground, and it is therefore theoretically unsafe to affirm the conclusion apart from the ground. But when part of the ground of inference is not affirmed, then we have really the case of the problematic judgment, and if the consequent is affirmed with omission of the supposed ground it can only be affirmed problematically, i.e. cannot be affirmed as true, or in the proper sense affirmed at all. The reference to reality is then incompletely mediated. But on a pure supposition no inference can be erected. The element of supposed reality is the element of reservation, and the element of real reality is the element of affirmation. A pure supposition would be all reservation and no affirmation.

Omission in inference is thus accidental and hazardous in various degrees. It is, as we saw, in one form (as omission of the condition or reservation in judgment) the mark of problematic judging. Omission however as here discussed

---

[1] This process has many degrees. The content of supposition may be real all but some very minute relation. The conclusion from the supposition can then be affirmed subject to a very minute reservation. The *main* content of the conclusion may depend on what is absolute fact. 'If that picture were $\frac{1}{2}$ in. to the left it would hang symmetrically with that other picture' gives the conclusion. The picture A hangs symmetrically to $\frac{1}{2}$ in. with the picture B.

is omission of matter relevant to the inference, or, which is the same thing, falling within the conclusion. In this sense, as within the relevant content, selection is the converse of omission, and is equally an accident of Inference. If you select, you omit; and if you omit, you select. But you need not do either.

iv. On the other hand, actual data must always present irrelevancies, and must be exhibited as transformed—not necessarily *be* transformed *de novo* by an act of discovery— in the inferential operation. Otherwise there could not be the circuit through the universal which we have taken to be the differentia of inference. It is natural therefore to think of Omission and Selection with reference to the *actual* data on which, as referred to reality in their crude form, a given inference depends. Within these actual data Selection is of the essence of Inference, but Omission depends on the existence of irrelevancies in the data, and although in theory these disguises and superfluities cannot be wanting, yet they may be reduced to an almost inappreciable margin, and the element of omission in that case becomes inappreciable also. There is then, apparently, selection without omission; there can never be omission without selection. *Omission of irrelevant matter.*

v. It has been maintained that the presence of three 'terms,' as required by the Aristotelian syllogism, is an accident of inference and does not touch its essence. I must leave this question, which is largely verbal, to decide itself in detail from our whole account of the subject. Here I will merely indicate the distinction on which in my opinion the answer to it depends. Of course an inference is constantly drawn by the combination of very numerous facts and conceptions. Aristotle's[1] or Lotze's Inductive *Three terms.*

---

[1] τὸ καθ' ἕκαστον is a term in both premises of the Aristotelian Inductive Syllogism. Obviously this means that each premise would be a conjunction of judgments, or a conjunctive judgment. Such a group of judgments would correspond to the so-called premises in Lotze's Inductive Syllogism, which 'premises' are really only a single premise, out of which Lotze takes his conclusion *per saltum*. If the other premise were filled in, his inference would show three terms.

syllogism, or a Sorites, or a Euclidean construction, are familiar examples of inference so drawn. The only question is whether these numerous facts or conceptions correspond to phases or elements in the logical act of Inference, and whether, if they do not, they can claim the title of logical 'terms.' Must there not always be (i) differences or parts directly referred to reality, (ii) the universal nature or continuous identity which binds these differences or parts into a whole, pregnant with a capacity of accepting and arranging further differences or parts, and (iii) further differences, identified as parts within the pregnant whole which controls the inference, and, on the strength of this identity, referred to reality? It may be observed that this last 'term,' moment or element of inference, may and ought to include the two former. But it contains them in another sense than that in which they appear as isolated elements of inference, and therefore is not superfluous nor tautologous. We may have a thousand observations of the places of a moving heavenly body, but these thousand data are not a thousand terms. The thousand observed places fuse into the law of the orbit, and the law of the orbit dictates the remaining places which form the path that the body traverses. Or, as the above instance really verges upon geometrical construction, we may take an example more cognate to what is commonly meant by Induction, though it is hard to find a good example of a process which does not exist. If typhoid fever attends a certain milk-supply through a large portion of its ins and outs, including many dozens of cases, then we shall no doubt be apt to suspect that danger attaches to that milk supply as a whole, and consequently menaces any localities as yet unexamined to which this same supply extends its operations. Here again the three elements of Inference are conspicuous, though, as we shall see, they are in any such statement exceedingly ill-defined and their connection ill-warranted.

The lower limit of Inference

3. I have thus far been speaking of explicit Inference, that is to say, of inference in which three or more 'terms' or

intellectual elements are consciously distinguished and combined. And it is true, as I said above, that the nature and phases of implicit Inference must really be gathered from the whole theory of judgment which I have stated in Book I. to the best of my power. But a few remarks and a few examples may be useful in throwing light on the modifications which have to be traced.

The function of which I have attempted, in the theory of judgment, to write the later history, is the activity of the universal in the mind, or in other words, of the mind as the universal.

i. I have at present neither space nor competence to enter upon psychological controversy with reference to the so-called Association of Ideas. But it is necessary to define my position by explaining that in as far as any doctrine of Association involves the hypothesis of reproduction by other ideas of ideas as separate particular units, i. e. the denial of real identity or of the active universal, I am unable to reconcile such a doctrine with logical phenomena. And logical phenomena, if we include in them the judgment from its very beginning, take in by far the larger part of the known phenomena of mind. I cannot suppose a discontinuity—in my opinion moreover wholly unmotived by experience—between distinctly logical phenomena and the quasi-intellectual activities of primitive and animal soul-life. And therefore I shall treat the fundamental activity of thought as the same throughout and as always consisting in the reproduction by a universal or a real identity, presented in a content, of contents distinguishable from the presented content, which also are differences of the same universal.

The reproduction of Ideas.

It may be that in early soul-life this reproduction is unconscious, and that its results, the images which it brings before the mind, are not used as ideas, i.e. are not distinguished from fact or known to be symbolic of a content other than themselves. The results of experience may be made available for the guidance of action in an animal through suggestion effected by reproduction, but not distinguished *as* suggestion from any presented reality. In this process we have something that does the work of judgment and inference, and that has the same fundamental nature with them. But it is not judgment, because the images which it causes to succeed one another in the mind, not being distinguished from any reality, as a mere meaning necessarily is [1], cannot be affirmed in qualification of reality. And *a fortiori* such early thought is not inference, because it is not judgment. Inference as we saw involves assertion.

To begin with, then, we may set down the lower limit of inference as at any rate not prior to the beginnings of judgment. Yet even this *prima facie* boundary is drawn subject to a large reservation on account of the primitive reproduction or redintegration to which I have just alluded. The unconscious extension of a sensation by reproduction fulfils some functions of inference.

General necessity of Judgment.

ii. And when we come to judgment in the strict sense, the task of drawing a line between implicit inference and what is not inference at all becomes an impossible one. Fortunately it is also, in this rigid form, an idle one. What we have to say upon it amounts to this. All Judgment, we are told [2] with emphasis, claims necessity. That is to say, every one who makes an assertion [3], though of course he has, as a rule, never heard of logic or of a ground, yet believes that he cannot think otherwise than as he asserts. In full-blown Inference he backs up this belief by a distinct allegation of separate but connected matters which he takes to justify his conviction. In implicit Inference we must distinguish the feeling that there *is* a justification from the incipient selection of definite matters as forming the justifi-

---

[1] When psychical images come to be employed for the sake of a meaning which they convey, *they ex hypothesi* are not treated as fact. And their meaning is not itself a psychical fact, but is an intellectual activity which can only enter into fact by being used to qualify reality.

[2] Sigwart, vol. i. pp. 193-4.

[3] A conscious lie is only a sham assertion, except in as far as the hearer is induced to judge it true.

cation. It is probable that, as Sigwart implies, the feeling of justification is in one form or another essential to judgment. An uneducated man or a child, if his perception or his memory is doubted, will sometimes merely reiterate his assertion. This reiteration implies on the one hand that he cannot formulate any inferential support for his original judgment; he does not know how to travel outside the content of his assertion in order to invoke external aid. Such a phase of the judging activity is well illustrated by the impersonal judgment, in which the place of the significant subject which develops into the pregnant genus-idea, or ground, or condition, is devoid of all content. Yet on the other hand such reiteration implies an effort and failure on the part of the speaker to get beyond the original content, and a consequent return to that content, which is the germ of the *motived* inability to think otherwise that constitutes the necessity of inference. In such a mind, we may suppose, imagination and conception do not fall apart, and his thinking satisfies the criterion of necessary truth which Mill criticised as defectively explained by Whewell, in that he cannot even *imagine* (not to speak of *conceiving*) the matter to be otherwise than as he asserts it to be.

An educated man makes a similar justification explicit when he tells us that he relies on the evidence of his senses. The phrase is perhaps primarily intended to be ironical, as implying that the senses give the fact and not mere evidence of the fact, but its irony fails because it is strictly true. Sense, though it is a fact, cannot give *the fact*, and is strictly, as the supposed speaker calls it, evidence—circumstantial evidence or datum, not 'testimony'[1] which implies assertion. The phrase 'evidence of the senses' then, if taken seriously, conveys the consciousness that sense-perception has an inferential character, and rests on a necessity arising out of combinations of elements among which sensation is but

[1] Evidence in this application may have originally meant obviousness or intuitiveness, 'Evidentia,' 'Evidenz,' and would then have no close connection with the common meaning of 'evidence' as = 'testimony.'

a part or datum. When this consciousness, which experience of illusions soon forces on reflecting men, is thoroughly attained, then the perceptive judgment is known to need justification, but it is not known in what this justification consists nor that it may lie in a connection of content apparently going beyond the observed conjunction. Attentive observation and precise interrogation of the memory are the engines which suggest themselves as securing the necessity of judgment at this stage. Of course these processes imply a reliance on certain principles. But the inference is so far formal and general, not material and specific. It is rather a general conviction that perception can be relied on, than an individual inference that this particular perception is rightly construed to give this particular content. And therefore the inference falls apart from the judgment as such, and cannot be taken as an element within it. When we pass this point, we come to something much more like Inference proper.

Specific necessity of Judgment. iii. Prior to Judgment, as we saw reason to suppose, the operation of the universal or the real identity which governs reproduction is unconscious. Of course it has a result in consciousness, but the mind is not aware of the limits and pervading ground of the process from which this result emanates. I cannot say on what definite stimulus my friend's name rises to my mind when I see him at a distance, not being yet aware that I have recognised him, nor what is the operative content which makes a certain room recall a long past incident which occurred elsewhere. In the phase of judgment which has just been alluded to this real identity emerges into consciousness as the meaning of sentences and as the active guide of perception and memory. In this capacity it is attended by a necessity at first actual and then perceived, which at least reveals itself (when men talk of the evidence of their senses) as a partly intellectual necessity. But up to this point the real identity or meaning has simply been suggested and affirmed, as this or that ideal content, to be true of reality, and has not within itself displayed any articulated or selective character. It has shown no systematic organisation to which thought could appeal as a definite individual compulsion prescribing the nature of the ideal content which it reproduced. The matters affirmed have simply been conjoined within a unity or identity, as philosophy and self-conceit may be conjoined in the same man. They have not been shown to cohere as parts in an intelligible whole, not, that is, as the third angle of a triangle coheres with two given angles and a given side, or as personal liberty in England coheres with the supremacy of law[1].

But a further principle makes its appearance, as we saw, with the judgments of individual character, of ideal measurement or of ideal enumeration. Here the universal takes on the character of a system, which governs its parts on the basis of its pervading nature. From this point onwards we have in fact the full essentials of Inference, and it is very much a question of convenience whether the inference takes implicit or explicit form. So long as we retain the form of direct synthesis our definition forbids us the title of explicit inference. For the identification of the subject-idea with reality is presupposed and not affirmed, and the qualification of reality by the predicated content is therefore direct in form, though indirect to a large extent in substance. 'To a large extent' only, for according to the view which I take of judgment the affirmation in all the more genuine and natural forms of assertion is both direct and indirect even in substance. If I affirm 'The Czar of Russia can throw Europe into a blaze by lifting his finger' I am judging both categorically of the historical individual, and necessarily or inferentially of the wielder of enormous forces. And the same holds good in some degree if I speak of the British Constitution, or of the force of gravity. The educated mind sees an argument in

[1] See Dicey on the Law of the Constitution. I may venture to remark that works of this class are a valuable study for logicians, because they illustrate forms of necessary connection which are not dependent on geometrical perception.

judgments dealing with these matters even without the help of vocal accent and inflexion which can be used to drive home the inference. From the individual judgment then, through the generic, as far as the pure hypothetical which has already been discussed in this context, we have implicit inference which verges upon explicitness in proportion as the operative ground or reason is more clearly set out in the subject-idea. The generic judgment shows the union of the two types in its fullest significance. The individual content here claims to be a presupposed qualification of reality, and therefore, as reality, has the predicated content *directly* identified with it; while the very same self-complete organisation which entitles the subject-content to be taken as real, also enables it to demand the predicated content as a necessary consequence, and to act as a middle term attaching this content *indirectly* to reality. ' Poetry is a form of art which employs ideas as the medium of representation.' Here we are at once qualifying a reality and drawing an inference.

The true immediate inferences.

iv. These principles may advantageously be elucidated by the example of what might be called the true immediate inferences, which may properly be mentioned here on the threshold of Inference. I refer to such processes as Recognition, Abstraction, Comparison, Identification, Discrimination. All these titles are obviously drawn from characteristics which in a certain sense no judgment or inference is without, and which reciprocally imply one another[1]. But they also can be and are used as names of processes, of cases of the judging activity, in which one or other of its aspects asserts itself *par excellence*. They are cross divisions to the progressive stages of judgment which were described in Book I, and might be spoken of, though not with equal appropriateness, as present in all these stages short of disjunction. They are separated from one another and from other forms of judgment rather by practical and methodological than by strictly logical distinctions.

[1] See Introduction, sect. 5.

α. Comparison is a good example. The Comparative Judgment, as described in Book I, fills an important place in logical evolution. The variations of a common quality between more and less are the simplest explicit case of identity in difference. But the reflective comparison of common life both stops short of and goes beyond what I have called the comparative judgment. Comparison in the ordinary sense is a name applied to the intentional cross-reference of two or more given contents, in order to establish, between those contents *as given*, a general or special identity, difference, or partial identity (likeness). And with the establishment of a relation of equality, or of quantitative difference which implies equality ($a > b$ implies $a = b + x$), popular comparison *diverges* into equation, in which the cross-reference is retained throughout. The equation is essentially *comparative*. You cannot say 'a is equal' any more than you can say 'a is the same.'[1] In Comparison, identity etc. is stated as a result, or else very strongly implied, in *an abstract form*. If it were made concrete and definite the cross-reference to the contents *as given* would be superfluous or impossible, other and profounder standards being introduced and the contents having no longer their original shape. The result required in comparison is such as 'A is like B.' If we say 'A and B are both red,' this too is comparison in virtue of the cross-reference implied in 'both.' But if we say 'A is red and B is green' we are passing out of the process popularly called comparison into ordinary investigation, aimed not at a particular cross-reference, but at developing the facts which may come to hand. And if we go to 'All a (including a and b) are coloured surfaces,' the original data have disappeared, and comparison in the popular sense has become impossible. When the process has justified in the concrete the abstract idea which guided it, it has put an end to its own *raison d'être* and passes into the normal operations of knowledge.

β. Abstraction, again, affords an example worth con-

[1] Cf. Sigwart, i. p. 69.

sidering. Abstraction in general is the necessary consequence of definite thought, and indeed of all definite activity. All activity has its restrictions and limitations, selects and omits, and is so far abstract. But though all thought is abstract, yet all thought need not be abstraction as a special process. Abstraction in this sense is a methodic activity guided by a special reflective idea, the idea of obtaining the part out of the whole by omission of other parts. The whole is theoretically always, and practically often, more knowable than the part. It is easier to say that $99 \times 5 =$ five hundreds *minus* five units, i.e. 495, than to multiply out ninety-nine by five. Subtraction may be regarded as the specific term for abstraction when the latter deals with the parts of a homogeneous or quantitative whole. The hydrostatic explanation of the cup which retains the juice in a fruit-tart is an example of abstraction[1] which obtains knowledge of one aspect of a heterogeneous whole by omitting all the rest. But the examinee who added that for the atmosphere to sustain the liquid within the cup it was necessary that the cup should not be more than thirty feet high had passed from mere abstraction within the given whole to independent consideration of the hydrostatic relation involved in the example.

Abstraction, then, like Comparison, when considered as a method *par excellence*, is one of the processes by which Reason, armed with reflective ideas, breaks into concrete data in search of the unity of the universal. The reflective idea which guides it is the equivalent in general knowledge of the mathematical axiom that if equals are taken from equals the remainders are equal. Withdraw a known relation from a known system of relations, and the relations which remain are known. It is plain that if the whole and its internal

---

[1] In saying this, I do not mean that the system of laws which an investigation, beginning with such an abstraction, ultimately brings to light, must be more abstract than the example which is the datum. The semi-logical and almost arbitrary character of these methodic processes as popularly limited is illustrated by the fact that abstraction, as in the case before us, so easily slides into systematic construction which leaves the example behind.

relations are really known so as to justify such a process, the withdrawal is a mere intellectual or ideal distinction. This is so even in mathematics. To know the difference between two quantities is the same as to know the greater as the sum of the lesser and the difference. An algebraical sum treats subtraction and addition as on a level. Abstraction would thus seem primarily to restrict itself to instances where, as in mere numerical conceptions, the withdrawal of a part leaves the other parts unaffected. But as this is never within any real whole theoretically the case, although by compensation or in loose-knit wholes it may seem to be so, the instances envisaged by abstraction occupy in truth no separate region from those which form the matter of all definite knowledge. Thus the guiding idea of abstraction is only a provisional idea. It amounts to no more than this, that within known wholes known changes may appear to leave remainders known *as unchanged*. For to say, as we said above, simply 'known remainders,' really lets in all that positive knowledge can tell us of the positive effects produced by the change on what remains. In this we go beyond abstraction. The supposed unchanged remainder, then, is predicated of the whole as modified by the withdrawal of some parts.

But really of course the abstraction is not what operates. Neither real nor ideal abstraction can help except by conferring or illustrating knowledge of the real whole in question. 'The Parnellites are chief men in Ireland, and were Ireland separated from England would be chief men still.' But *would* they? The abstraction puts the question, but does not answer it. The answer depends on our knowledge of Ireland. 'He has lost his wife and yet goes on much as before, therefore her loss has made no great change in him.' But perhaps in removing one motive to his habitual acts the loss supplied another. The inference even from this *actual* abstraction is utterly baseless except as a conclusion from our knowledge of the whole man, to which of course the new fact created by the actual abstraction must contribute. But had we had such knowledge before, we could have gone to the conclusion without the actual abstraction; and apart from such knowledge we cannot go to the conclusion on the basis of the actual abstraction.

From the difficulty of bearing in mind the necessity, often extremely obscure, of this circuitous route through the nature of the whole, and the inapplicability of mere subtraction in the complicated relations of non-mathematical reality, abstraction is perhaps the most fruitful in mistakes of all methods of knowledge. Knowledge in fact is one, and any method which consists in the exaggeration of a mere characteristic of knowledge is *ipso facto* hazardous.

Recognition.

γ. *Recognition*[1] is another of these curiously limited processes. In its complete form it appears to be reflective reproduction under the influence of an idea of identity, followed by comparison and identification of the content reproducing with the content reproduced. Recognition differs from Perception and from Inference as such both by dealing with a reproduced content, and by always ending in a direct comparison of contents. We do not speak of recognition either where there is no reproductive process, or where the process, though it may establish identity, does not end in direct comparison. When we meet a friend whom we see every day, there is no *process* of reproduction; the extension of the sensations is given along with them and the apprehension of his identity is a datum of perception. For true recognition to take place, it would be necessary that the first datum should create a second, on which two data the further process would operate. But in Inference the two data may just as well be given; and this is also the case of course with mere Comparison. On the other

[1] I restrict recognition to the elementary meaning of knowing *again*. The 'recognition' of a right or a principle, i. e. the admission of it, has interesting connections with the former case both in Logic and in Philology, and illustrates the ease with which these 'processes' pass beyond their normal sphere into knowledge in general. But it is truer to usage to regard this latter import as metaphorical.

hand, if I ask for a tune of which I know the name, but fail to recognise it when it is played, then I have inferential identification without recognition. For of course I know, supposing that I am confident in my recollection of the name and in the pianist's knowledge, that it *is* the same tune which I asked for; but, when played, it fails to reproduce the desired effect in my mind, and either there is nothing to compare, or if I compare the tune I hear with my idea of the tune I wanted, the result is distinction and not identification. Thus recognition is absent, though *inferential* identification is present. Inferential identification, however, though ever so circuitous, *may* set up a direct comparison ending in identification, and if so, then we have recognition. This is too common an experience to need illustration.

The reflective influence of the idea of identity may be active in recognition to very different degrees, and the idea itself may be suggested in very various ways. Probably these ways may all be included under imperfect reproduction. An interest in identification is necessary to make the idea work; but an interest can only operate in logical thought by attaching to a suggested content. Our interest in recollecting a man's name operates through the natural but unsuccessful efforts at reproduction, in which a prominent syllable of the name, or the like, occurs to us. And like the rest of these methodic processes, recognition loses its differentia when the abstract relation between the special contents in question ceases to interest. It is recognition to say 'That is the man who was with me in the train yesterday.' It may or may not be recognition to say 'That is Professor Huxley,' for this is a matter of fact which I may infer otherwise than by direct comparison, and which may not at all be meant to indicate an identity with a special content reproduced in my mind. And when I go deeper into knowledge and say 'Professor Huxley is one of the leaders of scientific thought in Europe' I have altogether got beyond recognition pure and simple, because

26   *The Nature of Inference.*   [BOOK II.

the interest is no longer that of mere identification but of concrete description.

Discrimination, etc.
δ. Discrimination and Identification, and many other methods or processes, might be analysed in the same way. All of them are in one sense characteristics of Inference or Judgment as such, and therefore enter into each other and into the various processes which have just been described. But each of them may also be regarded as a special though transitional method, guided by a more or less reflective idea of the result to be obtained, and subsuming under this reflective idea all matters in the content which are favourable to its purpose. Discrimination or Distinction is present in all judgment, in all inference, in all comparison, and in all recognition. But it would be pedantry to deny that we constantly set to work upon a presented content or two contents as yet unexamined, with the clearly envisaged purpose of making out a contrast or difference which we expect to find between them. Two Acts of Parliament on the same subject ought to deal with different aspects of it, and we may fairly set ourselves to distinguish the purpose and provisions of the one from the purpose and provisions of the other. What we have to keep clearly in mind is that the name Distinction is a title drawn from a merely dominant and not exclusive characteristic, that it therefore is not a desirable basis of logical discussion; and that the process of Distinction itself is transitory, because it can only continue as such so long as the result is abstract, and so long as our interest attaches rather to this abstraction than to concrete and material content.

Inference in above processes.
ε. There are thus two principles which limit the inferential and non-inferential character of the practical processes which we have been considering. As processes guided by reflective ideas, they must necessarily involve grounded selection [1] resting either on presupposed subsumption [2] or

---

[1] For the guiding idea operates through a selection within the content.

[2] When I recall a man's name on seeing him, this recognition is not based on a necessary connection of content. But the accepted identification or subsump-

on general connection of content. And when we have grounded selection, we have, as we saw, the essentials of inference—we have at least a suggested distinction between direct and indirect reference to Reality. On the other hand, the abstract and therefore accidental character of the controlling ideas renders it impossible that explicit inference should form the essence of these processes. The moment we really found our argument on an explicit ground going deep into the nature of the subject we get a conclusion that must go beyond mere identity, likeness, or distinctness, which with one modification or another, but always in more or less abstract form, are the guiding ideas and interests of these subordinate methods of knowledge.

ζ. If the above processes, including Comparison, are arbitrary and vanishing phases of knowledge, how do we come to speak of Comparative science?

Comparative Science.

The Comparative sciences are the sciences of organic and intellectual evolution through its varied series and ramifications. Their data are thus, in the first place, *actual*, independently of the operations of the science, and in the second place are essentially types relative to definite functions, and so not as a rule capable of being illustrated by the results of *direct*[1] interference. Hence it follows that the sciences in question (i) begin with cross-references between their actual data—the method of ordinary comparison —and (ii) retain their data untransformed in these crossreferences—a leading peculiarity of ordinary comparison.

tion of the man under his name in which I rest when the name is reproduced is as good *ad hoc* as such a connection. The reflective idea of identity guides me to select characteristic marks in the presented content, which I subsume under that idea. 'That gait, voice, gesture, is surely a help to his identity.' Then if I succeed in reproducing anything not present, this reproduced content goes up to fill up the idea of identity.

'That face of his I do remember well;
But when I saw it last it was besmeared
As black as Vulcan in the smoke of war,'—

and then a whole history comes up and mere identity gives place to description of character.

[1] Variations of animals under domestication are hardly for this purpose to be set down to *direct* interference.

On the other hand, the abstract ideas of identity, difference, etc. which guide ordinary comparison could not form the content of any science; and the comparative sciences go beyond 'comparison' by seeking for definite concrete principles of evolution and affiliation between the types with which they deal.

All science, of course, compares; but chemistry, for example, is not 'comparative' in the above sense. It does not begin by cross-references of mercury to carbon and of carbon to gold, as philology does with Latin and Greek, and Greek and Sanskrit. Chemistry has to create its regular series of phenomena by experiment before it can lay down principles that connect them, and each series at first concerns the nature of a single group of substances only. The data, as data of science, are not actual. And chemistry does not in its generalisations retain its data untransformed. The underlying principle, the molecular or atomic hypothesis, is the essence, the element of rationality and of interest. In its results, as at its starting-point, it would be sheer distortion to call chemistry a comparative science of elements and their compounds. It is an analytic enquiry into the fabric and behaviour of matter. The elements and their compounds have no individual or characteristic value like that of a language, or a polity, or a group of myths. In short, in the sciences which are analytic *par excellence* the rationality and interest are on the side of the underlying principle, while in comparative science the underlying principle serves rather to connect and illustrate realities which have independent functional importance. Science is one, and these distinctions are matters of degree. But even should chemistry ever succeed in representing its data as evolutionary products of an intelligible process and so as thenceforward challenging comparison *ab initio*, still this will be an ultimate achievement and not a method pursued throughout. Geometry, as we saw in treating of the quasi-generic judgment, mimics evolutionary procedure with some success. But its data in their pure form are really made, not given as realities of independent significance.

4. I will now attempt to exhibit in their true light some species of Inference, each of which has in turn been erroneously identified with its principle. *Species of Inference which have been treated as its principle.*

i. Induction in Mill's sense of the term, i.e. Induction by incomplete enumeration, or inference from particulars to particulars, is obviously to be identified with the species of inference in which a confused or implicit universal, indicated by a common name, is the ground in mediate assertion respecting concrete things or events. I do not mean to examine here the case of Induction by complete enumeration, which has in fact been sufficiently illustrated by the analysis of enumeration in Book I.[1] It is enough to remark that if this Induction really relies on the completeness of its enumeration, it ceases *ex hypothesi* to be Inference. If, again, it relies on some discovery made during the enumeration, then the *completeness* of the process is without influence on the result. *From particulars to particulars.*

In the Induction by incomplete enumeration, or inference from particulars to particulars, in which Mill finds the fundamental process of inference as such, there is apt to be at first sight nothing at all which binds these particulars together. The pervading identity or universal, which we affirm to be the operative power in inference, often appears in popular practice as in Mill's theory, to be simply non-existent. That is to say, it either creeps in under the shelter of a mere common name, or may even be absolutely ignored in the expression of our inference, because the common name which would express it is presupposed, or perhaps is not known or does not occur to us. 'Why do you think A likely to be a good scholar?' 'Well, because B and C and D are good scholars.' Here it is plain that something known to both speakers is presupposed and not expressed; perhaps for example the fact that A, B, C, and D were educated at the same school. But often the

[1] See Bk. I. chap. iv.

operative identity is left unexpressed not because it is clearly understood, but because we do not *think* it definitely at all. 'Why do you think that picture is by Mantegna?' 'Because it reminds me of some pictures of his in the National Gallery.' Here the words 'reminds me' appeal to a merely psychical fact, and express in doing so my inability to produce a distinct formulation of the ground on which I have gone.

Thus we are presented with something like an antinomy. Identity is necessary to Inference, but some Inference takes place without Identity.

The explanation of this contradiction, as distinguished from the logical justification of Inference from particulars to particulars, is afforded by what has been said about the ultimate nature of Inference. The 'particulars' are not particulars, but differences in a universal. The universal, however, which in elementary reproduction operates unconsciously, may in elementary inference be very far from explicit in thought; or, and this is by far the commoner case, there may be an obvious deep-seated identity in the nature of the concrete instances, which is not in its entirety relevant to the attribute about which we draw our conclusion. Then, in accordance with the principle of analogy, we follow the dominating identity, and come to a result the *precise* or relevant ground of which we are unable to ascertain. The conception of inference from particulars to particulars is thus an illusion arising from the activity in inference of presupposed, superficial, or unanalysed universals.

Subsumption.

ii. Subsumption is the complement of inference from particulars to particulars. I speak here as above of the natural and normal process, and not of the process by completed enumeration, which is devoid of inferential character. Subsumption is based on the conjunction of attributes in the actual concrete nature of a subject or subjects. The identity of nature which is implicit in inference 'from particulars to particulars' is here made explicit in the content of an individual or individuality. But this identity, though seldom wholly destitute of inferential significance, is in respect of the conjunction of attributes within it a confused and not a scientific concrete. The connection of the attributes is proved by it not as a principle but only as a fact. Of course, however, an inference which is really matter of principle may borrow the shape of subsumption, and in doing so may or may not continue to imply a principle that really goes beyond subsumption. The relation between inference from particulars to particulars and its complement subsumption is thoroughly illustrated by Mill's discussion of the subsumptive syllogism. Putting aside the notion of a *petitio principii*, which only applies when the major premise in Barbara is regarded as a complete enumeration, we find that the major premise consists in an explicit enunciation of the common nature which really warrants the conclusion. Mill regards this enunciation only in the light of a summary of particulars, and as we have seen, the facts of rudimentary reproduction and even of elementary inference bear him out in the view that it is not indispensable. The point however is, that though the enunciation itself is not indispensable, yet the operation of that identity which the enunciation formulates is indispensable. It is this which, in the form of an ideal content considered as a subject qualified by attributes, is the point of union in subsumptive inference. Here again the nature of the active universal determines the inferential form.

iii. Calculation is a divergent form of subsumption, in which, by passing through the stage of complete enumeration, the universal operative in the inference has been transformed from an ideal content existing *in* individuals to a totality where parts are units. The concrete individuality, i.e. the common generic nature of the individuals, has faded away by abstraction into a mere denomination of units, and the attributes which were conjoined within the generic content have also become denominations of the numerical wholes. These numerical wholes which have arisen out of the 'extension' of the ideal content by means of enumera-

[margin: Calculation and Equation. *]*

tion are related to each other as measurable parts and wholes in the system of number. Thus the subsumptive syllogism, 'All Englishmen are Europeans, all Londoners are Englishmen, therefore all Londoners are Europeans,' may be seriously taken in the aspect of extension, which through the affinity between the individual and the unit is always closely allied to the aspect of number. But to carry this aspect to a genuine result we must not simply say 'Englishmen = English Europeans,' etc. etc., for the insertion of 'English' in the predicate makes the sign =, which implies restriction to the aspect of number, superfluous and meaningless. And if we do not use =, but retain the copula 'are,' then the repetition in the predicate goes a long way to destroy the meaning of the judgment by reducing it to a tautology.

Calculation proper.   *a.* If we seriously intend to draw a conclusion from the relation of individuals as units, i. e. apart from their content except in so far as it distinguishes them into groups, we must first constitute each of our wholes into a numerical whole by complete enumeration, and then refer these wholes to one another in respect of their *measurable* identity or want of identity, i. e. equality or inequality, which latter, as we saw above, being assignable as an exact difference, involves the former. Then we should get something like Englishmen = $\frac{1}{20}$ Europeans, Londoners = $\frac{1}{4}$ Englishmen. That is to say, Londoners, *numerically considered*, are a part that repeats itself four times in the numerical whole of Englishmen, and Englishmen numerically considered are a part that repeats itself twenty times in the numerical whole of Europeans. Thus the same numerical whole presents itself as thoroughly identical with itself in its differences or different relations, whether as the number of Englishmen, obtained by simple enumeration, or as four times the number of Londoners, a relation obtained by comparison of enumerations and analysis of a sum into its parts, or as a twentieth part of the number of Europeans, a relation obtained in the same way as the last mentioned.

The quantitative universal, which is the same in kind throughout all its different aspects — not distinguishable as a subject controlling attributes and as attributes that severally do not exhaust the subject — is thus an embodiment of the rule, 'Things which are equal to the same thing are equal to each other.' Calculation is mediate judgment, in which, from the nature of the whole that operates, there is no distinction between subject and predicate.

It is obvious therefore that Calculation cannot be applied to wholes that consist of heterogeneous or non-quantitative parts, or at least, if so applied, can only deal with them in their aspect, probably a subordinate one, of homogeneity. If the number of lines in Macbeth is $\frac{1}{30}$th of the number of lines contained in all Shakespeare's plays together, what then? The relation of Macbeth to the other works of Shakespeare's mind must be expressed by other universals than this. There have always been logicians whose gaze has been fascinated by the simplicity and certainty of calculative processes; but it is idle to place the ideal of argument in a type which depends on the relations of identical units. The tendency to acquiesce in this ideal has no doubt been strengthened by the absolute reciprocity of the equational judgment, which has been explained above. This reciprocity anticipates, though at a long interval, a prominent attribute of notional definition or of any complete and concrete knowledge; and this anticipation of a characteristic which is rightly ascribed to the logical ideal has increased the attractiveness of computative or quasi-computative processes as types of logical method.

β. The importance of the Equational logic is so great that I will return for a moment to its principle, which has been cursorily alluded to on the previous page. The point of logical interest in regard to it is that it is not at first hand a calculus at all, though it is a calculus, and a very effective one, at second hand. In this respect it is of the same grade as the calculus of chances, with which it is closely allied. By saying that the logical calculus is not a calculus at first

Equational Logic.

hand, I mean that the judgments with which it deals are not judgments that embody numerical or quantitative relations as such, and therefore, as was shown above, have no fair claim to the sign = as copula. This is absolutely clear of the judgments which Jevons calls Partial Identities, in which the employment of the sign = is not in accordance with usage. It is not intelligible to say[1] that Iron = a metal, or that Diatomaceae = a class of plants, or that Mammalia = a class of vertebrates. These judgments are obviously subsumptive judgments, intended to express the conjunction of certain attributes in certain individuals, or else the identity of certain sets of individuals under certain different aspects or descriptions. But the sign = does not express this conjunction of attributes or identity of individuals, except as the attributes or identity of a quantitative whole, and as on the other hand the judgment suggests no obvious quantitative aspect, weight or number or value, in which identity can be asserted, it follows that the form of the judgment simply contradicts its content, i. e. the judgment is not intelligible.

With Simple Identities the case is somewhat different. It is not indeed intelligible to say that 'Lord Salisbury = the Prime Minister of England,' or that 'St. Mary's Church at Oxford = the University Church[2].' But it is intelligible —I now take Jevons' examples of simple identities—that 'The smell of a rotten egg = that of hydrogen sulphide;' and that 'The colour of the Pacific Ocean = the colour of the Atlantic Ocean.' And the reason why it is intelligible is this. It is possible to interpret these judgments as establishing identity of degree[3] in a quality capable of variations ; i. e.

[1] Principles of Science, p. 40.

[2] Unless we meant to affirm that Lord Salisbury when Prime Minister retains, for example, his normal height and weight; or that St. Mary's when considered as the University Church suffers no diminution of size. It might be urged that this is worth considering, for of Merton Chapel, if I remember right, a parallel assertion would be untrue, the choir being a college chapel, and the church as a whole a parish church.

[3] Jevons does not in the least distinguish true intensive equation, as in a colour match, from identification of individuals or classes of things in a sense

quantitative identity or an equation of colours or of smells. And by a metaphorical usage based on this fact identical *conceptions*, though not strictly quantitative, are sometimes said to be *equivalent*, and this equivalence is rudely symbolised by the sign of equality. But the point to note is that equivalence cannot be affirmed on the ground of individual identity. It means equal amount and kind *of intension*, and does not mean identity of component individuals. Thus it is simply false that 'Exogens = Dicotyledons,' for the meanings are not equivalent, though the individuals designated by the names are, *exceptis excipiendis*, the same.

In the first instance, therefore, the judgment as formulated by the Equational logic is not an equation, because it does not restrict itself to a quantitative aspect, but predicates individual identity, Although you say that Diatomaceae = a class of plants, you may not go on to say that this class of plants = another class *x* (meaning that the two are equal in number), and that therefore the Diatomaceae = the class *x*. The original judgment might indeed *happen* to justify this calculation, but in passing through it would have entirely lost its peculiar import.

The office of computation in the Calculus is not to compare quantitative attributes of objects, but to secure complete enumeration of possible judgments. In this office of secondary import it somewhat resembles the translation of a material disjunctive judgment into a numerical statement of chances. But the statement of chances gives a numerical result, whereas the logical calculus, after protecting itself by a computation of combinations, returns to a result in the shape of identification or identifications. Working as it does solely by the identification of individuals under different aspects, i.e. as conjoining in themselves different attributes, the equational logic is obviously

---

quite beyond quantity. He fails to distinguish Quality from Kind or Individuality. Hence ' Deal = Landing-place of Caesar ' is to him a ' simple Identity,' no less than ' Colour of Pacific Ocean = Colour of Atlantic Ocean.'

a species of subsumption, and rests ultimately on the subsumptive principle that attributes conjoined in the same individual are conjoined with each other. Thus in regard to the nature of the universal which is operative in inference through the calculus, there is little to say beyond what has already been said in dealing with subsumption. The only peculiarity of this species of subsumption is that in it the undefined capacities of subsumption as such for conveying connections of principles are cut down to the most abstract expression of individual unity, without being allowed to develope in the direction which such abstract unity naturally suggests, viz. that of participation in a numerical whole.

Construction. Physical.

iv. 'Construction' is a term frequently applied to a method or element of inference. a. It primarily indicates an auxiliary process employed in geometrical or mechanical reasoning. This process consists in making accessible to perception a geometrical or mechanical complex of relations which embodies a problem or theorem that is under consideration. The actual physical construction—a diagram on paper or a model or experimental machine [1]—though not ideal, but an object of sense, is nevertheless abstract in its sensuousness, being purposely cleared of the irrelevancies which encumber our ordinary perceptions. And further, the nature of space is so closely related to sense-perception, that ideal spatial relations can be adequately symbolised by actual figures presented to perception, although the ideal relation underlying a theorem is always both *more* and *less* than the visible or tangible lines and points. 'More,' because the visible lines can be but a case of the ideal relation; 'less,' because the perceptible lines, though reduced to black on white, still include errors and irrelevancies which the mind

---

[1] An excellent example of construction in this sense, the solution of a problem in actual physical embodiment, is the machine for drawing sound curves of any shape by combination of actual pendular oscillations. There is such a machine, I think, with actual pendulums, which thus does not merely *mimic* the curves (as the machine with cog-wheels may be said to do), but actually constructs them in terms of the theory.

in working with them disregards. The case of a working model or machine made to experiment with is at first sight different from that of a mere diagram. But the difference is only in degree. Both the diagram and the machine are really *in pari materia* with that which they represent to the mind; the diagram with ordinary perception, the machine with ordinary physical causation. But it is harder to say where the line is to be drawn between fact and representative of fact in the case of the machine, which shades off gradually into the ordinary operations of nature. Such a thing however as a working model[1] that illustrates the lever action of the limbs shows how the machine as such stands between natural process and abstract mechanics. It is the abstract *physical* expression for a natural activity, and paves the way for its abstract ideal expression.

Construction in this first and simplest sense is not even a case or species of Inference. The production of a visible material figure or object does not even, strictly speaking, *enter into* the essence of the inferential process. It is however a peculiar auxiliary method which depends upon and throws into relief the characteristic nature of the universal —the abstraction of sense—with which Inference is concerned in Geometry or abstract mechanics. The lines drawn on paper, though peculiarly adequate symbols, are nevertheless only symbols of the lines with which geometry actually works. And of course we do not draw the lines on paper at random, and they would be of no use if we did. We only draw them in accordance with the requirements of the universal operative in the inference, so far as these requirements are already known and can guide us from moment to moment. The aim is to aid intellectual reflection in fixing and following connections which suggest themselves within that universal; and as we have seen, the material lines or even cords, pulleys, levers, etc. *represent*

[1] A complete model of the ear or eye may seem not to be abstract, but only magnified; it is however abstract by its isolation from other parts, its fixity, and its capability of being taken to pieces.

an intellectual work already partly accomplished in the exclusion of irrelevant elements. But the material or physical construction *is* not the active element in the accomplishment of this work. This construction in the sense of actual drawing or model-making is a process *characteristic* of geometrical or mechanical inference, but not identical therewith.

Imaginative.

β. But this brings us to a secondary sense of construction—secondary not in logical value, but, as I think, in usage and the growth of meaning. Of course actual lines on paper are not essential to simple geometrical inference in which we can 'carry the figure in our heads,' and if so, the visible external figure cannot in theory be essential to *any* such inference. Professor Clifford, it would appear, was almost independent of external aids to realisation in considering geometrical or physical problems. But when we work with ideas of lines, and combine spatial elements *in our imagination,* and not on paper, is not this still construction, and yet is it not now of the essence of inference?

I fear that at this point a further refinement cannot be avoided. It seems to me obvious that the imaginative experiment is a different thing from the intellectual perception of unity. The imaginative experiment may be misdirected and void of result, as a line drawn on paper in addition to an actual diagram may be irrelevant and meaningless. The imaginary line projected on imaginary paper, though necessary perhaps to the intellectual apprehension, is it seems to me purely on a level with the external line perceived through sense. But when any line either given on paper or suggested in imagination has been intellectually grasped as symbolic of a relation relevant to the universal which we are developing, then it is taken up into the inference and has passed from a step in physical or imaginative construction to an element in necessary apprehension. In looking for that point in an ellipse in which the sun had to be placed in order that the ellipse might represent a planetary orbit according to the theory of gravitation it is easy either in imagination or on paper to select the middle point of the longer axis. The question as to the nature of the process is not whether I draw or only imagine, but whether in doing either one or the other I am guided by insight into the connection of the data and into the conditions of the problem. If I seem to myself to have such an insight, but am, as in the case above-mentioned, mistaken in the connection which I fancy that I detect, then I infer, but wrongly. If however, or in as far as, I put the sun in the wrong place or in the right place by an isolated act of sensuous fancy, then I may be constructing, but I am not inferring.

γ. The organised or articulated intellectual perception itself, in contrast with the physical or imaginative experiment—or rather taken as including this experiment, for the sensuous ideas cannot be dispensed with—affords a third meaning which may be put upon construction. Of course this perception has the effect of a synthesis, of a putting together as well as of a distinguishing. And especially when the relations thus put together as having their unity in one universal are spatial relations, readily symbolised by imaginative pictures, there is a plausibility in translating the Greek term 'synthesis,' which in technical logic expresses the unity of differences inherent in all intelligible judgment, into the term of Latin origin 'construction,' which may be held to express this same idea with the additional implication of *intentional* operation *in time*, by which elements of intellectual perception are put together like the parts of a machine. *Intellectual, in Geometry and Mechanics.*

Construction in this third sense, a sense largely insisted on by Kant, is a hybrid idea. I cannot doubt that it designates a true species of inference—inference dealing with the abstractions of sense—by a title actually drawn from and implying an accident of inference, viz. *intentional* combination, successive in time, of visible or imagined forms. Now the *intention*, except in as far as it is a general intention to infer correctly, falls outside inference.

40   *The Nature of Inference.*   [BOOK II.

In inference nothing can guide us but inferential necessity; and a special intention, such as that of drawing a line on a slate or on paper, or of constructing a model of a joint, arises in some motive external to the inference proper. And as with the intention, so with the fact of material construction. It is a mere accident of inference. Therefore the intentional combination of perceptible or imaginable elements falls outside inference proper except in so far as it is guided by inferential grounds. But it is true that, especially wherever we have novelty or discovery in inference [1], imaginative or perceptive construction is an indispensable auxiliary to thought.

<small>Intellectual, without limitation to Geometry, etc.</small>

δ. And finally, by insisting on the ideas of synthesis, of intention, and of the value of imagination in inference, we arrive at a fourth meaning of Construction [2], in which it is alleged to be an essential element or even the essence of *all* inference, as an *intellectual* combinative process, *not* confined to the region of geometrical or mechanical abstractions. Thus understood, Construction becomes a convenient expression for the distinct realisation in inference even of universals which are not numerical or geometrical, if they are more than subsumptive. Transferring a spatial metaphor to such universals, it appears to explain the definite necessity which unites their differences, by reference to the precise and unambiguous coherence which belongs to geometrical relations. But we have seen that even as applied to geometrical inferences construction is to a great extent a metaphor drawn from an accident of those inferences, and when we deal with universals which are not at all sensuous the simplicity of the expression becomes actually deceptive. It is easy to say, for example, that we intellectually 'construct' such a whole as the British Constitution out of isolated facts, principles, and accepted ideas, and then proceed to perceive its nature. But it is plain that anything valuable in the 'construction' is coincident

---
[1] See p. 8, supra.
[2] Bradley's Principles of Logic, p. 235, and passim.

with and guided by the growing insight into the nature of the content before us which constitutes the inference itself. We must distinguish from this usage that by which we speak of constructing a Utopia. Here of course we are ostensibly not inferring, though we have really to use inference. We are playing, employing the imagination according to arbitrary interests and motives, and not under intellectual guidance, until we begin to draw consequences from what we have said. And the root of the whole usage which we have examined is that in all inference, so far as it has novelty or is a process modifying itself in time, there is an arbitrary and external element which supplies guidance to the attention until the true principle and the relevant details have been disentangled, and operates throughout the inference by the side of the true principle which gradually displaces and finally ousts it. This arbitrary element may indeed be regarded as the universal itself in an imperfect form, but for this very reason it contains much in the way of suggestion or experiment[1]—much tentative synthesis—that has to be dropped and erased before the inference can assume its true and final form. And the name construction depends largely on the elements which, having been intentionally and therefore tentatively inserted, are ultimately dropped.

The outcome of our account of Construction then is this. Construction is a term drawn from moral, physical, and psychological adjuncts of inference. In the case of geometrical and mechanical inference these adjuncts are so far akin to the matter of the universal, that the term 'Construction' drawn from them may be held a fair designation of such inferential processes, e.g. of Kant's account of matter on the basis of attraction and repulsion. In the case of other and less sensuous universals this is not so, and Construction as applied to them is a mere metaphor and not even a case of Inference. Thus Construction should never

[1] Cp. the case above cited in which the focus of the ellipse was the point required, but the middle of the longer axis was the first point selected.

The Nature of Inference.

be assigned as the essence or as an essential element of Inferential activity.

The above account of four main cases [1] of Inference may serve as an anticipatory sketch of the course which our discussion will pursue in the following chapters. (See scheme annexed.)

SCHEME ILLUSTRATING AFFILIATION OF ARGUMENTS AS DESCRIBED IN BOOK II.

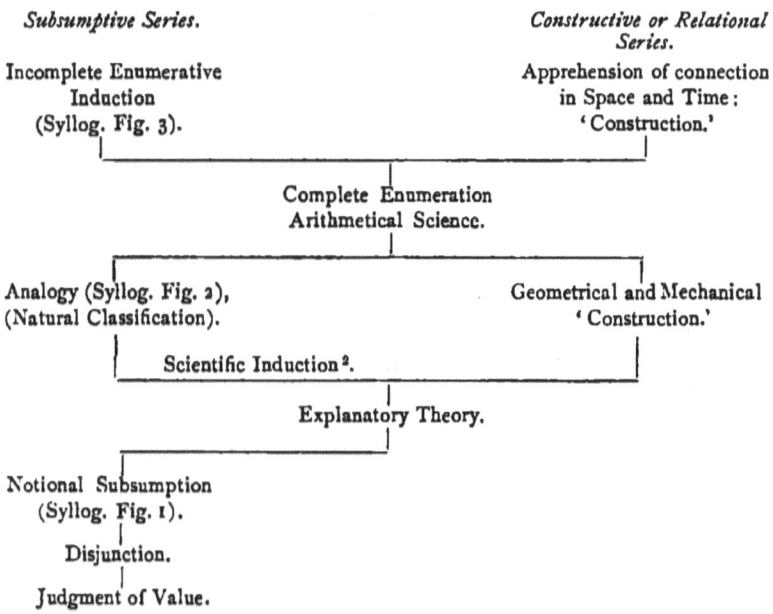

---

[1] Or five, counting among them the process which Construction in its fourth sense is abusively applied to designate.

[2] Scientific Induction is treated as a transition by which Explanatory Theory may be reached from the side of Analogy. The scheme is intended to represent each type of inference as a combination of that vertically above it with that with which it is connected by a horizontal line. This does not apply to the relation between Explanatory Theory and Complete Enumeration, which stand where they do merely as being intermediate forms.

CHAPTER II.

ENUMERATIVE INDUCTION AND MATHEMATICAL REASONING.

IN tracing the evolution and affiliation of the forms of explicit inference, we begin with a more developed phase of consciousness than that to which we went back in describing the rudiments of judgment. The judgment-form in which the universal first reveals itself as the simple unity of differences must have given place to the articulate perception of things, events, and relations, before we can grasp it as a system whose parts are in necessary connection. In other words, we have no longer to deal with the simplest judgments of perception—the impersonal and the elementary comparative judgment—but may go at once to the world of things with their characteristic identity, and to the abstract relations of number, space and time in which that world is constructed by the mind.

1. On the basis of a world of things and occurrences, which involves a language, i.e. a more or less systematised nomenclature[1], the articulate universal presents itself in the form of individual objects having characteristic identity, in which identity general attributes coexist. Language forces such coexistence on our attention through its natural classifications, and the first suggestions of inductive enumeration issue from language—which has in fact gained its significance by the same process conducted naturally and without explicit intention. Such suggestions are operative, as we saw, in the so-called inference from Particulars to Particulars, of which Incomplete Enumerative Induction is a form that has been made superficially rational.

Enumerative Induction

[1] Cp. Introduction, sect. 4.

Syllogism in Fig. 3.

a. Throwing this inference into the shape naturally prescribed by the tendency of the concrete individual thing to become the subject in judgment [1], and making use, as Aristotle also did, of the conjunctive judgment as representing a single step in inference, we obtain an inference analogous to the Aristotelian syllogism in the third figure :—

a, b, c, d, are rational ;
a, b, c, d, are men ;
∴ Are all men rational? or, Men may be rational.

The ground of argument being the characteristic unity of the unanalysed individual object or event, naturally takes the place of the subject in judgment—of the concrete individual which is taken as real—and therefore gives rise to that syllogistic form in which the middle term is the subject of both premises.

Experience bears out the view that some such type as this represents the simplest operation of mediate inference. All that is said for example by Stuart Mill about inference from Particulars to Particulars must really be taken as applying to inference of this type ; for it is impossible to state an inference in a shape that will even appear to be convincing, unless we supply by a second premise the element of unity between the particulars, always operative in the mind, which is necessary to bind the particular differences into the differences *of* a universal. The use of symbolic letters brings to light this formal necessity, which significant names satisfy without acknowledging. From '*a, b, c, d* are good books' to '*e* is a good book' no sort or kind of inference holds or is in any way suggested. The gulf between mere *d* and mere *e* is beyond the leaping powers of the boldest conjecture. These symbols are true particulars, and we can see from them how far true particulars will carry us in inference. But from 'Ivanhoe, Waverley, and Rob Roy are good books' to 'Guy Mannering is a good book' there is a self-evident passage by means of the identity of authorship, which is too obvious

---

[1] See on categorical and hypothetical elements in judging, Bk. I. chap. i.

to be expressed, but which would form a premise in any explicit statement of the inference. That this same ground would justify the conclusion 'The Surgeon's Daughter is a good book' is an illustration of Bacon's remark that enumerative Induction 'precarie concludit, et periculo exponitur ab instantia contradictoria.'

Speaking generally, the coincidence of several attributes ✓ in one or more objects, or of several relations in one or more events, is the usual starting-point of conscious conjecture and investigation. And this starting-point is all that the present form of inference embodies. Conjecture or pure 'discovery' differs only in degree from proof. Thus the conclusion may be fairly represented by a question or a modal affirmation: A, B, and C are great lawyers *and* had a classical education ∴ Has a classical education something to do with making great lawyers[1]? or 'A classical education may have something to do with making great lawyers.' In the case of events, which are designated more analytically, i.e. more with a view to an intended inference, than individuals can be, a single judgment is the natural form for elementary arguments of this kind. 'He killed his bird every shot,' i.e. 'Such and such times he fired; all those times he killed ∴ When he fires, he is likely to kill.' But in careful reasoning or experiment 'such and such' becomes an elaborate identification by marks.

β. In this argument by incomplete Enumeration we find Divergent a union of divergent tendencies. Plainly, it has no major Tendencies. premise; but no less plainly, the principle on which it primarily relies is the principle of subsumption. Its conclusion is therefore particular or modal, and affirms that in instances or under conditions which we are not in a position to assign explicitly, the attributes x and y are or would be united. For the premises neither express precise conditions nor furnish the basis of a complete inference by subsumption. In order to assigning precise conditions, the

[1] The disjunctive import of this question, as is natural with a rudimentary type of inference, is simply Yes or No.

form of subsumption, i. e. of identification in unanalysed subjects, must be surrendered. In order to furnish a complete subsumptive inference, the universal must appear in the form of Allness, i. e. in the form of a totality of examples enumerated up to a limit which its nature prescribes. Such an enumeration, or an allegation equivalent to such an enumeration—the allegation might be of mediate origin—would be the major premise in a pure subsumptive syllogism. In the present argument as it stands we simply formulate the first impression made by this discovery of an articulate[1] identity in difference, and the first suggestion towards completing the articulation of the universal thus indicated. This suggestion is most naturally to be taken, in accordance with the type of the inference, as quite abstract and superficial, consisting as it does in a single pervading attribute, chosen, so far as we are told, at random.

Individual Judgment in induction. γ. It is obvious that the study of inference must retraverse, in part at least, the path taken by the study of judgment. In the present form of inference the mind is at the same critical point at which it stands when in the Proportional Judgment it has become familiar with the identity of things beneath their attributes. Only in the study of Inference we see the actual process by which the judgment-forms pass into one another—in this case, in the sphere of enumeration, by the natural pressure of their own recurrence. Incomplete Enumerative Induction is an obvious result of recurrent individual Judgments, which accentuate the common distinguishable aspects prevalent in things and in their individualities—i. e. in their characteristic natures.

In Lotze's representation of an argument akin to this, he has set out the recurrent individual judgments as so many premises of the syllogism[2]; and, rightly recognising

---

[1] See distinction between explicit and implicit inference, in last chapter.

[2] Lotze, Logik, Eng. Tr. p. 100: 'Now it often happens that the same predicate occurs or does not occur not only in two but very many different subjects,

that the number of *such* premises is not limited, he has thereby cut the knot of the question whether inference essentially proceeds through three terms. It is not worth while to dispute about a matter of symbolic representation. So I have only to explain the relation of his scheme of the argument to that here given, by pointing out that his *entire set* of premises corresponds to either *one* of the two which I lay down, while the relation of the individuals P, S, T, etc. to the common attribute Σ forms the other of the two premises essential to the inference. The use of a conjunctive judgment in inference of this type is in accordance with the principles laid down in Book I[1] as regards the unity of the judgment, and with Aristotle's practice in his Inductive Syllogism, though not in the ordinary Syllogism in figure 3 which I have treated as the inductive syllogism. By using the individuals, not in a conjunctive judgment, but as subjects to several premises, Lotze has forced his inference into the second instead of the third syllogistic figure, the only common term being the common *predicate*, which therefore must formally serve as middle term though it does not operate as such. His transition from P, S, T to Σ is effected without an explicit judgment, and the whole process is more akin to the colligation of a conjunctive judgment into a singular or generic judgment as described in Book I[2], than to a process of Mediate Inference. It is obviously more convenient to use the third syllogistic figure, in which a common *subject* is the middle term, for Induction, and to reserve the second, in which a common *predicate* is middle term, for Analogy. This was the scheme followed by Hegel, and I venture to think that the deviation from this scheme [3], like other modifications which

---

P, S, T, V, W, and the question is what consequence can be drawn from the premisses PM, SM, TM, VM, ... which belong in form to the second figure of Aristotle..... Our conclusion runs as follows, " All Σ are M." '

[1] See Bk. I. chap. i. sect. 1. iii.
[2] l.c.
[3] See Hegel's Wissenschaft der Logik, ii. pp. 131, 148-9. Hegel, following

48   *Enumeration and Mathematics.*   [BOOK II.

Lotze has introduced into a logic largely resting on Hegel's ideas, is far from being an improvement.

The critical point which is involved in the inference before us is the point of divergence between the concrete and the abstract forms of the universal. This is fundamentally one with the divergence between subsumptive inference and the inference which depends on the systematic necessity of abstract relations. That these two types of inference unite again in the systematic and definite concretes of the higher sciences and of philosophy is obvious from the interconnection of the hypothetical and the disjunctive judgment. But for the greater part of their evolution they are distinct, though not fundamentally discrepant.

The abstract universal operates in all systems or totalities that can be regarded as aggregates of homogeneous parts, although this very word homogeneous indicates that the whole has a nature which is also the nature of the parts. All strictly mechanical science—all science, that is, which regards its objects in the light of number, space, matter and motion, is due to the operation of the abstract universal. And in a certain sense, as we shall see, there is nothing which does not in some degree correspond to these abstract relations; nothing, at all events, which in its analysis presents features discrepant with their abstract necessity.

The concrete universal follows the track of the individual totality, and displays itself, first, imperfectly, in analogical inference, and then in the teleological conceptions which govern the higher evolutionary sciences; especially in those sciences which have for their object-matter the achievements and the intellect of man.

Mathematical Reasoning. 2. To assign the directions of this divergence in terms of traditional logic is not so easy as to describe their real nature. Logic has been compelled to adapt its types of inference to the false directions in which it has looked for

the order which he finds convenient, calls Aristotle's figure 3 'figure 2,' and Aristotle's figure 2 'figure 3.' Is it possible that Lotze was misled by this?

Numerical Totality.

Thus in diverging towards the abstract universal leaving the track of true subsumption, but yet we following the path on which Formal and Quantifying gic have taught us to seek the perfectly regular sub-..mptive syllogism. Whereas by following the fortunes of true subsumption we lose all hope of attaining the genuine syllogism of Allness, and yet we go forward through syllogistic types—the second and third figures—which we have. been taught to regard as only demonstrable by reference to that syllogism.

i. The lines of advance *really* suggested by Incomplete Enumerative Induction lead to Analogy on the one hand and to complete Enumeration on the other. In the remainder of the present chapter I shall follow out the latter with its affiliated types of inference, and return in the following chapter with the discussion of Analogy to the central line of concrete inference which will take us to the end of our subject.

Number and Analogy—Divergence.

a. It is unnecessary to repeat the analysis of the Enumerative process which was given in Book I. It is sufficient if we bear in mind that complete Enumeration is the establishment of the universal as a numerical totality or aggregate of homogeneous parts, and therefore necessarily depresses the pervading nature or identity of the universal into a *denomination*, and its differences into *units*. By an extreme of abstraction all connection between the parts, beyond the fact that they are units in an aggregate, is done away with, so far as the numerical point of view prevails and the universal takes on the uniform attributes and modes of synthesis which belong to a numerical totality as such. It has been said by Mr. Ruskin[1] that two and two do not in fact necessarily make four, but more often make five. So of course they often may and do, but *not by the process of enumeration*, nor by calculation, which is a mere abridgment of enumeration. Nearly all fallacies and

Complete Enumeration as false ideal.

[1] I quote from memory, merely for the sake of illustration. I have no serious quarrel with the statement.

paradoxes depend upon a confusion of categories. It is well to be reminded by a man of genius that there are other spheres of knowledge besides calculation; but it would be wrong to take the paradox for a truth, and to impute to the system of number what is a simple omission of our own. Calculation is quite equal to the task of equating 2 + 2 with 5, if it is allowed to indicate the generation of an additional unit somewhere among the 2 and 2.

Complete Enumeration has been operative as a false ideal both in the doctrine of Induction and in the doctrine of the syllogism. Incomplete Enumeration naturally suggests an extension of itself up to Complete Enumeration. It is readily seen indeed that in dealing inductively with the ordinary objects of perception completeness of the process can never be attained, because the universal nature of an object is not comparable with nor reducible to an enumeration of individuals. Therefore such enumeration must fall into the Infinite series. And it is no less plain that if we interpret the universality of the syllogistic major premise in Barbara as depending on a complete enumeration, the inference is at once reduced to a *petitio principii* by the direct affirmation of the conclusion in the major premise. Yet though both these shortcomings are obvious, still the mere aggregation of instances always tends to obtrude itself as a feature of certainty in Induction; and syllogistic reasoning always tends to assume the shape in which mere extension, i.e. mere identity of individual units, is the bond of union between the predicated attributes. Instances of this tendency are to be found in the diagrammatic representations of inferences whether by circles included within larger circles, or by straight lines of varying thickness[1], in the quantification of the predicate, in De Morgan's numerically definite syllogism, and in the logical calculus. All of these treatments are founded on a view of reasoning which diverges from concrete determination by attributes, but stops short—except in the case of the numerically

[1] See Sir William Hamilton's Lectures on Logic, vol. ii. Appendix.

definite syllogism, which is simply calculation—of arithmetical inference by true numerical relations. All of these processes work well up to a certain point, being, technically, examples of quasi-subsumption—subsumption introduced into a sphere in which its concreteness is lost. All of them, finally, are cases of the tendency, so fatal in popular science, to accentuate at the expense of everything else any aspect of any content which affords the slightest prospect of reduction to a mechanical, i.e. to a calculative procedure. For calculation goes by fixed rules and according to regular series, and is *in that sense*[1] an easy process, whereas concrete enquiry into actual and material conditions or connections is inventive and creative—the very travail of the mind.

The real ground on which number of instances may be a source of certainty in Induction will appear when we treat of that process in its scientific aspect. No doubt the influence of Complete Enumeration as an ideal has operated in part through association with the Calculus of Probabilities. This calculus however is not the true warrant of Induction, and indeed in the case of an infinite series, which for the above-mentioned reason must always be the ultimate nature of mere enumeration of instances, the calculus can have no application.

β. But Complete Enumeration in its strict and proper sense leads up to Arithmetical Computation, and in due course to the generalised or symbolic forms of computation which are founded upon arithmetic. The judgment which corresponds to this form of argument is, as we saw in Book I[2], the equation; a type of judgment in which the predominance of the whole as determining the parts

Enumeration as Arithmetical computation.

---

[1] I am not so silly as to maintain that abstruse calculation is easy in the ordinary sense of the word. But I take it that its difficulties, though insuperable to untrained minds, are not of the same order as those presented by original investigation of actual conditions, in which the intellect is thrown entirely on its own guidance, and can gain but little aid from general rules. And it is not merely the logician but also the physicist who may complain of calculation from assumptions being substituted for investigation into them.

[2] Bk. I. chap. iv.

relatively to itself is no longer visible, conformably to the fact that we have left the field of subsumption, and are now dealing with combinations of connections devoid of subsumptive character. The nature of inference, which is common to such combinations and to subsumptive reasoning, has been explained in general terms in discussing the Essence of Inference, and will be more particularly examined when we have looked carefully at the type of Inference now before us.

In addition to what was said in the last chapter on the nature of Calculation, some more special remarks may be added here. Though Calculation may take the most varied forms, yet it must always depend in the last resort on the conception of a whole which is the sum of its parts. Enumeration is the synthesis of this sum out of, or its analysis into, the homogeneous parts or units themselves, through the correlative and all but identical processes of addition and subtraction. It is represented by such an equation as $3 = 1 + 1 + 1$. The changes of sides and signs in an equation exhibit the true relation of addition and subtraction. Multiplication and division are similarly correlative, and represent synthesis or analysis not by help of the ordinary unit, but by help of an artificial unit. The equation $100 = 10 \times 10$ represents multiplication and division alike, being simply an analysis or synthesis by means of a compound unit. Thus multiplication and division are more powerful than addition and subtraction, but less widely applicable, because the compound unit must be uniform. If you have ninety fives, the numerical system gives you the total in a moment as 450; but if you have such a succession of figures as 4, 5, 3, 7, 9, you have no identical compound unit, and must therefore proceed by the simple one, i.e. by addition.

In multiplying and dividing powers by help of their indices, the procedure (which governs I presume the use of logarithms) reverts to the form of addition and subtraction, that is, to the *apparent* enumeration of simple units instead of compound units. Thus the relation of 8 to 32 comes to be represented not by the *ratio* 1 : 4 (eight taken once compared with eight taken four times), but by the *difference* between 2^3 and 2^5. Multiplication proper was the construction of a quantity out of or. its analysis into an identical compound unit repeated so many times. Involution is the construction of a quantity out of or its analysis into a simple enumeration of the employments of a certain compound unit in multiplication by itself; that is to say in repetition of itself, or of a quantity generated by repetition of itself (the given compound unit), its own number of times. It is plain that as each step enumerated is a multiplication, or an employment of a factor in multiplication[1], in order to multiply or unmultiply (divide) one power by another we do not multiply or divide index by index, but simply count on or count off the number of acts of multiplication designated by one of the indices. Thus in dividing 2^6 by 2^3 we do not take 2^2 as the result, but 2^3— the *difference* of the two indices. In dropping from 2^6 to 2^3 we have counted off three multiplications by 2, and have thus reduced 64 successively to 32, 16, and 8. So far we are dealing with simple enumeration applied to a complex process.

It is possible of course to trace the same development further, and did the author's knowledge admit of his attempting the task, an interesting scheme of continuity in calculative processes might be obtained. When we come to powers of powers and roots of powers we are dealing with complex enumeration applied to steps consisting of complex processes. If the index of 2^6 is divided by the index of 2^3, the result 2^2 is obviously the cube root of 2^6; and if the index of 2^6 is multiplied

[1] To say 'each step is a multiplication' would *prima facie* mean that 4 should $= 2^1$ instead of 2^2. But yet it is not wholly false, for of course the difference between, say, 2^3 and 2^7 consists of *two* acts of multiplication by two, not of only one. In short, multiplication involves two factors, and would not be represented by enumerating only one to start with. In every further step the previous result is one factor in the process.

by the index of 2^3, the product 2^{18} is obviously the cube of 2^6. Here we are constructing by multiplication (complex enumeration) a quantity (18), the compound units 6 and 3 employed in the multiplication being themselves representative of simple enumerations of repeated processes of multiplication (complex enumeration).

Simple enumeration may of course itself be represented as the chronicle of a process, i.e. as consisting of units equal in number to the number of times the process has been repeated. Only in it, in arithmetical progression, the process, though applied to its own results, does not obtain the power of creating a progressive difference.

Calculation compared with argument.
γ. All arithmetical calculation, and therefore in the last resort all calculation whatever, may thus be reduced, I imagine, to enumeration, or, in some form, to enumeration of enumerations. And thus the entire method rests on the conception of the whole which is the sum of its parts—the universal whose differences, though distinguishable, are taken as equal and homogeneous. From the nature of this universal, in which the whole does not present itself as a concrete system, it is almost futile to enquire into the types and shapes which it assumes in inference. Is an Equation correlative to Judgment or to explicit inference? Is a combination of Equations necessary to explicit calculation, as a combination of Judgments is necessary to explicit Inference?

The Equation, it must be remembered, is a comparison of numerable relations in the *abstract*, and therefore corresponds not to any form of Singular or Perceptive Judgment, which are correlative to the simple Judgments of Enumeration, but only to a universal Judgment, and more especially to the pure Hypothetical. This is enough to show that the Equation is essentially of a synthetic or inferential character. And there is also a special reason why this character is more emphatically marked in an Equation than in a generic or hypothetical judgment. Every *judgment*—using the expression in the narrower sense in which it excludes equation—is liable if driven home to be accused of a fallacy *a dicto secundum quid ad dictum simpliciter*, for the concrete significance of the subject dwarfs and renders trivial the conditions under which alone the attribute can really attach, and some at least of these conditions are habitually omitted, or, if we prefer to say so, presupposed. But in the equation the whole content is homogeneous, and no one part can dwarf any other. We may not say that $99,999 = 100,000$. We must put in the condition, however trivial in real life, represented by $+1$ on the left of this equation, or -1 on the right. Therefore every equation, even the simplest, is not only hypothetical, but it is hypothetical on the basis of an explicit intellectual process or synthesis of differences. There is in this sphere no such thing as massing facts together, and leaving you to choose how you infer, or whether you really and conscientiously infer at all. To simply equate the whole with itself as a whole, as true Judgment, dealing with differences of attributes, may appear to do, must give tautology, and so nonsense, in Equation. Being debarred from even the appearance of such judgments as 'All Exogens are Dicotyledons,' the equation must always have on the one side or on the other an explicit synthesis of differences. It is therefore in itself a step nearer to explicit inference than the hypothetical judgment.

The Equation then exhibits an inferential connection more clearly than an ordinary hypothetical judgment. In respect however of not being a categorical assertion it is on the same level with that judgment, and only qualifies reality in virtue of the real element which underlies its hypothesis; i.e. pure arithmetical computation qualifies reality in as far as it expresses the properties of the system of number. $7+5=12$ means *If* five is added to seven we get twelve, and is categorical in as far as it involves the assertion, 'The system of number is such that "if five is added to seven," etc.' And as all prerogatives of a subject are absent (as is also the case with *pure* hypothetical judgments) no difference is more especially referred to Reality than the others. All are referred indirectly (i. e. through the system of number), and without priority.

The combination of equations bears the same relation to the single equation as the combination of judgments in explicit inference to the single judgment. In each case it is impossible to draw the line between the single act and the combination. An equation may be taken as involving any number of equational steps, just as a judgment may be taken as involving any number of intermediate judgments. In short, an equation, like a judgment, is the form of conclusion as well as the form of premise, and in ultimate analysis always partakes of both characters. But for this very reason there is no difference of principle between the single form and the combination, and it is sufficient in discussing inference to treat of the latter which has the advantage of being explicit. It may here be pointed out that as the equation is non-subsumptive, so the varieties and peculiarities of syllogistic figure disappear in the combination of equations. In every equated term or expression the whole is present in its entirety, and no form of it has any such peculiarity as we understand by the Universal, Particular, or Individual, —the subjects and predicates of the syllogism. This indifference corresponds to the nature of the numerical whole and renders arrangement and, apparently, number, of terms, in calculation a mere matter of practical convenience. But in every system of equations, *if bona fide treated as a single inference*, the three terms may be detected. Our insight develops along the chain of equation, and does not simply drop one term out and replace it by another.

Application of calculation.
ii. Lotze has treated of equational inference, i.e. of calculation, under the titles of substitutive and proportional inference, and of inference from the constitutive equation. I will comment briefly on the first of these forms at present, and will return to the others when something has been said of the matter to which they apply.

CHAP. II.]   *Equational Identification.*   57

a. The point of substitutive inference—which is described Substitu-
as a species of syllogism and as possessed of a major $\frac{\text{tive Infer-}}{\text{ence.}}$
premise—consists in substituting in the conclusion for the
middle term M the developed content of M as assigned in
the major premise, under the operation of a condition *s* representing the peculiar modification attaching to the minor
term S. The argument is thus written in symbolic form[1]—
    Major Premise $M = a \pm bx \pm cx^2 ...$
    Minor Premise $S = s\, M.$
    Conclusion $S = s\, (a \pm bx \pm cx^2 ...).$
This argument, in which a, b, c &c. represent any marks
within a concept, becomes efficient, as Lotze observes, only
when reducible to quantitative terms, because in other cases
the particular change effected by s in a or b is simply taken
from experience and is not really drawn from the form of
the argument, which might therefore just as well have
been thrown into an ordinary syllogism. But on the other
hand it is worth observing that if, in constructing such an
inference, we remain within the sphere of the *quantitative*
universal, then the relation of subsumption and the prerogative of the major premise necessarily disappear. We
have then simply two equational connections, related to an
identical whole, and therefore capable of giving rise to a
further connection. But M is not in that case generic, nor
is S specific, nor is the connection of S with $s\,(a \pm bx$ &c.)
known through their conjunction in and subordination to a
concrete individuality M. M is no doubt here the assigned
meeting-point of the relations, a form of the quantitative
universal which pervades the equational connection before
us, but S is no more a case of M than M of S. And indeed,
having once been led to observe the connection of S with
its development $s\,(a$ &c.), we no longer judge this true on
the mere ground of conjunction in M, but on the ground of
a systematic necessity revealed through M. S or s M, if it
is or has a true quantitative relation to M, cannot be *bona
fide* a *case under* M, an element in a concrete individuality

[1] Lotze, Logik, E. Tr., sect. 109.

or case of a generic nature M, and with this relation the whole idea of subsumption vanishes.

And the favourite and catching phrase 'substitution' must be similarly treated. Substitution is a consequence and not a principle of inferential relation. It arises from the identity of the whole with itself in all its forms, the discernment of which identity is the task of calculation. We may infer, to take a very elementary example, from $24 = 12 \times 2$, and $8 = \frac{24}{3}$, that $8 = \frac{12 \times 2}{3}$. We here 'substitute' 12×2 for 24, because we possess the connection which tells us that the former is a synthesis identical with the whole 24. To 'substitute' is simply to treat a whole as identical with itself.

This 'substitutive' inference then, in its mathematical shape, has no syllogistic character, no major premise, and no real dependence on a principle of substitution. It might fairly be spoken of as an inference by equational identification. It must include, so far as I can see, the entire range of strictly arithmetical computation, whether in algebraical or in arithmetical form, as contrasted with computation applied to geometry, mechanics, and physics. It establishes a ratio, for, logically at least, ratio is a genus of which equality is a species, but it does not *ostensibly compare* ratios, and therefore does not explicitly challenge problems in concurrent but heterogeneous series. But we must remember that *any* calculation which does not merely develop the properties of number depends for its meaning on *some* differences of real aspect correlative to the differences of numerical aspect. 'The shelf-space M of this shelf = the shelf-space required by thirty octavos.' 'I can have shelf-space which = 100 M, ∴ I can have shelf-space which = the space needed by 100 × 30 octavos.' Here no doubt we are dealing with homogeneous quantity—feet and inches—all through; but the wholes which are compared are differently motived, and these differences of motive—books compared with shelves, and one shelf with a library—are what give the inference its point. The next step is that these differences of motive affect the actual denominations of the units themselves. We come to deal in short not with simple equality—identity of number of the same units—but with equality of ratios, i. e. with *identity of the ratio* between the several quantities of a set, with that between the several quantities of another set or other sets. The unit of enumeration, in this case, must not be identical.

β. We must now break off somewhat abruptly to consider the apprehension of Connections in space and time, which must be treated for our present purpose as an independent root of knowledge, and must be investigated before we can proceed further with the analysis of calculation. Primarily no doubt the apprehension of these connections is an offshoot of the rudimentary judgment, which as we saw in Book I[1] must construct its world of Things largely under the influence of growing spatial and temporal discrimination. But starting as we have done in explicit inference with the developed concrete perception of the world of things, we have no choice but to assume also the developed abstract perception of relations in space and time. We reason from these relations or connections before we have subjected their elements to accurate enumeration or measurement, and it is the nature of non-numerical inferences from such relations that I now propose to consider[2]. 'A is to the right of B, B is to the right of C, ∴ A is to the right of C;' 'A is prior to B in time, and B to C, therefore A to C.' In such inferences as these, Mr. Bradley has told us, we first construct, and then perceive. I have expressed at length in another work, and briefly in the preceding chapter, my objections to employing the term construction as if it were a self-explaining account of an intellectual process. But I have conceded that when restricted to the sense of intellectual construction, neither imaginative nor physical, it affords an apt description of the peculiar work of inferential

Connections in Space and Time.

[1] Bk. I. chap. ii.
[2] See Bradley's *Principles of Logic,* p. 225 ff., which on this point I have followed very closely.

apprehension in the field of space, time, and motion. At all events we must, I think, agree with Mr. Bradley that in examples like those just given there is no *bonâ fide* major premise, and therefore no syllogism. The form 'A is to right of B, B to right of C, ∴ A to right of C' is so obviously the natural shape of the inference thus expressed, that we may be surprised at being reminded that, *qua* syllogism, it has the defect of four terms. To fulfil the syllogistic requirements we must set down as a major premise 'What is to the right of B is to the right of C,' or even 'What is to the right of B is to the right of that which B is to the right of.' In the latter case the entire content of the argument recurs in the minor premise 'A is to the right of B and B to the right of C.' Plainly this minor premise would carry the conclusion without a major.

It was the author's experience, when engaged in teaching elementary logic, that pupils had an invincible tendency to construct 'syllogisms' in one of these two types, the former of which is defective as a syllogism, and the latter unreal and ineffectual. In using the former, 'A to right of B, B to right of C, therefore &c.,' their instinct was just, so far as the argument to be expressed was not truly subsumptive. An extension of this just practice to subsumptive inference in which it becomes erroneous was no doubt the cause of Dr. Thomas Brown's remarkable view as described by Mill in an interesting passage[1]. The complementary error, to which also pupils are prone, is, in constructing a syllogism, to surrender the whole task of articulating the steps of the argument by simply putting as the major premise some syllogistic canon, in analogical argument some principle of analogy, or in 'constructive' argument such a general principle of construction as 'Whatever is to the right of B is to the right of that which B is to the right of.' It thus becomes necessary to mass the whole content of the particular infer-

[1] Brown thought the major premise *always* superfluous. See Mill's Logic, i. p. 225, sixth edition.

ence in hand within the minor premise. Wherever a syllogistic canon is taken as the ultimate major premise of inference, this error is committed. The error consists in taking out the active form of the inference—the intellectual function which the syllogistic or constructive arrangement expresses—and making this a mere portion of the content from which the inference is drawn. In drawing the inference the intellectual function is inevitably active, and the principle expressed in the major is no justification of the activity of this function, but merely a content on which it operates as it would on any other content, so that the explicit major really adds nothing to the argument[1]. *This* case, of subsumption under the principle of subsumption, needs itself to be subsumed under the same principle or another, and so on ad infinitum. Take 'A mark of a mark is a mark of the thing marked, growth is a mark of organic nature which is a mark of life, ∴ growth is a mark of life.' Here we have an act of subsumption under a principle of subsumption, which act itself falls outside the principle itself and needs justification in a prior syllogism, if the minor premise and conclusion needed justification in this.

On the other hand, subsumption does not allow the subject to be merely treated as a point of attachment, as is the case with abstract series in space or in time. If we tried to infer thus in concrete matter we should get something like Jevons' Added Determinants, which is an excellent example of inference that is almost necessarily fallacious, owing to the disproportioned effect of the same added determinant on two concrete conceptions. 'A child is a human being, A. B. is a big child, ∴ A. B. is a big human being;' 'Pericles rules Athens, Aspasia rules Pericles, ∴ Aspasia rules Athens.' The concrete subject in subsumption takes up the determinants into itself and transforms them in a way which we cannot predict. A woman's rule over her lover is not *in pari materia* with a statesman's

---

[1] See Bradley's Principles of Logic, p. 475; Hegel, Wiss. der Logic, ii. p. 151; and the Author's Knowledge and Reality, p. 275.

rule over a commonwealth, and a big child may be a very small human being. We must not try to read off conclusions from series in subsumptive matter as we can in space, time or number. Construction or abstract connection, on the other hand, deals with relations which bear on each other with systematic necessity, and which are not affected, or are assumed to be affected only within known limits, by the idiosyncrasies of the points of attachment. In 'A to right' etc. we take A to be a point or body in space; if not, the inference is unmeaning. Therefore in this sphere no premise has a prerogative, and the reciprocal modification of relations is constructed in the argument and not presupposed in the nature of the Subject. This characteristic of 'construction' applies to number, space and time, and to the mechanics of abstract matter.

The apprehension of relations in time needs no separate treatment in logic from that of relations in space. Apart from measurement, connections in time are not capable of any great complexity, seeing that they contain nothing that corresponds to a curve or angle in space. Mere succession is the relation of one set of changes to a permanent subject; but in this there is implicit from the first the idea of duration, which involves the elementary comparison by the permanent subject of two distinguishable sets of changes, each of which is *primâ facie* the measure of the other. There is no science of time in the sense in which geometry is the science of space. From this point of view it has been said that time is one degree more ideal than space; i.e. its essential character of successiveness falls outside the actual contact of events with sensation and exists for the most part in the ideal medium of memory. It is true however that the present has duration, and does not exclude succession. But in thus possessing duration, in spite of the fugitive character of actual sensation, the present of course displays an ideal nature which makes it continuous with temporal succession, a succession which pervades even the present itself.

CHAP. II.] *Pure Geometrical Reasoning.* 63

The intelligence in bringing order into the feelings begins by apprehending space or time and constructing its preconceived world in these forms. By developing them, however, into scientific characteristics of this material world, it further proceeds to idealise them into laws and proportions, and thus to take away their immediate and perceived character. The first step in this idealisation is the conception of absolute, standard, or uniform space and time, a conception which guides the process of measurement, but which is strictly speaking, in its common-sense form, an abstraction to which no real thing nor process corresponds. Constancy of ratio throughout the perceptible world is, as we saw[1], all that measurement can give us, and is what we really mean to assume. Uniform space or time, as embodied in a single series and not in a comparison, is a contradiction in terms.

γ. The apprehension of connections—even of explicitly mediate connections—in space and time does not necessarily involve the enumeration of parts with a view to precise measurement. Such apprehension begins, as we saw in Book I[2], with the perceptions indicated by 'Here' and 'There,' 'right' and 'left,' 'nearer' and 'further,' 'now' and 'then,' 'future' and 'past.' *Calculation applied to Geometrical Reasoning.*

But all these expressions involve a continuous series, and such a series is the beginning of measurement. The spatial elements however, the straight line, angle and arc, are not constructed by measurement but are given spatial relations, although the discovery of their properties cannot be effected apart from the comparison of quantities. I am not prepared to say that the identification of corresponding geometrical relations might not (in spite of the etymology of the word 'geometry') be prior to intentional quantitative comparison. Vertical angles, or right angles, or the triangles into which a rectangle is divided by the diagonal[3], might be seen to

---

[1] Bk. I. chap. iv.   [2] See Bk. I. chap. i.
[3] In elementary schools it is now the practice to familiarise young children with such relations as this, e.g. by folding square pieces of paper, first along

be *the same*, before numerical comparison was applied to sides, angular distances, and areas.

Apart however from definite history, nothing can tell us when an implicit character becomes explicit. It is certain that all developed consciousness of spatial and temporal connection must operate through quantitative comparison.

Geometrical and strictly mechanical reasoning is the endowment of the quantitative universal with control over the combination of homogeneous parts in space, or in space and time together. In this type of reasoning, though essentially 'constructive,' we are often reminded of subsumption by the peculiar working of the quasi-generic judgment.

The square and the cube are elementary and striking instances of the power of enumeration, i.e. of arithmetical ideas, to represent or to describe generically a purely geometrical relation. The 'square' of a number *is* not a square surface, nor does it, so far as I can see, display in itself the difference between the superficial and the linear unit. But such a number, or rather such a numerical relation, does indicate definite combinations of parts by which a square surface may be recognised or constructed, and therefore the numerical relation may for many purposes be regarded as equivalent to the surface. The *purely* homogeneous universal, *qua* homogeneous, already at this stage fails to grasp the nature of the content as such, whose structure is to be represented by the differences of the universal, but succeeds in a way unknown outside mathematics in presenting an adequate key to this nature.

I presume that the marvellous processes by which curves of all types have been subjected to the dominion of the equation must ultimately be regarded by logic in the same light as the relation of the square upon a line to the square

---

a line dividing them into equal rectangles, and then along the diagonal, thus exhibiting the equality of a right-angled triangle to a rectangle of the same height and half the base, both being halves of the same square. This is an equation, and so a measurement, but rudimentary in as far as unanalysed.

of a number. These processes do not, as I understand, exhaust the nature of the curves, but they exhaust a combination of directions and distances, referred to an assumed point, which can be given any required degree of accuracy in representing the curves. Hence, though numerical relations have not in themselves the aesthetic or mechanical attributes of the particular curves which correspond to them, yet the nature of space permits a curve to be adequately and unerringly constructed by putting together homogeneous parts, viz. distances, in accordance with these numerical relations. It is obvious therefore that by experience, if no otherwise, both aesthetic and mechanical attributes may come to appear as if directly legible in certain numerical relations considered as controlling spatial elements. In the case of curves these numerical relations or attributes are expressed in *constitutive equations*, and form by far the most striking examples of a transition from and through the homogeneous to the heterogeneous. But strictly speaking all the simple proportions which characterise e.g. the triangle or the square are examples of the same principle.

We spoke in Book I of this whole class of truths as 'quasi-generic judgments,' and insisted on the peculiar reversion which they display towards the type of concrete or organic totality. Never again in knowledge do we meet with such simple abstract and mechanical construction so unerringly analysing an individual and characteristic content. For this reason we are tempted to take the constitutive equation as the ideal of knowledge, and indeed *exceptis excipiendis* we are right in doing so. But the *excipienda* are serious. When we pass from abstractions like space, time and matter to the concrete evolution of the real world, to organisms, to political societies, and to human intelligences, not only is mechanical construction infinitely more difficult, but it is infinitely less adequate. A curve after all is a line in space, though it is not a straight line; so that it can be no such enormous leap to constitute a curve out of spatial elements. But a plant is hardly in the strict sense a phenomenon in space at all, and although a mechanical view of it, in a sense to be explained below, must certainly be aimed at by science, yet there will remain in it much to be *understood* which cannot be *constructed*— not *a part of its actions*, but *the whole result*.

If the constitutive equation is the type of quasi-generic judgment, it follows that Inference from the constitutive equation is the type of quasi-subsumptive inference. Such inference has two aspects. On the one hand it is pure calculation or combination of connections, like any mediate equation which has no meaning beyond the numerical system. It combines with a proportion between two changing quantities some particular values of these quantities, and follows out the modifications which result from this combination. This process is in itself, though more complex, yet not a whit more subsumptive or less purely calculative than to equate $2a$ with $3x$, and supplying any number as the value of a to fill in the number demanded by the proportion as the value of x. In such an expression a and x are merely generalised numbers, or numerical relations, or, if we like, names for a problem. There is no true major premise, but in its place there is the generalised description of an identical numerical whole in the two cases of being constructed with a factor 2 and with a factor 3, and the inference consists in exhibiting the construction of any such whole on the basis of these factors respectively.

If a and x represent distances in space defined by some further relations (e.g. perpendicular to each other or the like), and the whole expression has the effect of characterising a definite figure in space, then we have the germ of what I have called quasi-subsumption. The inference is still constructive in the narrow sense; it proceeds by enumeration of indifferent parts as in the case first considered. But it combines with this aspect another and a different one. It exhibits a particular portion of a particular curve in the light of a characteristic modification of a generic type. The curve may be closed or open, quick or slow, symmetrical or unsymmetrical. And these attributes, although they result from the construction, are not given within the construction. The spatial nature of the type of curve in question is the quasi-generic content through which the subsumption is made. It is not *pure* subsumption; for the construction would suffice in theory to draw out the *particular* curve before us and discover its properties, without ever giving it a generic name or observing that we are analysing the properties of something like a natural kind. And in fact, I presume, this is the usual order of procedure. Observations are obtained, upon which as data the curve is constructed, and its general nature is found only by means of this construction. But on the other hand, the mere fact that we know how to pass from an equational combination of numbers to a spatial figure shows that we are proceeding on a principle involved in the characteristic nature of such figures. The scheme of the argument is—

A spatial figure constructed on such proportions has such and such an outline;

This is a spatial figure constructed on *this* case of the above proportions;

∴ This has *this* particular outline.

The element of subsumption consists in the impossibility of passing from the ratio, which is only a generalised relation of numbers, to the markedly individual figure in space, except by identifying the subject in which the numerical relation and the characteristic curve-properties are conjoined as the nature of space, or, more closely, of a curve in space.

It only remains to mention that when we take in the unit of time, and thereby are able to represent motion as a length, and when we further erect the abstractions force and mass as correlative points of view from which motion is regarded as affecting bodies, we have all the *organa* of what may be called pure mechanism, or abstract constructive science—a complex and elaborate system, founded ultimately on the combination of three abstractions, space, time, and number. This abstract mode of consideration is true in so far as it applies to the characteristics of real things, but its application is obviously limited. The human body, for instance, is of course a case in which the geometrical and mechanical laws of space and motion have reality, but to a large part of its activity these laws in their purely abstract form have nothing to say. I proceed to discuss how and in what sense mechanism, and mediately, even *pure* mechanism, has a wider application.

Calculation applicable to Disparates. Proportion. δ. Lotze has spoken of inference from proportion as a limit of knowledge, and as assuming a type which from his description appears to be subsumptive, although he does not give it this name.

Homogeneous Terms. (1) I am unable to see that we have in proportion either subsumptive inference or a limit of knowledge, so long as the four terms of the proportion are either of the nature of abstract number, or are *in pari materiâ*, i.e. of the same denomination with one another. Numbers by themselves, it may be said, prove nothing, and computation in the abstract is not inference. But it seems obvious that the properties of the numerical system as such are worth establishing for their own sake. $2:4::3:x \therefore x = 6$ is not a worthless *type* of inference, although the example is one which has no interest. It depends on a relation within the numerical system, and is in itself, apart from its elementary character, as well worth establishing as any other consequence of an isolated abstract relation.

Or again, if we want to make a picture-frame of the same proportions with one that we have, but of different size, then all the numbers represent lengths, and we have, say, $16^{in.} : 24^{in.} :: x : y$; $x = 32^{in.}$; $\therefore y = 48$. In this example, however, the limit of which Lotze speaks is just beginning to make itself felt. All the numbers do no doubt in one sense stand for lengths in space; but they are lengths peculiarly related, in a way which falls outside the statement of proportion. *In the object to be constructed—*

this is the very reason for which we compare them—the one spatial length is to be at right angles to the other; or, in popular language, they are respectively length and breadth. Thus 16 and 24, and their correlatives x and y, are in one sense of one denomination, but in another sense of different denominations; and it is because they are of different denominations—or dimensions—that we have an interest in comparing them. Here moreover, as in geometrical reasoning, we come upon a trace of subsumption, because the essential identity which is the foundation of the inference consists in the nature of an object which has length and breadth, under which generic nature, as characterised by a certain ratio, we subsume a specific case of the same nature and of the same ratio. The meeting-point of the relations is a concrete and not an abstract, and this is the differentia of subsumption.

It would be easy to fill up many gradations of the appearance of heterogeneity in the terms of a proportion. First, the two *sets* compared cease to be measurable by any identical unit—whereas in the last examples both sides of the proportion *are* measurable as distances in space. Such are the proportions of times to distances and to areas, or of force to distance or to mass. And secondly, the several terms, either *in one set* or in both, cease to be strictly measurable by identical units. While this is the case with one side only, some sort of proportion may be supposed to exist, especially as the other side may present variations of a quantitative character, though not exhaustible by repetition of an identical unit. But when neither side presents a true ratio, i.e. when on neither side are the several terms measurable by an identical unit, then proportion is gone, and we are referred back or across to Analogy or Subsumption.

(2) Leaving the intermediate portion of these gradations for the reader to fill up, I pass at once to a class of proportions which prevail in a certain sense throughout the entire world of knowledge. I speak of related series of contents which might appropriately be designated '*a* and *a*' '*a* and *a* series.'

series. The examples which spring at once into the mind are the perceptions or sensations of light and sound, with their respective physical stimuli. It is true that in the connection of such series as these we come upon a 'limit of knowledge;' but it admits of question how far even in the most favourable instances of them we can be said to have proportional inference[1]. Perhaps the relation of angle to arc, which Lotze gives as an example, is about the extreme instance of true quantitative proportion which, although quantitative, includes heterogeneous matter.

When we look at the relation of musical sound to stimulus we find an ascertained parallelism between changes in the rapidity of periodic vibrations that reach the ear, and changes in pitch of the musical note which they generate in consciousness. And further, the changes in pitch are a continuous variation of a pervading quality and therefore are quantitative; and these are commonly measured by certain intervals of change taken to be equal in the sense of sharing certain attributes and capacities which remain the same for corresponding intervals in all parts of the scale. If we attempt to make out a proportional statement of these relations we may get some such result as a vibrations in second : 2 a vibrations in second :: note a : its octave a_1; a relation which admits of the quasi-subsumptive inference $a = 16\frac{1}{2}$ ∴ $a = $ a certain note x, and a_1 a certain note y.

[1] I suppose that 'irrational' in mathematical language designates a relation which cannot be expressed as a ratio, viz. as a relation between two numbers. It would seem then that 'incommensurable ratios' must be a contradiction in terms. The convenience of the expression in mathematics would not necessarily be interfered with by its self-contradictory character. Many conceptions which involve a more or less latent contradiction are employed in special sciences—quantitative infinity, or involuntary contracts, are well-known instances. It is interesting to notice that the reason of one science may be the unreason of another. Hegel complains that mathematicians call everything irrational in which reason begins to intrude—i.e. in which systematic heterogeneity begins to appear, e.g. in the relation between straight line and curve. Ratio is the reason of mathematics, and other systematic relations may be irrational *in this sphere*; just as ratio may be an irrational relation outside mathematics, e.g. in political science.

But this inference is by no means purely mathematical or quantitative.

First, we must notice the presupposed limitations, which do not exist in any purely mechanical or purely geometrical law. The vibrations must affect a hearing ear, and to affect a hearing ear they must be within certain limitations both of rapidity and amplitude, which from a mathematical point of view are wholly arbitrary.

Secondly, we must observe that not only, as in true cases of proportion such as that between the angle and the arc, are the two sets of terms incommensurable with one another, but also it is very doubtful whether the two terms represented by a and a_1 can be strictly called commensurable. In a sense no doubt the tones of the scale are units and serve as measures. But if we ask which note is 'twice' another, we are perplexed between the octave, which corresponds to twice the stimulus of the octave below, and the note, whatever it may be, which is next above the lowest audible note. For two of any identical unit ought to be twice one. But just as the zero of the common thermometer is not a zero of heat[1], so there is no sense in making the lowest pitch, or the point where pitch passes into separate sounds, a zero of pitch from which all its grades can be constructed by mere multiplication or superimposition. We may say, if we like, that the quantity is intensive, i.e. that the grades by which the greater is separated from the lesser amount do not persist in a distinguishable form beside or within the greater amount when it is attained. This, however, is only to say in other words that we are passing beyond a true quantitative relation. All true measurable quantity is extensive. In as far as it is *merely* intensive it is unanalysed, not referred to parts, and so not quantitative. Here we are between the two; we have *degrees* which are not parts, and of which the whole is in no strict sense a

---

[1] The idea of an absolute zero of heat does not matter for the present purpose, which is merely to illustrate the nature of a series which is not in a true ratio. See Mill's Logic, i. pp. 441 and 446.

multiple, but which not only exhibit an advance in themselves but *correspond* to parts of which *their* whole *is* a true multiple.

Then, thirdly, we are confronted here with something like a genuine subsumption. The correspondence of 33 vibration per second to a note x rests on a concrete relation, which we find but cannot construct, between an impact on the living person through the ear and a reaction in the soul of that person. It is by subsumption under this characteristic individuality that we justify the conjunction, not otherwise necessary, of periodic vibration and musical sound.

It should be noticed, too, as bearing on the concreteness of the operation which we are now considering, that loudness is a quantitative attribute of musical sound, and corresponds to a distinct feature of the sonorous vibrations, viz. to their amplitude, which I presume must on the whole diminish with increasing pitch. This ratio, and other analysable characteristics, fall within the same series of contents as that to which the correspondence between pitch and rapidity applies. We are thus in such a case far from being able to obtain a simple proportion between contents as wholes.

When we come to the colour-sensations, the individuality or disparateness of the *a* terms increases, and the quantitative relation, still traceable in sound, heat or pressure, becomes much more obscure if it does not disappear. Not to speak of the dark heat rays and the dark chemical rays, which mark differences in the action of the ether corresponding to no *saltus* in the ratio of vibrations, the transitions from colour to colour defy all attempt at quantitative expression. No one could mean anything by saying that central violet is twice or three times or five times central red, except in so far as colours may be characterised by an intensity of illumination which is a different thing from the peculiarity of their hue. It is needless to go into detail on this head. It is plain that while the variations in the mechanical stimulus, the *a* series, are still strictly numerable, the terms of the α series are altogether ceasing to present commensurable and therefore numerable differences in respect of their distinctive individuality, although various numerable differences may be traceable within their content. Then proportion in the strict sense wholly ceases to apply, because there is a ratio on one side only, and not on the other; and there cannot be equality of ratios unless we have two sets of matters with a ratio between the members of each set.

Nevertheless, there is in the colour series a uniform relation of a proportional character. 'Wave-length x : wave-length y :: violet : red' means not that red is such and such a multiple of violet, but yet that *in a series in which* wave-length x gives violet we can be sure that wave-length y will give red. And though these colours are not producible as multiples of one another, yet they are identifiable, on the assumption of correspondence to stimuli, by the process of colour-equation. Given the means for producing true spectral red, a problematic red colour can be equated with it, and the difference between the two stated in *terms of the stimulus.*

ε. We have here, it might be said, passed from Proportion to Analogy, which abandoning its original meaning of proportion has come to signify an *inexact* comparison of relations. But Analogy in the logical sense is not really an inexact form of proportion, but depends on other than quantitative considerations, as we shall see in the next chapter. And though we are now passing out of the region where equality of ratios would grasp and penetrate the whole essence of the subject-matter, yet there is no need to leave behind us either precision in the designation of relations, or such numerical attributes as accompany though without exhausting the individuality of contents. For these reasons it is better not to consider that we are here returning to Analogy, but rather that we are approaching, from the side of exact science, the hypothetical judgment,

Proportion, Analogy, and Hypothetical Judgment.

which forms the meeting-point between the concrete and abstract forms of inference. And the hypothetical judgment, especially when retaining a partially quantitative content, represents what may be called the wider or the philosophical sense in which mechanism prevails throughout the knowable world. In many regions it is not much that this view of things gives us; but it is always something.

It is needless to pursue this hypothetical judgment through all the gradations in which it embodies the idea of proportion throughout the sciences. Everywhere we have in the background the strictly numerable relations of space, time and mass. The exhibition of connected groups of contents as a and a series, in both of which the terms are as nearly as possible commensurable, is the ideal of natural science, or of *physical* science in the strict sense. How far in detail chemistry or biology may be reducible in this sense—for there is no other sense in which they can be—to molecular physics, is a question of fact and practice. At present it must often seem as if instead of a and a series we had rather a and x series, i.e. correspondences in which even the more quantitative series has hardly a true ratio between its terms, while the less quantitative series has no ratio at all. I have in my mind such correspondences as those between changes of temperature and allotropic phenomena in chemical agents, or again between changes of temperature and degrees of irritability in organic beings. But the changes of temperature themselves, considered as an a series, have behind them as a true a series their mechanical equivalents in the way of mass and motion (footpounds), and thus the whole phenomena, even those of allotropism, have ultimately a true correspondence with a genuine a series. Such a correspondence would form the content of a hypothetical judgment, under which quasi-subsumptive inference would be possible.

Consciousness and Conservation of Energy. ζ. It is under this modification of 'a and a series' that we ought to consider such a question as the relation of the physical changes in the human organism to the activities of consciousness. I am not now dealing with the sheer question of fact, whether in the human or other organism, considered as a machine, the production of work can be experimentally proved to be limited by the supply of mechanical energy. We know too well from daily experience that the output of work has gradations and a limit —a limit related at any rate *inter alia* to the supply of food. That this limit is prescribed by conditions precisely analogous to those which are embodied in the working of every machine, viz. by the constancy of energy, seems to be the natural assumption so long as no other principle of gradation and of limit is convincingly demonstrated.

But we now come upon a second difficulty. We assume that molecular change and muscular contractions in the organism must be taken as theoretically subject to the constancy of energy, i. e. that life or the soul so far as operative in or through the organism cannot create energy out of nothing[1]. These changes and contractions either are, or are reducible to, mechanical equivalents in motion and mass, and between them and the supply of energy a true a and a proportion might, if our knowledge permitted, be established.

But between either these organic changes or the expenditure of energy, on the one hand, and the states of consciousness which sometimes attend these changes on the other, no possible proportion could hold good. Here we have then a pair of series a and x (organic changes and consciousness) on the basis of a pair a and a (expenditure of energy and organic changes). It does not matter for our purpose here whether consciousness is independent work performed by the organism, or is an unaccountable

[1] I cannot think that Wundt, Logik, ii. p. 507, really means to deny this, though his expressions are bewildering. 'Hier (in the spiritual development) gilt vielmehr (as against the law of constancy of energy) ein Gesetz unbegrenzter Neuschöpfung geistiger Energie.' To judge from the Physiologische Psych. ii. pp. 461-3, he thinks that 'Geist' is operative throughout nature, and its 'creation of energy' must be a question merely of new *forms* of action. But I cannot thoroughly understand his view.

attendant upon such work which is not represented in its cost, or lastly, a consequence, or 'effect' if we like, of certain peculiar organic work, represented in the mechanical cost of such work, and inseparable from such work except by an utterly unmotived abstraction. In all of these cases we have, whether directly or through organic activities known to accompany consciousness, what may be called an a and a relation, or more truly an a and x relation mediated through a, between mechanical work and consciousness. But on the side of consciousness of course no ratio can be established, and therefore there is no proportion. We cannot safely say that to learn twenty lines of Virgil demands twice the expenditure of work that is needed to learn ten. We cannot say that to write the same letter requires the same exertion on one day and on another. We must however be on guard here. Interruption, a different state of memory, obstacles in the content, impair the reliability of what might seem a unit of mental work. But mere weariness of the organism which may lengthen the time taken and the apparent exertion demanded, seems only to affect the proportional and not the absolute work needed. What we have under such circumstances is merely a case of a weak machine doing slowly what a strong one does at one blow. The weak machine may however be destroyed by application to work too heavy for it, and in this sense even an identical unit of work has not always the same total effect.

If a unit cannot be obtained for the x or a series, what can our would-be proportion do for us? It enables us to say generally, though not precisely, that amount of even intellectual activity varies as expenditure of mechanical energy and is limited by the sources from which that energy is drawn; and further, to say precisely, though only as a hypothetical judgment of which the condition can never be entirely fulfilled, that if we could equate two amounts of intellectual activity, or if we could have the same intellectual activity repeated under the same conditions, we should find it had absorbed or had been accompanied by the same amount of mechanical work. There is, that is to say, a formal and constant correspondence between amount of mechanical energy and amount of intellectual work; but mechanical equivalence is so subordinate an aspect of such work that this constant relation tells us nothing by way of calculation, and only embodies in an abstract principle what we knew before—if he does not eat, neither can he think.

It may be objected that intellectual activity apart from molecular change, which latter is not intellectual, absorbs no work at all. But when any one can show us thought apart from an organism it will be time enough to speak of thought as an activity not dependent upon organic changes. *Prima facie* the complex molecular changes which accompany thought have thought for their natural outcome and consequence, and owe their high mechanical cost to this characteristic. That no mechanical expenditure goes directly to thought, but all goes to molecular change which is in some cases accompanied by thought, is only what we should naturally expect supposing thought to be conditioned by the activity of a physical organism. In any other case, i.e. supposing a contingent of energy to disappear into the thought-process and be unaccounted for in the balance-sheet of the body, we should have a proportionate amount of thought unaccompanied by material change, which is unknown in our entire experience and contrary to the whole analogy of that experience. All that we can say is that the *thinking being*, as we know him, is thus and thus conditioned. We cannot safely separate in theory what can never, to our experience, be separated in fact.

iii. Mechanism in the widest or ultimate sense is thus compatible with the disappearance of the ratio in both of the corresponding series. The principle of 'mechanism' is by this curtailment reduced to the law of Sufficient Reason, and simply expresses the point of view from which the

The Mechanical aspect of Knowledge.

scientific understanding necessarily and inevitably regards the world. This point of view is not a tyranny to be avoided, but a claim which must be satisfied. The Understanding is a necessary moment in the Reason. Instead of precise proportion, enabling us to construct or to predict by a formal process, we have in mechanical determination thus understood a conception which confronts us with a material problem. A man's character deteriorates, or the prosperity of a nation decays. The conception of mechanism or of sufficient reason entitles us to treat these phenomena as problems demanding explanation. They must not be miraculous, i.e. not isolated, ' cut off with an axe ' from the system of knowledge. We express this demand by saying that every change—or more generally, every modification—has its reason. It is only our tendency to illustrate the universal by the plural that makes us state the principle as if it necessarily applied to a number of examples in which the same ground has the same consequence. What we really mean is that every content is a consequent, and that every consequent has a ground. That the connection of ground and consequent is necessary, and therefore *if* the one is repeated without modifying circumstances *then* the other is repeated without modifying circumstances, is involved in the point of view from which we speak of ground and consequent at all. But what we primarily mean is objectivity, not uniformity.

Some uniformity, however, is for us a corollary from objectivity. The ultimate fact of knowledge, on which the objective relation of ground and consequent depends, is the existence of *systematic* connections. Now a system is a whole, a universal, an identity in difference. From the very beginning this is what we meant by something objective, something by which intelligence could agree with itself in the world of meanings. But such a system or identity, however heterogeneous the parts that enter into it, of course pervades all these parts as a common character. As we saw in the last chapter, if *a*, *b*, *c* are mere particulars, there is no bridge from the one to the other. A connecting quality there must be, although it need by no means take the shape of an immediate and simple quality. Thus in highly complicated matters we go back again to an earlier function of knowledge, and substitute equational comparison for exact enumeration. But the comparison is not here the ground of inference; the contents have the partly quantitative relation, which admits of such comparison, as a consequence of their systematic connection, but the grounds of inference lie in the systematic connection itself. Let the a series be the phases of the artistic individuality of a painter, and let the a series be a chronologically arranged series of pictures in which these phases display their effects. In such series we shall always have, among other processes of judgment and inference, a comparison by way of equation applied to pervading qualities as between phase and phase, and between picture and picture. No one would doubt that Turner's water-colour picture of Durham painted in 1836 has more of certain striking qualities commonly associated with Turner's art than that painted in 1802. But of course there would be no sense in saying that the one is twice or three times as ' Turneresque' as the other.

In series like these we have subsumption or abstract hypothesis—which latter is the bridge from mechanical construction to concrete systematic interference—according to the nature of the subject-matter. In tracing the phases of an artist's genius we have properly subsumption, the unity which operates being concrete and self-contained. But yet as regarded in the light of causal ideas the phase of mind may be distinguished from the picture produced, and the one regarded as the cause or ground from which, on the latent basis of a real individuality, the other necessarily issues. From this relative point of view the connection would be expressed by abstract hypothesis, ' If a_1, then a_2.' In this aspect everything in the universe may be referred to conditions outside itself, and nothing is free, complete, or self-contained. For to regard things thus is simply a phase or moment of knowledge, the phase which consists in determining every x in terms of some correlated y. Cause and condition, reason and ground, are only species of the generic idea which presides over thought of this type. But in ground we have as we saw[1] a conception in which the correlated terms tend to fall together, and to pass from being parts related within a system to being the system itself. The whole conception which we are discussing—the conception of 'sufficient reason'—is simply a corollary of or aspect in the ultimate nature of the universal, which is in other words the ultimate nature of thought itself. We have constantly reiterated that every universal is an identity in difference; and it is only the converse of this to say that every difference has a distinct and assignable place among the differences of a universal.

The statement of the principle of sufficient reason which was laid down above, 'There is no difference[2] without its reason,' may be illustrated by the formula in which Lotze[3] embodies it, $A + B = C$. This formula is intended to mean that a real subject A can only pass into a specific phase C under an assignable condition B. The 'proof' or analysis of the principle must be reserved for a later chapter. Here I am only dealing with its import. And we see its import reduced to the most abstract type when we are in a stage beyond proportion and yet have not returned to true subsumption, i.e. when we are dealing with the pure hypothetical judgment. For we have at this stage a *de facto* correspondence of which the ultimate ground is more or less latent, between the terms a and a, b and β, and so forth. What then do we mean by correspondence? We could not say that a and a correspond if a and a were respectively isolated occurrences of their kind. For what could possibly justify us in picking them out of the myriad

[1] Cp. Bk. I. chap. vi.
[2] P. 78, above. It is commonly worded 'there is no *change*,' etc., but I have attempted to show in Book I. chap. i. that change is simply a case of difference and needs no separate logical treatment.
[3] Logik, sect. 63.

complications of reality and attaching them together to the exclusion of other events and relations? Correspondence involves the recognition of a universal which fixes the relations of the terms that correspond. If the series a, b, c is to *correspond* to the series a, β, γ, then both series, simply in order to the possibility of selecting them, must be capable of being regarded as a_a, a_b, a_c and a_a, a_β, a_γ. If in a combination of musical sounds a slight harshness a is raised to a discord b, then the consequent feeling of pleasurable excitement a passes into a feeling of pain β. In virtue of being phases of the same combination the two sounds may be represented as a_a and a_b respectively; and the two phases of emotion, in virtue at any rate of relation to the same series of sounds, may be represented by o_a and o_β respectively. But neither sounds nor feelings, of course, are terms between which a ratio subsists. What we can infer is, by a process which is half-subsumption and half-hypothetical judgment, 'In a pair of series where the sound a_a causes the feeling o_a, the sound a_b will cause the feeling o_β.' When we develope any such doctrine as that the source of pain is intermittent irritation of sense, of which musical discord is a species, we pass into subsumption of the higher kind, which has absorbed into itself what can be done by mechanical construction.

The point of view which we have been considering—that of reflection and relativity—is the point of view which has been distinguished by Kant and Hegel as the standpoint of the understanding. It is not separable in kind from the mode of consideration which the same thinkers have designated by the term Reason. Nor is it an intelligible contention, even if favoured by the language of Kant in dealing with practical philosophy, that Reason could be actual and operative otherwise than as completing and containing the understanding. That the understanding must have its rights is one of the cardinal principles of Hegel, which Lotze has but laboriously and ingeniously illustrated in his analysis of the pervading mechanical aspect of the world. The real prophet of the understanding, however, was Schopenhauer. His treatment of the principle of sufficient reason as at once the fundamental axiom of human science and the innate source of its illusions, forms an ultimate and irreversible criticism on the aspect of intelligence which consists, to sum up its nature in a popular but not inaccurate phrase, in explaining everything by something else—a process which taken by itself is necessarily unending and unsatisfying.

In returning from the consideration of abstract necessary relations to that of concrete real totalities, we must remark that ideally speaking every concrete real totality can be analysed into a complex of abstract necessary relations. Were this not so, as it is Wundt's and Lotze's great achievement to have shown in detail, teleology itself would vanish. For adaptation disappears if the end can dispense with means, and a universe which had no necessary connections between its parts could have no definite or significant structure as a whole. In the remainder of the present Book I shall attempt to put these relations in a clearer light.

CHAPTER III.

ANALOGY.

WE now take up the thread from the end of sect. 1 of the last chapter, and returning into the track of concrete inference, we have to ask ourselves how we go forward in inference from a simple enumerative Induction when we do *not* accept the task of completing the enumeration. In this case we no longer count the examples, but we weigh them. We turn the focus of attention upon the concrete content which as subject of both premises, as a real thing or things, formed the middle term of Induction, and endeavour to deepen it by observation, and to define its relations by analysis. The first effect of this procedure is to transform the content in question from a subject into a predicate, as no longer a qualification tacitly presupposed of reality, but as an attribute explicitly referred to it and under process of definition and extension.

1. As regards the relation between Analogy and Enumerative Induction, we have to remember that Induction only gave us a problem or suggestion; and consequently we cannot arrange the two types of inference in a simple concatenation by taking the Inductive conclusion as the analogical premise. Rather we have in Analogy to go back upon the suggestive process of Induction, and repeat it with the requisite difference. Suppose that the Inductive Inference or grounded conjecture has been— {Analogy and Enumerative Induction.}

The poor people *a b c d* are pauperised *x*;

The poor people *a b c d* are constantly cared for by charitable persons *y*;

∴ Being cared for by charitable persons *y* may have to do with their being pauperised *x*.

If now we desire, as we ought, further to examine this

suggestion on the basis of the direct experience which generated it, we shall still make this experience—the cases *a, b, c, d* —the middle term or ground of inference, but we shall divert our attention from the number of the examples to their nature, and shall therefore put their nature as an attribute in the place of a predicate common to both judgments. Thus we obtain an argument having a form akin to that of the Aristotelian second figure. And the premises are now no longer conjunctive individual judgments, but are passing into generic judgments.

In the pauperised type x, what strikes us on further examining the cases is the loss of independence (A as common content of *a b c d*);

In the charitably-cared-for type y, what strikes us on further examining the cases is the loss of independence (A as common content of *a b c d*);

∴ The type y has a fundamental feature A akin to the type x and the two are thus closely coherent.

We are apt to think that in analogy we must conclude from old instances to new instances. But analogy is essentially an argument about the significance of a type, or of what in botany are called characters. Of course however this inference, like all others, has the aspect of discovery as well as the aspect of proof. The deeper theoretical need is to find the link and limit of connection between the characters x and y sometimes observed in conjunction, i. e. to *prove* the one of the other. But the reality of the distinction between x and y which gives interest to the inference makes it practically certain that in some examples we shall be first struck by y and in some first by x, and that we shall often need to make the circuit through the identical nature A before we can even detect or have ground to believe in the remaining character x or y. This is the aspect of discovery. Proof overcomes logical disconnection, discovery overcomes apparent presented disconnection. Thus our account of Analogy can really satisfy the popular idea that inference is, here as in Induction, from particulars to particulars.

I subjoin one or two simple examples, in order to illustrate the connection of proof and discovery, and the working of the process.

Enumerative Induction (*or* observation in single instance).
Almost all animals have some power of self-movement;
Almost all animals have some degree of sentience;
∴ Sentience may be intimately connected with self-movement.

Analogical Enquiry.
Self-moving creatures are creatures in need of special nourishment and protection (*qua* living creatures);
Sentient creatures are in need of special nourishment and protection (*qua* living creatures);
∴ Sentience is connected (by the requirements of animal life) with self-movement.

I may give another instance which shows the transition from Induction to Analogy just *not* made. Newton guessed[1] that a diamond was combustible because of its high refractive index relatively to its identity, a feature which he had observed in many combustible bodies.

Enumerative Induction.
Oil, Canada balsam, &c. are combustible;
Oil, Canada balsam, &c. have a high refractive index relatively to density;
∴ High refractive index may be connected with combustibility.

In the case of the diamond the combustibility had not been observed, so that when applied to it the conclusion was a prediction or discovery. But the essential import of the conclusion would have been just the same if no new case had been in question.

The next step would have been to say—
'Combustibility has to do with such and such attributes of oil, Canada balsam, &c.
High refractive index has to do with these same attributes.

[1] See Mill's Logic, ii. p. 88. I write merely on the faith of the place in Mill. The instances by which I illustrate Newton's guess are therefore of my own invention.

∴ High refractive index is fundamentally connected with combustibility.'

But this step, which would have constituted an analogical inference, has not, as I understand from the passage in Mill, been taken.

We may now look at an instance drawn from the relation of natural kinds.

Enumerative Induction.

> The exotic Pelargonia have a peculiar herring-bone structure in the petals;
> The exotic Pelargonia have the same kind of seed-vessels as our wild geraniums;
> ∴ In flowers with the peculiar seed-vessels of our wild geraniums it is worth while to look for the herring-bone structure in the petals.

Analogy.

> The herring-bone structure is conjoined in the Pelargonia with the characters of Geranieae;
> The flowers with such seed-vessels as our wild geraniums have the characters of Geranieae;
> ∴ That these flowers, e.g. our wild geraniums, should have the peculiar herring-bone structure[1] is exceedingly probable.

Botanical classification might almost be said to rest wholly on analogy. The above guess, like a thousand and one such guesses which every field botanist is continually making, is verified in fact. The eye that can detect the dominant habit of a natural *genus* or order in an unfamiliar species is constantly inferring in analogical form, on the ground of generic identity, to hundreds of details, which as as a rule confirm its diagnosis on more minute inspection. And the term diagnosis, logically applicable, but not

---

[1] As a matter of fact, all the Geranieae which I have examined possess this structure. I might have mentioned this verification immediately after the Induction; but this would really take us into mere enumeration of instances. It is the coherence with the properties of a natural kind that alone gives any help towards a general conclusion.

customarily applied, to botanical science, reminds us of another great province of knowledge in which analogical inference is our guide and counsellor. As in the normal so in the abnormal activities—the diseases—of the organic world, it is analogy that is the chief clue to what is taking place and to what we must anticipate. Diagnosis is to symptoms what classification is to characters. And finally we may here mention the class of examples to which we shall shortly return as throwing the strongest light upon the true *rationale* of analogy, although or because they tend ultimately to pass beyond its province. I mean our judgment of the actual use or even of the intentional object of mechanical adaptations of every kind, whether in nature or in the work of man. Thus we may infer by Analogy,

Cutting-tools have edges, and places for handles;
These flints have edges and places for handles;
∴ These flints are cutting tools.

Here we go at once to analogy, without passing through the observation of conjunctions as a *first suggestion*. It is not simply from seeing handles and edges conjoined in knives or chisels that we know a cutting-tool must have a handle and an edge. We know this from extraneous considerations, especially from the texture and use of the human hand. But nevertheless we might never have discussed the coherence of these attributes if we had never seen them in conjunction; and further, in the new instance of the flints, we have had to go through a process of observation which told us that here too there were both edges and handles or places for handles. Thus the present example illustrates at once the true nature of analogy, and the ground and degree of its dependence on Induction. The observation 'Flint tools have edges, flint tools have handles,' does not linger in the stage of induction, simply because we are not dependent on the nature of flint tools to tell us the connection in use between a handle and an edge. We leap at once to this notion of cutting-tools, and compare the flints with them in respect of the conjoined attributes which we try to deepen and define.

Logical criticism of analogy.

2. The logical nature of analogy may be analysed as follows.

Undistributed middle in fig. 2.

i. As a formal syllogism in the second figure, having an affirmative conclusion, the analogical argument has the fallacy of undistributed middle. We need not indeed trouble ourselves at this stage with questions of distribution involving the extension of the judgment. Nevertheless a fault in the extensional relations of an argument infallibly indicates something which is *primâ facie* a fault in its connection of content. In the present case the fault is this—that what is materially the ground of Knowledge, the content which underlies and links together the two matters which demand explanation, is, *qua* predicate or characteristic, in its wrong place, the place of a *consequent*. Now according to the ordinary interpretation of the judgment, of which we have frequently spoken and which holds good for our present level[1], the same consequent may have any number of independent grounds. . There is therefore no formal necessity whatever for the two grounds or antecedents which in this case possess the same consequent to have any connection with each other beyond the fact that they do possess it.

But on the same ordinary interpretation of the judgment if we deny the formal consequent of either of the grounds while affirming it of the other, we can then deny that the two grounds in question are connected through the universal suggested in the premises before us. Thus the negative argument escapes the formal defect which attaches to the affirmative. About any further or other connection that they may or may not have the denial tells us nothing, and therefore it is really a denial not of all or any connection, but of a particular connection through a particular middle term. The customary omission in the conclusion

[1] For the judgment is not purged of irrelevancy till it has passed through *scientific* induction.

to specify the excluded connexion is a fallacy *a dicto secundum quid ad dictum simpliciter*. It may be said that the denial takes on the absoluteness of the assertion on which it rests. 'Every Tory is a good man; He is not a good man; ∴ He is not a Tory.' If the major is true without reserve the conclusion is true without reserve, and in logic we are to suppose our premises true. But still we must consider what the judgment means, i.e. what it really is. And no judgment is absolutely meant. The conclusion does not really represent the inference as a concrete thought unless we repeat in the conclusion, 'He is not a Tory, so far as his not being a good man prevents his being one.' This refinement has no exclusive relation to analogical argument or to fig. 2, for the negative argument falls into fig. 1 as readily as into fig. 2, the ground and consequent in negation being reciprocal. In order to give the criticism a peculiar relation to analogy we must say, 'He is not a Tory, so far as the peculiar way in which he is not a good man prevents his being one.' This positive way is variable.

Except then for the purpose of negative inference, which is not purely analogical, the form of analogical argument in fig. 2 is at variance with its matter, and represents no inferential necessity at all. Inferential necessity is either subsumptive or constructive. In order to obtain subsumptive necessity one of the premises would have to be converted and become a major premise. And this conversion would have to be material, not merely formal; for a formal conversion of an affirmative generic judgment would destroy its generic character and make it incapable of standing as a major premise. The Analogical inference as it stands shares with enumerative Induction the peculiarity of being a subsumptive inference without a major premise—an argument from a concrete content without the assertion that this content is absolutely dominant for the purpose of the argument. Again, in order to obtain constructive or abstract necessity the relations of the contents must be reduced into abstract and mechanical relations akin to the universals embodied in the pure hypothetical judgment or in the equation. The formal defect of analogy as it stands is expressed by the 'probably' inserted in the conclusion, which indicates a coherence under conditions not precisely known.

Real value of Analogical Argument.

ii. Seeing that the form of analogical argument is *prima facie* inconclusive, on what does its value really depend? It represents, we said, the phase of thought in which we no longer count but weigh the examples. It might be said therefore that analogy is a material and not a formal inference. This is so far true that the value of analogy depends not on a formal conjunction of attributes in a subject, but on the material governing power or essentiality of a predicate. Everything turns on the 'importance' of the character which forms the common predicate, and this 'importance' is closely bound up with completeness of definition. I will return directly to the question of the importance of characters; but it is necessary first to point out that an inference without assignable form is no inference at all, and that therefore it is not correct to say that analogy is a material and not a formal inference. Every inference has a form, in the sense of a definite relation between the differences of the universal which the inference exhibits. I do not however mean to say that such a form can be laid down antecedently for every inference. It is this relation, as we have seen, which varies with the nature of the universal, and which by its variations dictates the main types both of judgment and of inference. We need not here take refuge in the form of complete subsumption through the conversion of one judgment. When that is possible—and no doubt analogy is on the road to it—we are already beyond analogy. But the form of analogical argument is to be found in the neglected aspect of the ordinary judgment, its strong *implication* of a value in the predicate. If all judgments were taken as reciprocal, analogy would be *ipso facto* an argument from ground to consequent, *besides* being as it is now from consequent to ground. 'Two grounds that have the same consequent *ought* to cohere,' is the form as it stands. 'Two grounds that have the same consequent are consequents of the same ground, therefore *must* cohere,' is the *implied* form, or, as we said above, the matter of the inference. This form might be identified with fig. 3, and so take us back to Enumerative Induction. But the content being changed from instances into their defined nature, we are rather taken forward into the hypothetical judgment as used in constructive inference, or to complete subsumption in fig. 1. With reciprocal judgments the syllogistic form becomes indifferent; and the premises of analogy are implicitly reciprocal[1]. That their reciprocity is implicit and not explicit is in accordance with the nature of analogy, which is as we have agreed only a method of problematic conclusion, not a method of absolute and precise determination.

I now return to the question of the material 'importance' of characters, the attribute on which the implicit form of analogical inference depends. It is possible, and is verified in daily experience, that a character or group of characters from which the remaining properties of an object cannot at present be derived by mechanical analysis may either amount for inferential purposes to a ground, or at least may serve as an unerring index of the qualities of the object. Such a character or group of characters, and I may add such a symptom or group of symptoms, has logical 'importance.'

I will commit myself at once to the opinion that this importance rests in every case on a presumption drawn from

---

[1] The explicit form is A is B ;   The implicit form is B is A ;
    C is B ;   B is C ;
    ∴ C is A.   ∴ C is A.

But the implicit form deals not with mere instances as in Induction, but with *that* B which was found to be essential in A and C. Therefore the whole implied argument is—

If B, then A (which is also a sign of B);
If B, then C (which is also a sign of B);
∴ If C, then B and therefore A.

what I may call morphology, or from teleology; these two ideas being regarded as secondary and primary forms of the same conception. In all objects or institutions made for a purpose by man, at least while their nature corresponds to the intention embodied in their structure, there is true teleology. In all organisms, parts of organisms, objects or structures that live a life or have in any way a being that is to our eyes individual and distinctive, there is morphology or *de facto* teleology. I am aware that a *de facto* teleology is a contradiction in terms. Purpose implies more than actual result. But as a description of a result in language borrowed from a result of another class—from human operation—the phrase though contradictory may pass; and it is in this sense alone that I employ it. If there is a peculiar principle underneath this ambiguous class of results, it is at least not, within our knowledge, a principle of intentional adaptation by a foreseeing consciousness. But I repeat that every universal, every persistent identity in difference, just because it is a synthesis of differences in a universal, may be regarded as a concentration of means in a distinguishable result. How far such a view is 'subjective' or in what sense it renders a real aspect of the nature of things is a question to which I shall return.

It is on this characteristic of all universals that anticipation by analogy rests. Where we have a constitutive equation, i.e. an absolute rule for the synthesis of the differences, we can construct without teleology and without analogy. If, again, according to Bacon's dream, science could arrive at 'forms' or underlying qualities, capable of doing the work of constitutive equations for every natural attribute and every natural object, then in presence of such a form we should not need analogy. Or where complete concrete subsumption prevails, where we have actual conscious teleology, e. g. in the philosophical analysis of laws, institutions, opinions, logical activities, we should never need analogy but for the all-important fact that all these contents are determined by growth and history in a way of which those who make and use them are not aware, and which they cannot control. Hence all such matters have an organic and almost a mechanical side, and can be treated by comparative science—analogy, as well as by philosophy —analysis. No actual law or institution or idea has its form exclusively determined by its explicit purpose. All of them are loaded with inherited matter which may in part be an incumbrance, but in large part serves purposes wider and not less essential than the purpose which consciousness is able to recognise. And in human affairs there is a bridge between the unconscious and the conscious function; for the latent purpose—which as latent is not a purpose at all—is actually one side of the explicit purpose and is continually emerging into explicit consciousness, so that the *de facto* operation of human energy in one stage *characterises* the explicit purpose of that stage itself and *enters into* the explicit purpose of the next. Thus philosophy can deal with even latent or unconscious significance partly as an aspect and partly as a condition precedent of conscious significance. The history of religion or of any achievement of man's intelligence is inexhaustible in illustrations of this principle. Precise knowledge, however, whether affirmative or negative, whether constructive or subsumptive, excludes anticipation by analogy, for analogy is a stage on the road to precise knowledge [1]. This condition satisfies the popular requirement [2] that in Analogy we must know neither necessary connection nor necessary exclusion.

To explain the connection of Analogy with Teleology, I will at once take the strongest class of examples.

We are on the border between analogy and a higher form of inference when we argue from a presumed genuine teleology to the conjunction of qualities in the content that it governs. We are so far already outside analogy that the argument must consist largely of judgments upon actual mechanical adaptations, the *de facto* use of which is a matter of precise knowledge and not of presumption. We

[1] Compare however p. 231 supra.   [2] Mill's Logic, ii. p. 88.

are not wholly outside analogy, because the *de facto* nature of these adaptations is not enough, in the case supposed, to carry our conclusion, which needs the actual and intentional purpose. This, in inferences of the type supposed, can only rest upon presumption. If we find, near a known seat of stone-age inhabitants, some flints of peculiar shape and make, it is a mere judgment on a matter of fact to say whether they *are* adapted for use as knives or as hatchets ; but to say what they *were* meant for, and so actually used for, and therefore whether we may expect to find near them chips of wood or bones of animals, is a question for analogical inference based on the nature of the country, on the known or supposed habits of the people, and on any convergent indications in the adaptations of the flint tools themselves. Any character in such a connected group of characters, that gives the key to the pervading purpose of the whole content under examination, is an 'important' character. 'Importance' is relation to the purpose or pervading nature, the 'import,' of any system. If both qualities to whose coherence we conclude are directly derivable from the presumed purpose, then we are so far beyond analogy, but the element of presumption which consists in ascribing true intention or purpose is still analogical. If one or both of the qualities to whose coherence we conclude are not derivable from the pervading purpose, then we are more completely or quite completely in the region of analogy, and the inference will simply be that identity of purpose is probably both a ground and also a consequent of uniform structure.

In the former case, both properties being derivable, we have :—

The flint knives *are* adapted for cutting wood ;
Cut logs and chips *are* connected with cutting wood ;
∴ Cut logs and chips[1] will probably be found near the knives (i. e. *if* the adaptation which we observe in the knives is a true index of the use for which they were

---

[1] I omit, merely for brevity, to say anything about the possibility of the chips &c. having been removed.

really made, and to which—a further presumption—they were actually put.

Or again :—

A telescope with the eye-piece at one side of the tube is probably a reflector;

Lord Rosse's telescope is a reflector;

∴ Lord Rosse's telescope probably has the eye-piece at one side of the tube.

In the latter case we have, one or both properties being not directly derivable from the presumed purpose,—

A clock with a watch movement is a carriage-clock;

A clock with plate-glass sides is a carriage-clock.

∴ A clock with plate-glass sides is probably a clock with a watch-movement.

There are pendulum clocks with plate-glass sides, so the analogy is not made out. There is a reason why a clock with a watch movement should be a carriage clock, viz. that it is a mechanism which the motion of the carriage will not disturb. But there is no reason that I know of for the second premise, which rests on mere custom and turns out to be a precarious basis of argument.

Or again :—

A horseshoe-stand is a common shape of French microscope-stands;

A very simple stage is common in French microscope-stands;

∴ With a very simple stage one may expect a horseshoe-stand;

The horseshoe shape is not the best for securing steadiness, so that there is no direct connection between the two properties of which the conclusion alleges the conjunction, and the purpose indicated by the name microscope-stand. And I have purposely introduced a limitation referring to the character of the conditions under which the purpose is carried out, ' *French* microscope-stand,' in order to illustrate the boundary-line between genuine conscious teleology and mere characteristic individuality. Probably in this example the two join hands; French makers must have, or have had, an idea that the horseshoe shape and the simple stage best secured the purposes of the microscope.

The former set of examples, with both properties derivable from the purpose, illustrate the general type of analogical inference affecting attributes connected with self-preservation in the organic world—chief or fundamental attributes. The latter, with one property or neither derivable, gives the general type of analogical inference affecting attributes which are not vital, but which have in heredity or otherwise their own degree of constancy. But these examples, though illustrative of organic relations, are by their connection with conscious teleology upon a higher level than those relations.

A further class of inferences, to which the last example prepared a transition, is intermediate between conscious and merely organic teleology. I allude to the enormous class of daily inferences relating to time or locality of origin or to authorship, in the case of literary, artistic, or mechanical productions. Obviously the conception of the presumed period, place, or person, as significant of peculiar characteristics, may itself be the presumed ground of inference in virtue of which the coherence of certain properties is analogically expected; or the individual characteristics stated explicitly may be the ground, and the name may be inferred by analogy. Supposing a single conjunction (Inductive in its nature) to have furnished the suggestion 'This design which is beautiful is by A. B[1],' then analogical enquiry will infer in the form 'The beauty of this design is drawn from nature yet original and full of thought; A. B.'s designs are drawn from nature yet original and full of thought; ∴ The beauty of this design is probably the beauty of one of A. B.'s designs.' The reader can construct further variations of this very common type of argument for himself.

The common analogical inferences which run throughout

[1] In the form: 'This design is beautiful. This design is by A. B.'

our treatment of organic and even of inorganic nature rest practically on the existence of natural kinds, that is to say, on morphology or on *de facto* teleology. I may explain the distinction of degree which I attach to the two expressions by reference to the general conception of self-maintenance or self-preservation. Where self-maintenance means simply any reaction of a distinguishable agent against or upon an influence approaching it from without, I should speak of the distinguishable individuality of that agent as morphological, i.e. as consisting simply of a formal or recognisable self whose unity is charged with no especial interest. Where on the contrary there is a self maintained or preserved which exhibits the attributes of life, or, however partially, of consciousness, I should say that the facts, and not our own choice, demand that we should apply the paradoxical idea of an *actual purpose*, or *de facto* teleology. It is obvious that the conception is one varying in degree and not limited by any despotic necessity to the range of the organic world. After all, it is a plain fact that elements combine in processes; and the moment we single out part of a process as a result we introduce the conception of *de facto* co-operation on the part of means towards an end. Every distinguishable persistent content may thus formally be regarded as an end, without, of course, any implication whatever of an aim pre-existing in a foreseeing consciousness. That from a purely mechanical or analytic point of view such constituent relations are absolutely indifferent to the whole which they co-operate in constituting is a necessary consequence of regarding such relations in their isolation. But without the further aspect supplied by an interest in the whole as such, not merely ethical and aesthetic judgment, but scientific judgment itself, loses all power of discrimination, and therefore all objectivity. Even to name, as we saw in the Introduction, is to select and to identify.

Analogy then rests on the 'importance' or significance of attributes, an idea well illustrated by systems of true conscious teleology which happen to be but partially known to us, but really dominant throughout the various grades of actual self-maintenance and individuality presented by the organic and inorganic world. Analogy is never demonstration. A thorough mechanical nexus and a subordination to a conscious purpose in an intelligent being or rational system both *pro tanto* exclude it.

<small>No ratio of Identities to Differences.</small>   iii. The obvious truth that *ceteris paribus* the predicate with more meaning has a deeper grasp of the import of the reality which it qualifies, and so is the safer ground of inference respecting that reality, has introduced the fatal fascination of the ratio into the doctrine of analogy. I quote from Mill[1] a complete account of the idea so generated: 'Since the value of an analogical argument inferring one resemblance from other resemblances without any antecedent evidence of a connection between them depends on the extent of ascertained resemblance, compared first with the amount of ascertained difference and next with the extent of the unexplored region of unascertained properties; it follows that where the resemblance is very great, the ascertained difference very small, and our knowledge of the subject-matter tolerably extensive, the argument from analogy may approach in strength very near to a valid induction. If, after much observation of B, we find that it agrees with A in nine out of ten of its known properties, we may conclude with a probability of nine to one that it will possess any given derivative property of A. If we discover, for example, an unknown animal or plant, resembling closely some known one in the greater number of the properties we observe in it, but differing in some few, we may reasonably expect to find in the unobserved remainder of its properties a general agreement with those of the former; but also a difference corresponding proportionately to the amount of observed diversity.'

This passage gives us the valuable suggestion of negative analogy, to which I shall return below. But as to the idea

[1] Mill's Logic, ii. p. 90.

of ratio, we must be faithful to our principle that in analogy the examples—or the properties, it matters not which—are to be weighed and not to be counted. Mill's idea is in fact that by counting the properties you weigh the examples. And every one must be struck by the verisimilitude of the view which the above passage propounds. But on pressing the matter home we see that at least the form which it gives to the right idea of insisting on the depth of the common predicate is a wholly unreal form, and takes us into the wrong track. There is no ratio without a unit; and, to begin with, a 'resemblance' (a point of identity) is not as such a content that can be employed as a unit. It is impossible to say what is a point of identity and what amounts to many such points. Identity is systematic through and through, and its 'points' derive their value from their relation to a system. It is impossible to break up such a system into numerable parts and points without prejudging the very question—the question of their respective values as index-qualities—which the enumeration is supposed to be a straightforward method of solving.

It is worth while to illustrate this point. Suppose that we are asked to compare two given plants of different species in order to determine their botanical affinity on analogical evidence — on the evidence of observed resemblances or points of identity matched against observed differences. In order to meet the retort that affinity in botany is what we like to make it, by the arbitrary value which we attach to the characters, I will assign to affinity the definite meaning of relationship by descent as indicated through the accepted natural classification. Thus the actual fact to be discovered by analogy, put at its lowest value, is how the plants in question are classified in the accepted natural classification, and put at its highest value is how the two are related by descent. Let one of these two given plants be a shrub six feet high, with branches and stalked leaves, with its inflorescence in branching masses, without any 'bract' or small leaf at the base of each mass, with white flowers, with nearly black fruit, and when young having its leaves covered with silky hairs. Let the other plant be herbaceous, six inches high, not branched, with no stalks to its leaves, its flowers in heads which do not branch, but which have four conspicuous yellowish 'bracts' at the base; the flowers are purple, the fruit red, and the leaves have only a few hairs on them. Add to these differences that the general look and habit of the plants are very different. Now set against the above differences such points of identity as number of parts of the flower, structure of the flower (polypetalous with inferior ovary and epigynous stamens and petals), the structure of the fruit, the partly identical growth of the head of flowers (an 'umbel' in the small plant, and a 'cyme' in the large one), and certain peculiarities of the leaf surface, such hairs as there are being closely appressed, and the nerves having a peculiar prominence. Perhaps it is rather easier to make out a long list of identities between the two plants than to make out a long list of differences. But we might really lengthen either list to infinity by subdividing in detail characters which have been mentioned in the abstract. I have little doubt however that in microscopic structure of petals, pollen-grains, etc. there would be some striking identities, hardly compensated by differences. Still we can see at once that no ratio between number of identities and number of differences can be constructed which will tell us anything—the number on each side is *almost* purely arbitrary. The *value* or *importance* is what we have to consider.

In what does the value of characters consist as a basis of natural classification or as a proof of common descent? Largely no doubt in their connection with the number and general arrangement of parts. Evolution only accounts for essential changes and their consequences, and though it may modify the number of parts and their arrangement, at first superficially and in course of generations more profoundly, yet an older general arrangement survives long beneath the modification and can as a rule be traced there[1]. The arrangement of those four or five whorls of leaves on a shortened stalk which we call the flower, is thus one dominant feature in the analogical estimate of a plant's affinities. Its inferential value is the same whether we call it one point of identity, or five, or twenty. It will be observed that in considering a plant in the light of evolution we have a combination of the higher and lower forms of teleology, related negatively to each other. Just as in the example employed above of the 'French microscope-stand,' we have here within the basis of analogy *both* a definite purpose suggesting definite means, *and* the mere tendency of individual or racial characteristics to perpetuate themselves. The local manufacturers' custom is *gradually* modified towards the better mechanical adaptation, as the organism is *gradually* modified towards the better mechanical adaptation. At any moment a manufacture or an organism is a compound of recent useful change, and of survival, some of which survival is obsolete, and some, the major part probably, has never ceased to be useful.

Thus, in the establishment of common descent, there is a special value in what recent evolutionary modification is likely to have spared. This would include both underlying arrangements which evolution would take very long to touch, and trifling details which it would have no reason for touching.

The account which I gave of the differences between the plants in question is the account of a common observer; the account of their identities is the account of a botanist. This, it may be said, is enough to vitiate the argument against a ratio, for of course knowledge and judgment are to be used in making the enumerations. But the idea of enumeration gives us no right to employ botanical know-

[1] See Darwin's beautiful verification of the modifications of the orchid-blossom by following the spiral vessels which indicate the position of the original petals in the modified corolla; Fertilisation of Orchids, p. 289 ff. Homology is an analogical conception.

ledge. It is only the idea of a presumption resting negatively or positively on teleology that enables knowledge to operate in assigning value to index-characters. Thus in judging of the plants in question we have to distinguish the element of heredity, or self-maintenance in the lower sense including the deeper and also the more trivial survivals, from self-preservation in the higher sense (though even here not involving conscious intention) in the set of recent differentiations introduced by evolution. Even thus we omit much that is most interesting and important. Evolution can for example assimilate plants of different origin as well as differentiate plants of the same descent, and we ought properly to show that any identities on which we rely cannot have been initiated by such assimilation[1]. We have so far anticipated this demand by requiring the identities to refer to matters with which evolution is not likely to have recently interfered.

The plants of which I have been speaking are *Cornus sanguinea*, common dogwood, and *Cornus suecica*, the Swedish or dwarf cornel. They are in fact species of the same genus. But the four yellowish bracts round the flower-heads of the dwarf cornel have the appearance of petals and form a striking superficial difference between the two plants, not to mention the enormous disparity in size. And now, possessing the names of the two plants, and having thus opened to us what is known of their local distribution, we can confirm our analogical estimate based on passive self-preservation or heredity, by a presumption drawn from the coherence of the modifications which that estimate ascribes to active self-preservation, i. e. to evolution since the divergence of the species. The smaller plant is sub-Alpine and Arctic; the larger belongs to southern England and to temperate climates. This fact suggests that the smaller plant, whether driven northwards by a change of climate, or simply main-

---

[1] Such identities are called in biological language 'homoplastic,' as opposed to 'homologous.' The daisy, for example, is a head of flowers that mimics the appearance of a single flower.

taining a portion of its old habitat, has been dwarfed or has not grown larger, and has compensated for its smallness by the brilliant simulated flower. Its distinctive leaf-growth and flower-growth may be summed up as a dwarfed or at least as a miniature growth, stalks and branchings having disappeared or not appeared. How the contrast between the inconspicuous small dark purple flower of the small plant and the larger white flower of the large plant is to be explained I am unable to suggest. But it is hard to suppose that the petal-like bracts of the small plant are not in some way a compensation for the inconspicuousness of its flower.

iv. Before reducing this example to regular form it is worth while to remark that, by assuming the two plants to be given us to compare, we presuppose the work of enumerative induction to be done to our hand. And in fact, where a subject-matter falls under an existing science, we are already in general beyond the stage of Enumerative Induction, though it may of course operate in particular unfamiliar instances. But speaking generally, the abstract ideas which guide Comparison are active in every special science as precepts filled with a content capable of guiding elementary observations. We approach an element, or a plant, or a part of speech, just as the state approaches a taxpayer, with a schedule in which the heads of our requirements are already jotted down, forming an abstract analysis of the predicates with which, in the class of cases in question, we are concerned. But if, supposing ourselves unfurnished with such a schedule, we construct a conjunctive Induction for the case before us, it would run in some such fashion as this:— *Concurrent Analogies. Negative Confirmation.*

These two plants[1] have similar berries;
These two plants have similar leaf-nerves;
∴ The conjunction of similar leaf-nerves and similar berries may not be an accident[2].

[1] 'Plant' here = species. This equivalence itself rests on analogical argument, which however is presupposed in any highly developed language, though not for all classes of objects. See above on Individual Judgment, and Lotze, Logik, sect. 14, on 'first universals.'

[2] In strict form, 'Similar leaf-nerves perhaps are (involve) similar berries.

Then the Analogical argument would fall into some such shape as—

Having similar berries is conjoined in these plants with a pervading identity of underlying (and so long inherited) structure;

Having similar leaf-nerves is conjoined in these plants, &c., &c.;

∴ Having these similar berries is connected by an underlying (and so long inherited) structure with having these leaf-nerves.

And, as we saw, two further analogies would confirm this:—

The resemblance in the berries is conjoined in these plants with trivial identities of structure (e. g. closely appressed hairs on the leaves) not likely to be modified by evolution;

The resemblance in the leaf-nerves is conjoined in these plants with trivial identities, &c., &c.;

∴ These attributes are connected with each other by attributes probably hereditary.

And contra-positively, giving affirmative content to the negations, but leaving them their negative value in inference:—

What is not identical in the fruit-growth (e. g. the clustering and the isolation of the fruit) is not a property likely to be remotely hereditary (because obviously modified by alteration of length of the stalks, i. e. by dwarfing);

What is not identical in the flower-growth (e. g. the presence and absence of the four white bracts) is not a property likely to be remotely hereditary (because obviously related to the inconspicuous flower, i. e. to dwarfing);

∴ What is not identical in the flower-growth of these plants is united with what is not identical in the fruit-structure as parts in a set of properties not likely to be remotely hereditary.

The true relation of these arguments to each other would be

that they should form a single analogical inference, in which each positive premise and the positive conclusion should be *materially* defined and limited by the corresponding negative judgment. When this reciprocal adjustment was completed, we should have analysed each of the plants into two related systems, in respect of one of which systems the two plants would coincide, and in respect of the other of which they would differ. The one system would point to the construction of a common ancestor; the other would point to the evolutional history of the species since their divergence. As their boundaries would precisely fit each other we should, in arguing on the basis of either, be supported by the defining influence of the other; that is to say, every judgment A is B would be supported by its converses Not-A is not-B, and Not-B is not-A. But though such negative relation of positive contents is valuable in analogy as elsewhere, yet to be fully effective it presupposes great accuracy and exhaustiveness of analysis, which is not usually to be obtained where analogy flourishes, and which, if obtained, takes us beyond analogy. By its negative aspect such inference leans over to Scientific Induction, while by its appeal to the coherent nature of a system it tends to pass into definite or philosophical subsumption.

v. Analogy, like Enumerative Induction, is a critical point from which two tracks of knowledge diverge. In assigning the coherence of attributes within a system we cannot but be confronted with negative relations, which are the conditions of all precise determination and of all causal or necessary inference. This feature of deepening analogical consideration points forward to scientific induction—the analysis of the teleological whole, or, *a fortiori*, of the unformed datum of perception, into its definite and necessary constituent relations. The goal of this path is the abstract Hypothetical judgment which forms, as we have seen, the point of transition between inference by combination of abstract relations and inference through the nature of concrete subjects.

On the other hand, if we continue to regard the concrete

Divergent tendencies in analogy.

subject from the point of view of its totality, which has begun to dawn upon us in analogical inference, our principle of inference tends to assume the shape of a *concrete whole, understood as a synthesis of abstract relations*. Such a subject combines within itself, in perfect equilibrium, the two aspects of the universal which have occupied us throughout—the aspect of concrete reality and that of abstract interconnection. Inference based upon contents of this nature may take the shape of the complete subsumptive syllogism in fig. 1, or, when more adequately expressed, of inference under a disjunction, or finally of the *explicitly* teleological inference respecting beauty or goodness.

It is plain that to employ in inference such a subject notion as I have just indicated presupposes a detailed mastery of the abstract relations which enter into it, and therefore presupposes the advance, which was above described as a divergence taking the direction of the hypothetical judgment. The subject can be known as an embodied purpose only by inference based on its necessary constituent relations. Why then should we regard the abstract hypothetical judgment as belonging to a track that diverges from the direct high-road of concrete knowledge? The reason is simply that in the formation and combination of Hypothetical judgments we sacrifice reality for the sake of necessity, and lose an element which was present in Analogy. In other words, the Hypothetical judgment with the combining inference that belongs to it is itself an apex or climax of one whole tendency of knowledge—of the mechanical view of the world which considers necessity apart from reality, and to which disease is as orderly a sequence as health. This is the view of the eye of *purely* physical science, which in a catastrophe that should extinguish life on the surface of the globe might see 'no more disorder than in the sabbatical peace of a summer sea[1].' This aspect of knowledge has been suffi-

---

[1] Professor Huxley in Contemp. Review, Feb. 1887. For a further consideration of this point of view, see chap. vii. below.

ciently analysed and discussed in our treatment of mathematical inference which is its purest form. My excuse for constantly recurring to it must be that a thorough understanding of its range and consequences is the primary condition of any clear thinking on the subject of the reign of law, which, as thus isolated, is absolutely indifferent to the purposes and interests that give reality its relation to mankind. The apparently self-dependent completeness of this analytic view of the universe gives it a right to an independent development, although this right of independence which it claims may also be regarded as a limitation to which it submits. Science, professing to be purely physical, has, as we have partly seen and shall more fully see, in our own day at least occupied itself with ideas which fall outside the categories of abstract necessity. And this was hardly avoidable; for we have seen over and over again that necessity must rest upon reality, and that therefore the self-completeness of the mechanical view of things is in this ultimate instance merely apparent.

CHAPTER IV.

Scientific Induction by Analysis.

THE moment we begin to demand precise definition of relations and to attempt analysis, we are, as the development of analogy proved to us, face to face with inference from negations.

Negative Inference. 1. I will now speak shortly of the nature of this inference, and will then attempt to explain its function in inductive analysis.

Its general nature and conditions. i. All inference depends on the relation of differences within a universal; and negative inference, in its fundamental nature, does not deviate from this principle. It may be laid down at once that the ideal of negative inference is to be looked for in Inference under Disjunction, as the ideal of negative Judgment is to be looked for in negation under Disjunction. Our discussion on the connection between bare negation and significant negation will have prepared us for this conception.

But negative inference in this sense is not a peculiar or separable form of reasoning. Negation and Affirmation in disjunctive or precise thinking are respectively double-edged; and though this character which thought acquires from being imbued with negation is pre-eminently distinctive of thought that has reached the stage in question, yet it does not admit of being ascribed to negation as contrasted in the abstract with affirmation. It is for this reason that in treating of calculation and of geometrical reasoning it has been unnecessary to devote special attention to negative inference. Negation appears no doubt in mathematical principles and theorems, e.g. in the definition of parallel straight lines, or in the theorem that if two circles cut one another they shall not have the same centre.

But as a general rule—I will not venture to say universally—it is easy to substitute for a negative expression of this kind a definite though not thoroughly particularised positive expression, which possibility goes to show that the negative expression was adopted rather for some rhetorical convenience—e.g. for brevity—than because a positive expression was unattainable. Often, as in the second of the above examples, the negative form of a conclusion arises from the employment of an indirect proof. And an indirect proof can only operate under a disjunction. True, in the present example the disjunction *seems* to be merely formal,—i.e. to consist simply in a positive judgment and bare negation; 'have the same centre,' 'have not the same centre.' But 'have not the same centre' in spatial matters means 'have different centres,' the relations of which are easily seen in general from the content of the indirect proof itself. In mathematical or pure mechanical reasoning there is no room for anything approximating to bare negation—the excluding motive must be definitely demonstrable, and contains the idea, though not necessarily the particulars, of an assignable quantitative difference between the excluding and the excluded content[1]. Incommensurable quantities are, *so far as incommensurable*, not quantities at all. Throughout this region of inference therefore negation and affirmation have as a rule their ideal complementary position, and no ground is given for a special and separate treatment of negative inference. For this same reason, however, *where* and *in as far as* negative inference formally occurs within this sphere, it *formally* falls outside the character required of combining inference, and must be technically referred, not indeed to subsumption, but to a special genus which also includes any negative reasoning that may arise within the limits proper to subsumption.

But when we turn from calculation with precise scales of difference to the traditional form of the subsumptive

[1] So that we need not say 'is' or 'is not,' but 'differ by a yard,' 'the same to a yard.'

syllogism, the inherent paradox of negative inference immediately stands in our path. The syllogistic rules undoubtedly contemplate inference *from* bare negation, and also, so far as they are concerned, inference that has bare negation for its conclusion. But all inference, we have been insisting, rests on an identical nature or a pervading universal, which prescribes a relation, whether definite or indefinite, between its differences. How can a universal prescribe a relation between itself and a content which falls wholly outside it, and is absolutely disparate and alien to its nature?

We were met by this difficulty in the discussion of the negatively infinite judgment, and of the ultimate indemonstrability of the negative *as such*. Where there is absolutely no connection it is impossible for denial to be intelligible; and what is not intelligible cannot convey a truth. Denials which though frivolous seem true have some shade of assignable meaning beneath them [1]. Therefore the only true meaning of an inference in Celarent is e.g.—

To be a man excludes being a monkey (in virtue of a certain universal nature which *including both* assigns an intelligible difference between the two);
Socrates is a man;
∴ Socrates is not a monkey.

But the ordinary graphical representations of the extensive syllogism slur over this difference, and leave us to suppose that from an *utter* absence of connection together with an assignable connection we can infer an absence of connection, which is to introduce the infinite judgment into inference. It is worth pointing out, however, that even the true reasoning in Celarent, considered as starting with its conclusion as a suggestion to be proved [2], *begins*

[1] For examples, see Bk. I. chap. vii.
[2] I am confident that this is as a rule the most instructive point of view from which to analyse inference, corresponding best to the vital process of thought. The essential question is, what difference is there in the conclusion as a judgment, before and after, or in and out of the inference.

with something nearer a bare denial, and *ends* with an intelligibly motived exclusion. 'Socrates is not a monkey;' 'Socrates having the nature of a man, cannot be a monkey.'

Thus in syllogistic negative inference we find (1) the erroneous idea that negation is utter disconnection, and that negation in this sense, bare negation, can be intelligibly asserted and inferred. And we have (2) the true idea that negation in order to be significant must fall within a controlling identity, although its ultimate shape is indemonstrable, and *qua* indemonstrable or irrational falls into a genus by itself, and outside both subsumption and construction. And as a testimony to the inevitable power of formalism in any symbolic scheme of inference, we may point out (3) that the accepted syllogistic rule that there can be no inference from two negative premises is really an offshoot of the idea of bare negation.

ii. If we have two bare negations or mere disconnections —negatively infinite judgments—nothing follows, because nothing is said. And as two negations will always present the external appearance of two mere disconnections, and will be ambiguous in interpretation, concealing their positive aspect, it is well to maintain this rule in a symbolic scheme of inference. Once at least in every inference, the rule says, you must show your hand, and develope your universal in terms of its positive content. Then, with one positive relation of content before us, we shall not be far out, it is implied, in interpreting the denial which is subjoined to it.

No conclusion from two negatives.

Nevertheless, it must be maintained that the negative syllogism acquires scientific value just in the degree in which this rule is disregarded and in which the syllogism is consequently informal. If negative inference has any value it is the establishment of exact and self-consistent boundaries between the species of any genus, or the modifications of any principle.

The rule that two negatives give no conclusion has been

impeached by good authorities[1] in respect of the third figure—the figure which we followed in our account of Enumerative Induction. This figure is obviously adapted for the expression of a positive instance, or of an exception —of an instance which comes under the condition of a rule but of which the consequent annexed by the rule to its condition does not hold good[2]. Why should it not also express a true *negative instance*, i. e. a negation which does not conflict with but corroborates the rule by coming neither under the condition nor under the consequent? In insisting on such a principle as 'Whatever gravitates is matter' we may often find ourselves relying on such instances as 'Light is not matter; Light does not gravitate; ∴ Something which is not matter does not gravitate,' or *vice versâ*, making in favour of the contra-positive converse either of 'Whatever gravitates is matter' or of its reciprocal 'Whatever is matter gravitates.'

It has been objected against this case of a conclusion from two negations that either the argument has four terms or one of the premises is affirmative. If the two premises are mere denials, then neither of them can furnish the negative predicate required to be subject of the conclusion. For this subject must be a positive content merely determined in one aspect by a negation. A bare negation cannot be subject in any judgment. If on the contrary in one premise such a positive content negatively determined is the predicate, and the fallacy of four terms is thus avoided, then that premise is affirmative in form and the conclusion is not drawn from two negatives.

This objection is not only sound in form, but has substantial justification. It is well known that to attach the negative closely to the predicated content has a tendency

---

[1] Lotze, Logic, sect. 89; Bradley, Principles of Logic, p. 254, quoting Jevons.

[2] Or in case of a reciprocal judgment, also *vice versâ*. Even in a rule which is not reciprocal, a great extension of the consequent beyond the condition is always suspicious.

to transform the idea so negated from an excluded content into a positive opposite. A form like 'not-moral' cannot maintain itself in living thought. It must advance to 'immoral' or fall back to 'what is not moral.' And if we admit in the third syllogistic figure that the same judgment can be both affirmative and negative—for accepting the above case of inference amounts to accepting this—it is hard to say why the same double character should not be adopted, and conclusions from two negatives introduced, in the remaining figures as well. In the second figure we should be tempted actually to take an affirmative conclusion from two negative premises; but as the ambiguous term is here the middle term, and not the subject of the conclusion, we cannot do this without treating both premises as affirmative (to secure an identical middle) and thereby reducing our conclusion to a problematic judgment[1], thus,

> Good workmen do not complain of their tools;
> My pupils do not complain of their tools;
> ∴ My pupils are probably good workmen.

Or again,

> Not good workmen are not satisfied with their tools;
> Not-my-pupils are not satisfied with their tools;
> ∴ Not-my-pupils are probably not good workmen.

Our treatment of analogy would also be illustrated by the case in which Not-A and Not-B join in a positive C. But as both premises would then be formally affirmative, the case does not come under the present head.

It is impossible to deny that arguments like the above may have material weight. Their value rests on the possibility of gathering up the phenomena just bordering on a

---

[1] Both premises must be taken in the same way, though both may be taken as either negative or affirmative. It is only the contrast of exclusion with assertion that can give a certain result in the figure.

system we are investigating into a system of their own, a, β, γ, limiting and limited by the former A, B, C at every point. We nearly achieved this—rudely of course—in our comparison of *Cornus sanguinea* and *Cornus suecica*. We then obtained two systems, A, B, C and a, β, γ, such that A, B, C were respectively not-a, not-β, and not-γ, while a, β, and γ were respectively not-A, not-B, and not-C. B and β, the two dominant or middle terms, stood, it will be remembered, for 'inherited from before divergence of the species' and 'modified by recent evolution' respectively; and the object was to attach all the peculiarities of the two plants systematically to one or other of these conceptions. Obviously in such a case it depends merely on our point of view whether we take as premises 'Not-A and Not-C are Not-B,' or 'a and γ are Not-B,' or 'Not-A and Not-C are β,' which are the various forms suggested above.

In the same way it might be argued in fig. 1 that

No mere animal has language;
A deaf mute is no mere animal;
∴ A deaf mute has language.

Horrible as these arguments must appear to any one conversant with syllogistic rules, I do not see how they are to be kept out if the argument from two negations in fig. 3 is admitted.

There is however an indispensable condition on which alone any value can be ascribed to these inferences. This is that the negation of a content should in all cases be merely an aspect of a positive content[1] which is really in question, and this we know to be the case in all significant negation, although not reckoned upon in the technical rules of the

---

[1] There is a puzzling inconsistency in this identification, because the treatment of 'man is not-mortal' as an affirmative judgment, which I have regarded as making 'not-mortal' a positive or significant content, was historically, as reference to a *class* 'not-mortal,' the origin of the 'infinite judgment' which is the very type of bare negation. The interpretation employed in the text regards 'not-mortal' not as a fictitious class but as a positive attribute excluding mortality.

CHAP. IV.]   *Scheme of Negative Instance.*   115

syllogism. Moreover, we have seen, that we are not bound to omit in the conclusion of inference any relevant matter given in the premises. But if not, we can in any case secure the positive significance of the denial of a content by supplying in the conclusion the middle term of which it is denied. Thus in one of the above examples we may conclude 'Light is something which does not gravitate, and is not material.'

iii. We have now obtained the logical formulation of the Negative Instance. Like the Exception, it begins in Enumerative Induction, and is capable of development through Analogy. I shall assume throughout my examination of its working, in order to avoid uninstructive complications, that the rule or law suggested by Enumerative Induction, of which the negative instance is confirmatory, has come to begin with from affirmative instances, and is expressed in an affirmative judgment. Then we may formulate the cases supplied by mere Enumerative Induction, with their sequels in Analogy, as follows:— {The Negative Instance.}

AFFIRMATIVE INSTANCE suggesting	EXCEPTION against the *prima facie* rule that B is probably C.	NEGATIVE INSTANCE confirming	Symbolic scheme of Instances.
A is C; A is B; ∴ B is or may be C.	A is not C; A is B; ∴ B may not be C.	a is not C; a is not B; ∴ Not-B may be Not-C.	Enumerative Induction.
C is $x y z$ R^1; B is $x y z$ R^1; ∴ B is for good reasons likely to be C.	C is not $x y z$ R^1 (i.e. is $x, y, z,$ R^2); B is $x y z$ R^1; ∴ B is not exactly C.	Not-C is $x_1 y_1 z_1$ R$_1^2$; Not-B is $x_1 y_1 z_1$ R$_1^2$; ∴ Not-B is Not-C (i.e. C is B).	Analogy.

[1] Analysis of A.
[2] The analysis of a, which is not-A, i.e., not $x y z$ R.

116 *Scientific Induction by Analysis.* [BOOK II.

Example of Instances.	AFFIRMATIVE INSTANCE suggesting	EXCEPTION[1] against	NEGATIVE INSTANCE confirming
		the flower-structure in these two plants probably is characteristic of a common descent shown also in the leaf-structure.		
Enumerative Induction.	In these two plants there is similar leaf-structure; In these two plants there is similar flower-structure; ∴ The flower structure may be an element in an inherited group of qualities to which the leaf-structure also belongs (or, in brief, may be at bottom one with the leaf-structure).	In these two plants there is not wholly identical leaf-structure; In these two plants there is wholly identical flower-structure; ∴ Flower-structure seems not to be generically connected with leaf-structure.	In some aspects of these two plants there *is* a difference, e.g. of leaf-stalk; In some aspects of these two plants there *is* a difference, e.g. of flower-stalk (umbels v. cymes); ∴ The difference of leaf-stalk may be connected (through those aspects of the two plants) with the difference of flower-stalk.
Analogy.	The leaf-structure in these two plants can be connected with a whole set of identical generic properties; The flower-structure in these two plants includes a whole set of identical generic properties; ∴ The flower-structure in these two plants probably is characteristic of a common descent shown also in the leaf-structure.	Leaves have not the same stalk-arrangement (i.e. are sessile in one case and stalked in the other); Flowers have the same stalk-arrangement in both plants (i. e. are stalked in both); ∴ Flower-structure does not follow variations of leaf-structure (in these two plants, i. e. species).	The difference of leaf-stalk belongs to a connected set of aspects[2] of these two plants *not* concerned with their remote hereditary properties; The difference of flower-stalk belongs to a connected set of aspects[2] of these two plants *not* concerned with their remote hereditary properties; ∴ The difference of leaf-stalk is connected with the difference of flower-stalk by a relation *not* concerned with their remote hereditary properties.

[1] The Exception of course cannot be made successful if the Negative Instance is to be so. I have therefore treated the Exception as a mistaken interpretation of the facts which the Negative Instance interprets rightly.

[2] Viz., the recent dwarfing of one plant.

2. The object of Scientific Induction is, *given a suggested* Scientific *coherence*, ' B may be (probably is) C,' which has become Induction. through analogy a hypothesis in germ represented by an 'importance' attached to the mediating content $x\,y\,z$ R, to bring such a coherence into the form of one or many pure Hypothetical judgments. The outward and visible side of this process is to modify the rule, i. e. the contents B and C with their connecting content $x\,y\,z$ R, so that there shall be no exceptions 'B is not quite C,' and that the two contrapositive converses 'Not-C is not-B' and 'Not-B is not-C[1]' shall be true when filled up with positive contents precisely excluding B and C respectively. The inward and intellectual side of the process however simply consists in grasping a necessary relation based upon some fundamental reality. This essential activity of the scientific spirit can only be characterised beforehand in respect of its most general attributes, which are embodied in the external process to be described as Scientific Induction. We can affirm from the known nature of the logical universal that it must be purified by exceptions and finally limited by negations. But as all data presented to us are thoroughly concrete, it follows that there is an endless possibility of erroneous abstraction and construction in all adjustment of contents to one another, so that the outward and visible side of induction, though knowable in respect of certain essential phases, can never assume the character of a mechanical method or royal road to knowledge. In the same way the ultimate necessity of the law or principle at which we arrive can be guaranteed by no general considerations. It depends in general, we know, on the systematic necessity of the negations, which, representing its relation to the reality within which it falls, hedge it in on every side and exhibit it as no longer itself, but as transformed, whenever and in as far as their limits are passed. But the specific necessity of

---

[1] The contrapositive converse of C is B, which affirmative judgment, and therefore its contrapositive converse, must be true if B is C is to be a pure or reciprocal judgment.

individual truths cannot be assigned by any general theory of science.

Induction and other Inference.

i. Induction then in its most general sense consists in satisfying the principle of sufficient reason by an analysis of experience, directed to revealing the true coherence of differences within universals. But as soon as this is stated, a difficulty arises in distinguishing Induction from Inference as such, which has precisely the same object. And this difficulty has, historically speaking, prevented the range of Induction from being consistently defined. As in Jevons' theory of Induction, the most recent and, so far as I know, the most thorough and appreciative account of the operation, so in Mill's famous analysis of the four methods of experimental enquiry, we are dealing with processes essentially deductive. On the other hand, if we try to confine ourselves to what has been termed 'Inference from particulars to particulars' we cannot meet the requirements of Scientific Induction. The name Scientific Induction is indeed something of a contradiction in terms. Induction *is meant to mean* the treatment of instances. In this meaning the idea of enumeration and even of the calculus of chances is confused with the idea of an analysis of observations—a confusion all the harder to disentangle, because number of observations does as a rule assist analysis and contribute to eliminating error. Scientific analysis as such, however, does not deal with instances, but only with contents. When we speak of a scientific treatment of instances, we mean a precise determination and skilful resolution *of their content*.

Therefore the distinction between Induction and other forms of Inference, erroneously described as the distinction between Induction and Deduction, is chiefly a distinction of *aspects*, largely based on a confused idea of Induction, but yet in some degree justified. I have just spoken of the confused idea in virtue of which Induction is regarded as a treatment of instances pure and simple. I need only add that a semi-numerical content may often have to be added to an inductive analysis of causes, where our knowledge of conditions falls short. Here we *really* fall back on number, on ratio of instances to instances. If a self-fertilised flower is fertilised 90 times in 100 cases, and an insect-fertilised flower only 20 times in 100 cases, then the number of cases strengthens the unlikelihood of any exceptional *variety and relevancy of unknown conditions*, and we take self-fertilisation to be the more effective process, because there are fewer unknown conditions which stop it, or more which assist it. This helps the confusion which regards Induction in contrast to Deduction as an affair of number of instances.

Again, Induction does not exclude Deductive processes. All Induction whatever is guided by principles; and Induction as considered in Jevons' theory essentially consists in processes of mediate Inference, which he explicitly calls Deduction, and which operate by deriving data deductively from hypothetical premises. And usage bears him out. The verification of hypothesis has been considered from Bacon downward as an integral part of scientific induction. And nothing can be more deductive than the connection of a hypothesis with the consequences by which it is verified.

But the distinction, as one of aspects, is justified. It is nearly akin to, but not identical with, the distinction between discovery and proof. This distinction indeed we refused to recognise, because what is not proved is not really discovered. Nor does Induction coincide with discovery. For discovery may include as in mathematical science construction and proof, which no one would call inductive[1].

But in a deeper form an analogous distinction to that meant to be drawn between discovery and proof does hold good between Induction and Deduction. We may take Induction as Inference viewed from the side of the differences, Deduction as Inference viewed from the side of the universal. In Induction *par excellence* the Real presents itself in con-

---

[1] There may be and indeed must be true induction in mathematical matter in so far as instances suggest underlying laws. The case of gravitation, to be discussed below, illustrates the degree in which this is possible.

crete and more or less isolated data, in virtue of which universal nature, or the system of further differences charg with the universal nature, is referred to reality. In Deduct*par excellence* the Real presents itself as qualified by intelligible system—e.g. by mathematical attributes; ai further differences are referred to reality as construct(by and out of this system. It may be doubted wheth Newton's discovery of Gravitation was Inductive or Dc ductive. That in process it was largely deductive there of course no doubt. The popular story however, abo the falling apple[1], would indicate, if true, an inductive aspect—that of a problem set by concrete data, and resolved by analysis and hypothesis. But we must not suppose Newton's mind to have been as empty of mathematical generalisations as our own. He probably brought a systematised qualification of Reality, drawn from elements in the researches of previous mathematicians, to meet the facts that demanded explanation. In this example the aspects of Induction and of Deduction are about equally balanced, and we see the whole principle involved in the distinction together with its merely transitory importance. The relation of the universal to its differences is not affected by the order in which they have presented themselves to us as qualifications of Reality. But it is this order alone which furnishes the differentia of Induction.

Regarded as relations within a system, i.e. in the light of the principle of Sufficient Reason, all inductive explanations point beyond themselves. They demand in the first instance the explicit statement of the system from which their necessity is derived, and thus they appeal as we have seen from the pure Hypothetical judgment to the Notional or Disjunctive judgment. But the underlying real systems themselves are in various degrees limited and incomplete, and in virtue of their finite nature, as we have seen to be the case with space and time, demand explanations which go

[1] For comments on this and for an excellent criticism on popular notions of Induction, see De Morgan's Budget of Paradoxes, pp. 49, 81.

further and further afield in accounting for the boundaries which persistently present themselves. The task of explanation imposed upon the mind by the principle of sufficient reason is therefore an endless task. The principle of sufficient reason, as Schopenhauer says, is not like a cab which you can send away when it has brought you to your destination. Nothing is isolated, but as the connections which debar isolation reach to infinity, nothing is complete, nor has what it requires in order to justify its existence. This is the standpoint of relativity, which applies in a degree to all known matters. How far we can escape from this standpoint, which has been called the standpoint of the Understanding, and which as thus stated is merely an abstraction of our own minds, will appear when we return to more concrete forms of thought.

Two observations may be made about the account here to be given of Scientific Induction. I shall not speak in it especially of Causation. I have attempted to show in Book I[1] that cause is a merely popular idea, indicating one or another ill-defined grade in the process of inductive explanation. The only distinctive peculiarity of Cause contrasted with Reason is that it refers to operation in time. I believe that all which has value in this idea will be elucidated by our account of inductive explanation, taken together with the analysis of the idea of Cause to which I have referred.

And I do not propose to give any account of inductive disproof. Disproof is for the theory of Inference only a form of correction or modification. If at any point we are unable to perform the processes necessary to correction, then we have *pro tanto* a disproof—if e.g. we fail in accommodating a suggested rule to actual exceptions, or actual exceptions to a suggested rule. But for theory such a failure is not a positive phenomenon. We must suppose that there is a true rule, which, if we could but hit upon it, would cover the facts and appear as a correction of our disproved rule. The failure to light upon a hypothetical

[1] Chap. vi.

rule fulfilling these conditions is a mere delay in making the required correction, of which theory need take no account. Bacon's complaint that the 'axioma distinctione aliquâ frivolâ salvatur' is, but for 'frivolâ' which is its sting, an account of the sole and inevitable process of knowledge.

In order to exhibit distinctly the variations which impede a clear definition of Induction, I propose to speak separately of Induction as perceptive analysis and of Induction as inferential explanation. These two varieties, together with Analogical Inference and Enumerative Induction, are all confused together in the popular idea of Induction as opposed to Deduction[1].

Induction as perceptive analysis.

Symbolic expression of the problem.

ii. Induction in the narrowest sense is perceptive analysis.

a. We suppose ourselves to have obtained from any source whatever, all such sources being ultimately reducible to analogy, the problematic judgment that the attribute or occurrence B in virtue of a nature $a\,b\,c$ R, has probably a necessary coherence with the attribute or event C. This is so far only a presumption arising from the value for cognition which we have been led to attach to the nature $a\,b\,c$ R—a value depending, in all the higher and truer applications of analogy, on the ultimate identity of human purposes and necessities[2], and in the lower walks of inference on the identification of self-maintenance or self-preservation with some such idea as that of purpose. I follow Lotze in employing an expression of the type $a\,b\,c$ R in which a, b, c may be taken to stand respectively for definite attributes or relations and R for the residual nature of the concrete whole before us, considered as only contributing its normal support to the operations of $a\,b\,c$ and not as actively inter-

---

[1] Compare Mill, ii. 25 ff. He tries to separate Hypothesis from Induction, but really includes, though he denies doing so, much Hypothesis in Induction. His test seems to be that where you have a *vera causa* you have Induction, not Hypothesis. But he admits that in Induction the *vera causa* may not be known to be present in the case under investigation.

[2] The process of learning a foreign language, and ultimately of understanding language at all, is an excellent example of this. We are guided throughout by the assumption that identical aims and feelings underlie the different systems of expression.

fering to modify them. It is worth mentioning that Mill's account of the Experimental methods, otherwise at least suggestive, is rendered terribly perplexing by his use of corresponding letters A and a to indicate from the first the several antecedents and consequents underlying concrete phenomena. The result is that his first statement of every problem presupposes in symbolic form its explicit solution. When the phenomenon can be resolved into antecedents A B C and consequents $a\ b\ c$ the work is already done. Mill, no doubt, does not *mean* to have determined by his expression the fact that a particular element A of the given content is from the first known to correspond to another particular element a. He intends A and a to be empty forms, indicating the problem which our analysis has to solve. But the correspondences of the symbolic letters are undoubtedly misleading.

I mention this question partly because it illustrates our present task. The *problem* is just to break up B into $a\ \beta\ \gamma$ R, so that we can say of each element in turn, 'If a R, then a R; and if a R, then a R.' In each case we must understand all the elements which we are not observing to fall back into the mass of R. This neglect of the other elements is capable of two interpretations. Either the other elements may be taken to retain their normal relation to the a under investigation, and are not especially and abnormally operative upon it under the conditions of the observation, or they are actually inoperative and might be removed. This latter interpretation can never be justified without special proof, which must address itself to a definite analysed R. For every conjunction of conditions whatever is *an* R, i.e. an inexhaustible concrete, even in the most precise experiment, and all that can ever be done in the way of isolation is to exclude some portion x of the whole concrete R, by substituting for it an element y which has the effect of turning R into R_1. We have then excluded x, but not R as such, i.e. we can only exclude R in as far as we can analyse it.

And to end the subject of symbolic expression, I may point out that for simplicity's sake I shall not consider the whole analogical suggestion 'B is probably connected with C, both being conjoined with *a b c* R,' but shall confine myself to one member at a time, as we should have to do in a practical investigation, e. g. to 'B is conjoined with, and probably coheres with, *a b c* R.' This is not an inadequate treatment. It would be easy to add C as a character to *a b c* R, indicating that their conjunction must be taken subject to unknown conditions; and in any case the investigation of B in relation to *a b c* R is certain if pursued to the end to lay open the track of coherence between *a b c* R and C. The defect of symbolic modes of expression in these higher forms of reasoning is that not only are all elements of the content most variously interconnected, and far from being on the same level in value, but also every element of the content is undergoing transformation from the beginning to the end of the whole process. Therefore, as Mill no doubt really intended, corresponding symbols like *a* and α represent a pair of series or a pair of continuous developments within the inference rather than a pair of fixed contents.

Establishment of Ordinary Hypothetical Judgment.

β. I will begin by analysing at some length an example of perceptive analysis conducted *chiefly* through observation as opposed to experiment—though experiment was at times applied—and in respect of its content just on the borderland between analogy and scientific induction.

It might be suggested without doing violence to facts that the Linnaean classification in botany corresponds on the whole to the stage of enumerative or conjunctive Induction; the mere natural classification to Analogical Inference; and the analysis of plant-structure and evolution in the light of the Darwinian hypothesis to scientific induction—to perceptive induction where we deal with the visible adaptations of particular species, and to generalising or reflective induction when we lay down universal conditions as controlling the evolution of the organic world.

Let us suppose that Analogy, the habit of ascribing what I have ventured to call *de facto* purposes to adaptations in the organic world, has made it probable to us on inspecting the flower of the Bee Ophrys that it (B) is adapted for self-fertilisation (*a b c* R).

Here the expression 'adapted for,' in consonance with the notion of *de facto* purpose, refers not merely to the mechanical adjustment of a contrivance, but to the fact of that contrivance actually achieving in normal use the purpose which it suggests. A case in which we cannot make out this additional element of meaning will be mentioned below, and in it the purpose will not rank as established by Induction.

I should observe, too, that the element C which we usually spoke of in analogy and which we mean to omit here for the sake of brevity may in the present example be identified with any peculiarity the conjunction of which with the general appearance B might have first attracted our attention to the flower B.

Of course my analysis is only rough and typical. I select two or three prominent characters out of a whole apparatus of converging contrivances.

The object is now to analyse the flower B in the light of *a b c* R. We may attempt this roughly as follows :—

(a) Caudicles (stalks of pollen-masses) are of the right length to (*a*) reach the stigma.

(β) Anther-cells open of themselves, and (*b*) let the pollen-masses fall to the level of the stigma.

(γ) Hanging pollen-masses oscillate in the wind till (*c*) they strike the stigma.

R in this example has the significance that the remaining parts of the flower and plant are necessary to give the process its value, and to make it possible for the contrivance to operate, by nourishing and mechanically supporting the flower. But all this is involved in the nature of a plant, and therefore assuming a, β, γ to be in a living plant, and that, of course, the right plant, R need not be further considered in the analysis *at present*; i.e. until it in some way interferes with the possibility or reality of the action we are investigating.

The very important relation of γ to c in the above analysis assumes the operation of an external cause, and requires a confirmation without which the whole analysis is futile; for as the pollen masses when liberated do not fall on the stigma, but only hang like a pendulum on the level of the stigma, it is incumbent on us to show how they can be and are brought in contact with it. There is a further interest at this point in affirming or denying the action of insects, which are usually necessary to cross-fertilisation, but the need for whose intervention would impair the certainty which is the purpose of self-fertilisation. Here we have recourse to the negative instance which, here as usual, contains an element of experiment. For the essence of the negative instance is to obtain a positive content equivalent *ad hoc* to an exclusion, and this can only be done by a disjunctive limitation of possibilities, and an exact ascertainment of the reality within the possibilities so limited. The limitation of possibilities consists, not in removing all R, which is impossible, but in securing an R analysed and believed to be passive; and artificial combinations give the best chance of obtaining this condition. And the exact ascertainment of reality consists in observing a positive or negative condition, or both, whose nature we can exhaustively analyse. Here again artificial production gives the best chance. To test the connection of γ (movement by wind) with c (contact with stigma) Mr. Darwin put a spike of Bee Ophrys in water in a room. Thus he secured an R, residuary conditions, which he could ensure to be passive (absence of touching by animals or by any unknown cause of motion), and having thus limited the possibilities he was able to observe with certainty and with a high degree of exclusiveness *the absence of wind*, not-γ, which resulted in *absence of contact*, not-c, the pollen-masses continuing to hang freely in front of the stigma. Thus he obtained the confirmatory or true negative instance 'not-y is not c,' which is the contrapositive converse of 'c is γ,' i. e. 'contact arises from wind.' We have here left the ground of formal logic [1], in which 'not-y is not c' could only rest on the knowledge that 'c is γ.' In the process now considered 'c is γ' actually rests on the knowledge that 'not-y is not c.' The corroborative power of the negative instance in induction depends on the fact that it has a positive content within the same *ultimate* system as c and γ, and, within that system, related by way of definite negation to them. Thus the negative instance is capable of *independent agreement* with the positive case. 'Not-y is not c'='Free caudicles without wind give no contact.'

But it will be said that we have gone too fast. We read the 'free caudicles in a room give no contact' as 'not-y is not c.' But it was probably also 'Not-G (no insects) is not c,' 'where no *insects*, there no contact,' i. e. in searching R we have found a not-G, an absence of a condition, which, it is suggested, may not be, as R was meant to be, indifferent. We may treat this as a positive suggestion from analogy, 'G is probably c;' for in the absence of such a positive suggestion we should have no more cause to note the absence of insects G from the experimental R than to note the absence of direct sunlight L or extreme changes of temperature T. But there is plenty of analogy for insects fertilising plants; so 'G is probably c' demands attention.

Mr. Darwin provided against this suggestion by exposing some of the flowers under a net, which excluded insects but admitted wind. In the cases so treated contact was effected. We may read this off as an *exception* in the form 'not-G is c' against the suggested rule 'G is (probably) c,' or 'insects (probably) produce the contact,' and as at the same time a positive instance in favour of the suggested rule 'γ is c,' 'wind makes contact.' This double-edged character, proper to a negated content at this stage, is justified by the experi-

---

[1] See vol. i. pp. 322–4. What is true of the double negation is true of the contrapositive converse which implies double negation.

ment above-mentioned which might be read off as 'R γ not-G is c;' R standing for the mass of conditions presumed to be indifferent, not-G for the exclusion of insects, γ for the presence of wind, and c for contact.

<small>Establishment of Reciprocal Hypothetical Judgment.</small> γ. And this connection γ is c (wind acting on the pendent pollen-masses produces contact with the stigma) has been defined and confirmed—i.e. *re-inferred in a precise form*—through the two conjunctions claiming to be connections, R-not-γ is not c (pendent pollinia without wind[1] do not touch the stigma) and R γ-not-G is c, i.e. pendent pollinia with wind and without insects[2] do touch the stigma. From not-γ is not c (R being disregarded as the common basis) we infer c is γ, i.e. 'contact comes from wind,' the reciprocal of 'wind produces contact.' And by 'γ-not-G is c' we confirm this reciprocal 'contact comes from wind' by overthrowing the suggestion that G may be the operative agent in c, and consequently that *either* wind *or* insects may be concerned in the contact.

It is true, however, that we have not obtained, against 'G may be c,' the more fatal exception 'G is not c' (in presence of insects no contact is effected); the exception which we obtained is strictly an exception against the reciprocal of this, viz. against c is G or contact comes from insects, i.e. against the suggestion that insects are the *only* agency in producing contact. Thus we have not strictly *proved*, as against insect agency the only suggested alternative, that wind is the *exclusive* agency in the self-fertilisation of this flower, for when wind was excluded, insects were probably (in the room) excluded with it. In fact the γ with which we began included G, and was really 'wind-or-insects,' and it is of *this* γ that the reciprocal 'c is γ' was proved by the experiment not-γ is not-c. But we subsequently make it probable that this γ *ought* to mean wind only, by making

---

[1] Experiment of the flower in a room.
[2] Experiment of flowers under a net in the open air. This experiment goes far to give the pure judgment '*only* γ is c,' which no ordinary Judgment-form will express for Logic, except the clumsy equivalent 'All c is γ.' I have written it 'γ-not-G is c.'

it certain that it may mean wind only. This shows the transformation which a content undergoes in course of an inductive inference.

And for the kind of matter with which we are dealing this conclúsion is perhaps sufficient. We are studying the use of an adaptation, which use any normal agency suitable to it will suffice to establish. We could not hope to prove that no insect, or that no human hand, has ever fertilised a Bee Ophrys by pushing the pendent pollen-masses. When we know that the wind can do it, and does it without other aid, and that wind is a common occurrence, and that in the absence of wind (though in the absence of other things at the same time) the adaptation fails, then we are justified in saying that here we have the only agency which is normal enough to account for the growth of a contrivance adapted to it. Logically, these considerations are represented by the claim of every judgment to become reciprocal, which formal claim has different values and interpretations in different kinds of matter. Here, for instance, we might make our judgment truly reciprocal—and purely truistic— by transforming the content of γ into simply 'a sufficient cause of motion.' This would suffice for a mechanical construction of our problem, but not for an organic explanation of it. An organic adaptation demands for its explanation a definite regular agency to which it is adapted; it *need* not exclude agencies of diverse origin ; but it is pretty certain to shape itself on some one well-defined type of operation. Thus in speaking of agencies to which evolution has adapted structures, the claim of any actual and normal agency to be *the* exclusive agency is *prima facie* very strong. To make it absolute we should proceed by analysing c as we have analysed B itself, and showing that γ, wind agency, as $\xi \, \upsilon \, \zeta$, is the *only* agency corresponding to c as $x \, y \, z$. But this I at all events am unable to do, further than by pointing out that 'normal' and 'general' in γ correspond to 'gradual growth' and 'need of a reliable agent' in the contrivances concerned in c.

Thus far we are left with B as $a\beta\gamma$ R is abc R or S. The flower of the Bee Ophrys as having flexible caudicles of the right length and self-opening anther cells, and considered as acted upon by wind, is adapted for self-fertilisation by the pollinia falling to the level of the stigma and oscillating till they touch it.

Conversion or Generalisation. δ. In formal logic the affirmation of one attribute can have no influence on the affirmation of another about the same subject unless an explicit contrariety between the two affirmations is within our knowledge. In short, difference does not justify negation. To say that a flower is self-fertilised does not formally warrant us in denying that it is cross-fertilised. But in science every content claims to be treated as a system, and every attribute must either quarrel with any other attribute suggested of the same subject, or must make peace with it on definite terms. Therefore the inductive conclusion B is S, 'The Bee Ophrys is self-fertilising,' which we have thus obtained, contains in its claim for reciprocity, i.e. for predominance or essentiality on the part of the attribute, a further suggestion to which in material or actual knowledge we are bound to pay attention. We cannot indeed expect to show that every self-fertilised plant is a Bee Ophrys; i.e. we cannot reduce self-fertilisation to mean solely the adaptations of the flower in question, nor can we extend our idea of the flower in question to include all adaptations that in any plant might ensure self-fertilisation. The attribute 'self-fertilisation' is not sufficiently concrete and specific to be identified in this way with the nature of a particular species of plant. But though we cannot reduce self-fertilisation as such to mean simply and solely the fertilising contrivances of *Ophrys apifera*, we are confronted by the reciprocal tendency of judgment with another problem which Darwin, with his usual exhaustiveness of apprehension, has frankly stated and discussed. We saw that B is S, or, to prepare for our present enquiry, B is b S, i.e. The flower in question is characterised by its own peculiar contrivances for self-ferti-

CHAP. IV.] *Difference and Antagonism.* 131

lisation. Can we convert this judgment materially? Can we say 'Self-fertilisation S, not cross-fertilisation F, is *the* characteristic of this species,' or in hypothetical form, 'If S pure and simple, then B'? This suggestion might be embodied with more formal correctness in double negation or in contra-position, as 'B is not not-S,' or, 'If any not-S, then not-B,' and the question would thus arise whether F (cross-fertilisation) was not-S in the sense of being incompatible with S in B. But Simple Conversion without limitation (formally impossible) expresses the guiding idea more effectually, in demanding that an *essential* attribute of a subject shall be the *sole* attribute in the relation to which it belongs. Here however this suggested reciprocal is not true. The contrivances which have their meaning in subserving cross-fertilisation, the viscid discs, sinking caudicles, and elastic threads tying up the pollen-masses, are present in the Bee Ophrys without the least trace of becoming aborted, and therefore a strong *analogical* inference holds, to show that B being def is F, and so is not-S in as far as not-S is identified with F ; in other words, that S, and not-S in the sense of F, are not contrary or incompatible in B, and so if we like that F is in this case not to count as not-S, or else that B is both S and not-S, to which, if not-S only means different from S, there is no objection.

A certain methodical gain is drawn from affirming this conjunction of S and not-S, although unintelligible to formal logic. Having failed in Conversion, we are driven to Generalisation. For though S and F form no logical contradiction, but are *prima facie* quite compatible with one another, yet ultimately and from the point of view of a harmonious theory there is a contradiction *until we reconcile them.* Difference without a reason,—i. e. difference in the same relation, or difference of means [1] to the same end *qua*

[1] Apart from the insufficient amount of the one means, which therefore may need supplementing by another. If the one means is as easy to provide as the other, this reason falls away.

K 2

the same,—*is* a contradiction. We express this problem justly by saying, 'The flower B is self-fertilised S, and apparently may also be cross-fertilised Not-S.' We are here in need of a further suggestion by which to generalise S and not-S into one conception. This suggestion cannot be mechanically obtained, but must be drawn by analogy from our general knowledge of the organic world. Combining what Darwin says in the place under discussion with his views in other works, we might give this suggestion the form, 'Σ (healthy preservation of the species) demands some F (cross-fertilisation) at least;' under which we may infer by analogy from 'B has besides S some F (not-S)' that 'B the special adaptations of the Bee Ophrys have for their all-embracing and determining nature the tendency to Σ the healthy self-preservation of the species, including both S and not-S.'

Beyond analogy, in this final inference, we cannot go, for cross-fertilisation is not, according to the passage upon which I rely, affirmed of Reality as a datum in the content of *Ophrys apifera*, but is itself only inferred from analogy; and therefore the general conclusion, though a suggestive concurrence of analogies, cannot be considered as a truth resting upon scientific induction. The operation of the contrivances by which the self-fertilisation of this flower is secured may on the other hand be regarded as made good by precise perceptive analysis at every point.

In establishing this positive attribute of self-fertilisation considered as significant of a *de facto* purpose, we have about reached the limits of perceptive analysis. In establishing the probability of cross-fertilisation we have in one sense gone beyond the limits of perceptive analysis into the region of hypothesis, if in another sense we have retrograded into mere analogy. Such a hypothesis as we have just recommended by analogy, if drawn out into a variety of precise details and supported by their precise verification as real data, would be the essence of reflective, mediate, or generalising Induction. We must however bear in mind

CHAP. IV.] *Mediate Inference in Induction.* 133

that hypothesis was present in a germinal form throughout perceptive analysis, throughout analogy, and even throughout enumerative induction, where it was represented by the content of a common name; so that there is no *saltus* between these phases of inference. The fascination which attaches to the researches of the great masters lies just in their power of absorbing, by exhaustive analysis, the mass of perceived data into intelligible conceptions.

iii. In order to estimate the logical character — the position in the evolution of thought—of such a process as this which I have attempted to describe, three special points must be briefly treated. These are, a. What is the essence of the inferential process concerned? β. What is the purpose of the symbolic representation of it by letters? γ. What part in it is played by number of instances? _{Logical character of Perceptive Induction.}

a. Ordinary mediate inference, either subsumptive or constructive, may be detected in every step of the process which we have examined, as in any complex judgment of perception. As we analyse, for example, the flower into its parts, and its parts into mechanical adaptations, we obtain the material for a three-term inference by which the adaptations in their mechanical aspect would be formally brought home to the flower. Or again, the contra-positive conversions and the ideal reciprocity of the judgment, to which we have so freely appealed, may be held to require explicit proof through syllogistic or disjunctive argument based on abstract principles. The mediate inference thus involved is of two kinds. _{Its essence as Inference.} √

With regard to the mediate inference involved in every *complex* judgment of perception, and therefore in every *precise* one—this is *really* present in the Induction of which we are speaking, and may sometimes need to be explicitly drawn out in order to correct the results of an overhasty perceptive analysis. Especially this is the case when we are employing experimental apparatus which embodies whole chains of reasoning and concentrates on a single datum a multitude of precisely determined conditions. The observer e. g. with a microscope must always bear in mind what it is that his instrument does in virtue of the principles of its own construction, and in many classes of observations is liable to be thrown back on constructive optical inference, in order to determine the interpretation of the appearance presented to him,—whether it means a true line or an interference-line, whether an elevation or a depression, whether absence of structure or complete transparency of structure (in which latter case the use of polarised light will sometimes detect the illusion). Such mediate inference as this is really and genuinely present in the processes we have been considering, being concerned with material principles relevant to the special subject of the inferences. But yet such mediate inference does not belong to the differentia of Induction, but is shared by all Inference whatever, being inherent in the nature of Judgment.

On the other hand, it appears to me that mediate inference from abstract principles of knowledge, such as principles of disjunction, of causation, or of sufficient reason, is not a genuine element of scientific Induction at all, although it may be the duty of the logician to point out a relation between inductive inference and such principles as these. The active form of thought, to which these principles belong, loses, as we have seen[1], its active nature if it is made a mere content within an inference. The relation, for example, of the judgment that embodies a 'negative' instance to the affirmative judgment which it corroborates is a case of the active form of negation engaged in acquiring a definite content within a certain complex system. We should gain nothing in such a case by erecting an argument to the effect that What is not A is not-A. The problem is, given the forms A and not-A, the positive and its limit,

---

[1] Cp. chapter i. of the present Book.

to bring these two forms into material agreement in respect of the matter to be organised.

To reject abstract argument from principles of knowledge is however a different thing from the omission to exhibit the material of inference as permeated and articulated by the active forms of thought. Such an omission I hold to be unjustifiable. I have argued elsewhere that Mr. Bradley goes too far in holding that an inference *qua* inference is not bound to exhibit its principle or *rationale*.

The essence of induction in this, the perceptive stage— and beyond this stage it more and more transcends mere induction—is in the peculiar parallelism between the positive connection which suggests, the negative connection which defines in corroborating and corroborates in defining, and the 'exceptional' connection which modifies either itself or the affirmative connection. I have explained[1] why I do not take account of the sustained exception which overthrows. The logical peculiarity of the process is in the positive and consequently independent value of the negations, which are established without being derived from the affirmations, but operate on the latter through the formal interdependence of negation and affirmation. The process is of course not mechanical. Mechanical Induction is an idle dream. The reciprocal adjustment of the negations and affirmations consists in the revelation of intelligible systematic ideas which are thus inferred to be true of reality.

β. The symbolic representation of these processes by letters may seem to have an external affinity with the processes of equational logic. But the two systems are to be regarded in precisely opposite aspects. In the above discussion not-*a* and not-*a* have been employed to designate contents which are positive, but have, towards *a* and *a* respectively, a boundary or negative side. The only object of such designations was to emphasise, for theoretical purposes, the negative relations subsisting between certain

Theoretical purpose of representation by symbols.

[1] p. 42, above.

inter-connected positive contents. But for practical use the events or attributes in question must be taken in their concrete form, upon which everything turns. By manipulating them in the shape of abstract symbols no progress can be made in the task of Induction, which is a problem of material suggestion and adjustment. '*Just* where' and '*just in so far as x* fails to be *a* it fails to be *a*;' this is the meaning of the inductive 'not-*a* is not *a*.' And no handling of symbols[1] can express or can warrant this 'just' and 'in so far as' which are the whole essence of the process. What warrants these expressions of definite relation is and can be nothing less than a ground or real system containing parts which negatively determine each other. It is the business of Induction in the form of perceptive analysis to initiate the disentanglement and reciprocal determination of elements within such systems, in the light of ideas—germinal hypotheses—suggested by analogy. Analogy, in fact, does not cease to operate in Induction. Induction is Analogy fortified by negative and precise determination.

<small>Part played by number of instances.</small>
γ. Induction, we saw, is popularly identified with proof by instances, and owes its recognition as a distinct method of inference to this identification.

<small>In perceptive analysis proper.</small>
(1) But scientific induction does not depend on or in any way deal with instances as such, i.e. particular occurrences or observations with reference to their particularity—their number or recurrence. Here we have an antinomy, to which at the present stage we need only draw attention, as it has really been solved by the distinction between Enumerative Induction and the subsequent diverging phases of the Inductive process. All that scientific Induction demands is a content referred to reality; in how many observations or cases or occurrences the content is presented is a matter of entire indifference to science. If, to put an extreme supposition, the entire content, positive and nega-

---

[1] Of course this remark does not extend to true calculation, which has been independently treated and does not fall within induction. The two processes have some common ground in statistics, as will appear from γ below.

tive, employed in the above analysis of the Bee Ophrys, could be observable in a single flower, that single flower would, subject to one reservation to be mentioned presently, form a sufficient ground for all the conclusions that were then drawn. What characters can be and what cannot be united in a single or continuous observation is a question of the nature of the object concerned, and not of logical theory. The same flower cannot be both fertilised, and ultimately not fertilised at all. It can be both fertilised (later) and not-fertilised (up to a certain point of time). Or it can be both self-fertilised, and not-self-fertilised in the specific sense of being cross-fertilised. The first of these three comparisons requires two 'instances'; the two latter need only require one apiece, or indeed one between them. And then is an 'instance' a plant or a flower? If a plant, one instance would probably do all we should demand.

(2) There is, however, one case to be distinguished to which the above remarks do not apply. The self-fertilisation of the Bee Ophrys, Darwin says, is markedly 'successful.' The Bee Ophrys, which is self-fertilised, in many dozens of plants had a capsule (seed-vessel) for every flower[1]. The Fly Ophrys, cross-fertilised by insects, had only seven capsules in forty-nine flowers. This is again '*a* is *a*,' 'not-*a* tends to be not *a*.' And here number of instances is essential to the result, *because we are dealing with the operation of conditions not fully known*. This throws us back at once into enumeration of instances, statistical methods, or even the statement of chances. We proceed by the comparison of hypotheses explanatory of observed ratios, as we saw in discussing the statement of chances. If, to use an extreme illustration, we could say 'Fly Ophrys is exclusively insect-fertilised,' *and* 'the observed plants of Fly Ophrys are in a place inaccessible to insects,' then we should not need a single instance to fortify the conclusion that all these plants must remain unfertilised. But as we do not know with precision what conditions are operative,

Known effects of unknown conditions.

[1] *Exceptis excipiendis*—deformed flowers.

and to what degree, in securing or hindering the approach of the right insects to the flower at the right moment, we are reduced to enumerating observed instances in order to obtain an actual ratio between successes and failures, upon which we may base an estimate of the nature of the cause or causes, whether in the flower or outside it, which would probably have produced the observed ratio of successes to failures. We have as data, say, forty-eight cases and forty-eight successes in self-fertilisation, compared with forty-eight cases and only six successes in cross-fertilisation by insects. We have to conjecture or construct the kind or type of causes which are most likely to have produced these two observed series.

Supposing indeed that we take into account *all* unknown conditions whatever, no question can be raised, for it is a mere transcription of the series to say that the one flower is less adapted to the conditions which *have* acted on it, than the other to the conditions which *have* acted on *it*. And supposing that Darwin excluded interfering causes in counting both his sets of instances, as he did in one, there is no more to be said. The self-fertilised plant meets the unknown conditions wholly and the other does not. In order to compare probabilities we must have a suggestion as to some special kinds of causes that normally operate with an assigned frequency[1], and for the sake of illustration I will assume that obvious accidents have not been excluded. As every adaptation has its limits beyond which conditions become abnormal to it, i.e. are accidents, I am able by this means to suggest the idea that the two kinds

[1] We must in short take by way of hypothesis some 'natural cycle,' or what comes to the same thing, some cycle external to that observed, otherwise there are no two ratios to compare in respect of each observed series. See Book I. chap. viii. We might indeed compare the probabilities that each series proceeded from a supposed cause, and from chance (unknown independent conditions) respectively, but this would be, where we know some of the conditions operative, to forfeit the use of knowledge which we possess. If we wished to reckon the probability of either series occurring by chance, I suppose we should have to take (*faute de mieux*) the chances of failure and success as even for each flower.

of flower may be equally well adapted to normal conditions, but that *in the observed series of cases* the Fly Ophrys may have been the victim of a set of disasters which destroyed the flowers inspected, by causes lying outside the limits of adaptation of either flower. Abortion of the flower or destruction by insects before maturity may easily prevent seeding in one flower out of four. Now of course in the first place it is an impossible assumption that Darwin would not have noticed any extraordinary prevalence of abnormal interfering causes confined to the flowers of the Fly Ophrys. In order to obtain a useful 'not-a is not *a*' the two negative contents must diverge from the positive a and *a* only in a-ness and *a*-ness. They must be, as we have insisted, within the same real system; i.e. the R of general conditions must be the same in both, or in the same relation to both[1].

But in the second place, making this false assumption for the sake of illustrating our point, we will suggest that one flower in four of the Fly Ophrys is *on the average* destroyed by accidents which no adaptation could avert. And then it becomes not impossible that in a given series of forty-eight inspected flowers, these accidents have been heaped together by unknown causes; and that the flowers, though adapted to *all* normal conditions,—i.e. as successfully adapted as those of the Bee Ophrys,—were nevertheless in forty-two cases out of a given forty-eight hindered from being fertilised by a series of extraordinary accidents. We have then to compare, as regards the Fly Ophrys, the hypotheses of maladaptation to normal conditions, such as to cause failure in forty-two cases out of forty-eight, and of perfect adaptation to normal conditions, hindered of its effect by abnormal conditions in forty-two cases out of forty-eight. The possibility of making this

---

[1] It is not indeed fair to say that in order to a just comparison the Fly Ophrys must have its insects as the other must have its wind, because the question is whether the Fly Ophrys was wise to rely on so capricious an agency as that of insects. But there must be no extraordinary influence known to be keeping the insects from it.

comparison by calculation depends on our being able to assign an average ratio of operation to the abnormal causes. Taking them to produce on an average established by general observation one failure to be fertilised in every four flowers, and excluding probabilities derived from the non-appearance of extraordinary hindrances in the instances of the Bee Ophrys, we have to determine the probability that in forty-eight independent flowers, with three favourable chances and only one unfavourable for each flower, we should obtain a set (in any order) of forty-two failures and only six successes. I presume that this problem is the same as to estimate the chances of drawing a black ball exactly forty-two times in forty-eight out of a box containing only four balls, being three white balls and one black ball. These chances would be expressed I suppose by $(\frac{3}{4})^6 \times (\frac{1}{4})^{42}$—the chances of six successes in drawing a white ball on *assigned* occasions—multiplied by the combinations of forty-eight things taken six together, in order to add together the number of independent ways in which six successes and forty-two failures can be realised.

This probability, which must be very low, owing to the enormous number of failures required, with the low chance $\frac{1}{4}$ for each, has to be compared with the high probability with which the assumption that, *normally*, insects only visit one flower in eight, and that therefore the flowers are maladapted to seven sets of conditions in eight, would give as a consequence the ratio of forty-two failures in forty-eight flowers. This would I suppose be the same as the chance that out of a box containing seven black balls and one white, forty-two black balls should be drawn in forty-eight trials. The combinations remain the same as in the former case, and the factor supplied by the fractions expressing the chances would be $(\frac{1}{8})^6 \times (\frac{7}{8})^{42}$, involving a high power, the forty-second, of the very favourable chance $\frac{7}{8}$. The comparison of these probabilities would be our warrant for deciding, on the assumptions which we have made, that Fly Ophrys is much worse adapted to normal conditions than the Bee Ophrys. In fact, our conclusion is much more certain than on these assumptions, for it is certain that any violent interfering cause which destroyed one flower in four would have been noticed and excluded by any such observer as Darwin. But in as far as we rely on the exclusion we are ceasing to rely on number and are going back to analysis of content. The exclusion, however, in such varied and uncertain conditions is probably imperfect, and therefore, in our actual inference, I take it that we eke out our reliance on Darwin's accuracy of comparison by a reliance on the probability of a normal feature in the conditions (viz. a degree of unsuitability to the flower) as against the very low probability of a variety of accidental conditions which Darwin did not exclude. We shall illustrate this particular application of the inference from number of instances directly.

The above case may serve as a type of all Inductive processes in which number of instances, as number, plays an essential part. Their essence consists in selecting as most probable that cause or class of causes which would produce, as an alternative bearing the largest proportion to the sum of possible alternatives, the ratio actually observed among the phenomena. Apart from the assumption of any particular cause, every additional instance enormously increases the improbability of *every* single definite succession by making every such succession one among an immensely increased number of possible alternative successions (or conjunctions). If therefore any cause can be alleged or supposed, which would give that particular definite succession which exists in reality as sole alternative or as one of a comparatively small number of alternatives, the principle of impartial ignorance urges us to decide for that cause as giving to the actual observed succession the nearest approach to its actual position as real—i.e. the largest share of estimated reality. Or if two or more causes are suggested, from which each component event of the actual observed succession can be derived as one out of different numbers of alternatives respectively (e.g. as one out of three alternatives in one case and as one out of twenty alternatives in another), then we compare the probability of these two causes just on the same principle as that on which we compare the probability of a single imputed cause and that of the total absence of any single cause at all, forming a case in which the actual succession must be attributed to a succession of what we call accidents. *A particular class of accidents* however, such as that assumed above as destroying one flower in four before maturity, is of course a class of causes, and may be defined and treated for purposes of calculation as 'a cause.'

Number of instances thus operates by increasing the improbability *per se* of every particular conjunction or succession of phenomena, and therefore increasing the probability of any cause which can be proved capable of producing the given conjunction or succession as one out of fewer alternatives than the number derivable from any other suggested cause or from the whole series of instances treated as accidental. Probability is estimated by counting, on the basis of impartial ignorance; hence the opposition between enumeration of instances and analysis of content.

The case of so-called elimination of irregularities by accumulation of instances may readily be exhibited as an application of the above principle. A class of causes, or common element in a variety of active conditions, is for our present purpose a cause or ground. If, on the accumulation of instances, there appears in the observed succession or conjunction any feature, e.g. of recurrence in certain cycles, or *a fortiori* of persistence in a single character, which can be hypothetically referred to any common element in the wholly unknown conditions; then the accumulation of instances progressively increases the relative probability of causation by this common element, by progressively decreasing the probability of every conceivable sequence, including the one observed if considered as the result of accident, i.e. of independent causes[1]. In other words, it

---

[1] See below, p. 175, on Kirchoff's proof of the presence of iron in the sun.

becomes more and more probable that, the unknown irregularities notwithstanding, the unknown conditions include a common element, however composed, relative to the persistent feature of the observed conjunction or succession, and uninterfered with by the unknown irregularities of the unknown conditions. Material considerations of content, suggesting an approximation to exhaustiveness in the enumeration of kinds of instances and consequently of kinds of conditions, are almost invariably present to reinforce in some degree the argument from sheer probability.

iv. Experiment is observation under artificial conditions. What is artificial bears to a certain extent the impress of human intelligence, and is, to this extent, abstract and idealised. Human action, in virtue of the human thought which directs it, is definite and selective. And 'artificial' means produced or arranged by human action. The difference between observation and experiment therefore is in the degree of definiteness and ideal selection which is present in the material conditions of the latter process. *Observation and Experiment.*

a. It is obvious that natural conditions would serve the purposes of enquiry as well as artificial conditions on the assumption that they were exhaustively known. And if exhaustive knowledge of natural conditions were in no case possible, observation could not exist as a scientific process. But it must be noticed that in giving effect to the knowledge which guides it, observation itself tends to take on the character of experiment. The transition between the two processes is therefore gradual. Experiment would usually be considered to begin where we pass from intentional selection of our standpoint and from the use of contrivances auxiliary to perception, to actual analytic interference with the object under observation. Before the line is reached, however, observation passes into something which may properly be called 'natural experiment.' I quote an excellent passage from Jevons[1] in illustration of this point. *Natural Experiment.*

[1] Principles of Science, pp. 400-1.

'It may readily be seen that we pass upwards by insensible gradations from pure observation to determinate experiment. When the earliest astronomers simply noticed the ordinary motions of the sun, moon, and planets, upon the face of the starry heavens, they were pure observers. But astronomers now select precise times and places for important observations of stellar parallax, or the transits of planets. They make the earth's orbit the basis of a well-arranged *natural experiment*, as it were, and take well-considered advantage of motions which they cannot control. Meteorology might seem to be a science of pure observation, because we cannot possibly govern the changes of weather which we record. Nevertheless we may ascend mountains or rise in balloons, like Gay-Lussac and Glaisher, and may thus so vary the points of observation as to render our procedure experimental. We are wholly unable either to produce or prevent earth-currents of electricity, but when we construct long lines of telegraph, we gather such strong currents during periods of disturbance as to render them capable of easy observation.'

Observation with accurate instruments.

β. There is a further point connected with this transition which calls for remark. We habitually speak of telescopic, microscopic, or even of spectroscopic observation. Considering what an enormous artificial interference the instruments thus employed exert upon the image of the object to be observed, it may seem strange that we call the result an observation and not an experiment. The instinct which guides our use of language is however just, at least so far as concerns the ordinary applications of telescope and microscope as magnifying instruments. An apparatus which merely brings the object nearer our perception is *par excellence* an observing instrument. In the compound microscope the image is variously transformed, and often goes through some degree of chromatic dispersion, *in transitu*, but as it is reconstituted before reaching the eye, these transformations do not amount to experiment. This question turns on the employment of interference not

CHAP. IV.] *Phases of Condition and Result.* 145

merely to make an object accessible to us, but to analyse its content. Thus the moment we modify the object under observation itself, e.g. by applying heat, electricity, or chemical reagents on the stage of the microscope, we say that we are experimenting. When we use spectroscopic devices to observe the real prominences of the sun, without waiting for a total eclipse, we are really analysing the solar image, though not the sun, but strong analogy from the general use of optical instruments makes us still say that we are observing. In actually compounding coloured lights with a colour-box for the purpose of equation, however, there is no doubt that we are experimenting. The fact is then that experiment is not merely observation under artificial or determinate conditions, but *observation under determinate conditions which constitute an integral part of the image or product to be observed.* Thus common dissection is not experiment, though it introduces conditions in the way of separation and demarcation as definite as anything can be; but vivisection is experiment, because the determinate conditions it produces enter as factors into the action of the organism observed.

γ. Returning for the sake of brevity to the symbols which we used before, we may say that the function of experiment is to exhibit both a and not-a as determinate cases of β, γ, δ, &c. which form the ultimate analysis of R so far as R is relevant to a. The cases of $\beta \gamma \delta$, &c. obviously may include zero values of any one or more of these factors, and apart from a special hypothesis to be tested—or rather if the hypothesis to be tested is merely that $\beta \gamma \delta$ are concerned in a—all possible combinations of values of the three or more series must be tried. a moreover is certain to be continuous, and to admit of variation within itself; for no phenomenon is utterly atomic. But in order to secure a distinct correspondence between phases of condition and of effect, it is well to treat every appreciable phase a, within the general a, in turn, as a bounded by not-a, so as to identify its condition a, viz. a phase of $\beta \gamma \delta$,

Experiment expressed in logical symbols.

with absolute precision, as being on both sides bounded by not-a, viz. other positive phases of $\beta\gamma\delta$ excluding that which is a. The goal to be attained, if the experimental conditions admit of it, is a reciprocal Hypothetical judgment; consisting of an affirmative hypothetical judgment in the form, 'If a (a determinate phase, or series of phases, of $\beta\gamma\delta$), then a,' supported by its *simply* corroborative equivalent, 'If not-a[1], then not-a' (viz. determinate phases of $\beta\gamma\delta$ excluding the phases a), and by its reciprocally corroborative equivalent, 'If not-a, then not-a.'

Can this reciprocal, equivalent to 'If a then a,' be justified by experiment, which can at best take the shape, 'in order to remove a you must remove a,' and not 'by removing a you remove a'? It can be thus justified on the assumption that a considered as a phase of $\beta\gamma\delta$ is an ultimate analysis of R. For in this case all possible combinations of the ultimate components of R have been exhausted, and we can lay down throughout them all the demarcation between a and not-a. But if we take R in its primary meaning, of which we cannot stop short without special justification—viz. as the entire system of the universe—this assumption can never be true except in virtue of a consistent abstraction by which it is taken as true.

Such an abstraction is the source of mathematical necessity. I will not say that in mathematical construction we are secure from the irruption of any conditions beyond those which we have put there, because we may be guilty of omission or oversight on mathematical ground, and the fact that discoveries can be made in mathematics seems to show that such omission constitutes the gradually receding limit of the science. But it may safely be said that in mathematical construction we are secure against

---

[1] Not-a under experimental conditions is of course itself positive and exclusive of a. If there are different not-a's, as is quite possible at first sight, they determine different a's. E.g. aerial impulses too slow to be heard as musical sound, and discord, are two not-a's as against a's in musical sound.

any conditions which do not fall within the definite general type of those which we have put there.

Apart from such an abstraction, the assumption that we have a perfect analysis of R is always erroneous, and the postulate that we must express a and not-a in terms of the ultimate analysis of R is theoretically incapable of being fulfilled. The approximate or presumptive fulfilment of the postulate depends chiefly on our general systematic knowledge of the course of things, which enables us, as we think, to draw a line between R_1 the whole irrelevant residuum, R_2 the real basis of both a and the positive not-a which make up the phenomenon *prima facie* in question, and therefore *as such* irrelevant to the distinction between a and not-a, and R_3 the limited number of precise positive conditions on the combination of which, including their reciprocal interference, the precise distinction between a and not-a depends. R_3 is finally reduced to the general a. It is obvious that R_3 has its roots in R_2, and R_2 in R_1, so that the distinction between these remainders cannot be pressed far except on the ground of specific knowledge. Gravity for example belongs to R_1 in relation to an acoustical experiment which I purpose to describe presently. No doubt gravity is essential to this experiment in the same sense in which it is essential to all that takes place on the surface of the globe. But the variations of gravity within their actual limits do not affect the experiment appreciably or at all. Thus general systematic knowledge operates through confining the immediate problem to R_3 or at most to R_2 and R_3, by setting down R_1 as for this purpose not-R, viz. not a residuum within the problem, but one outside it. R of the problem (viz. R_2 and R_3) is related to not-R of the problem (viz. R_1) just as a is related to not-a in the immediate experiment.

And secondarily, in as far as R_1 is *not* materially known, but is an unknown residuum, a presumption of its irrelevancy may be supported by the *number* of instances in which R (as R_2 and R_3) is a sufficient R for the experiment, i.e. presents a and not-a as required. This confirmation of the line drawn between the R of the problem and the not-R of the problem is precisely the same in kind as the confirmation by number of instances of a material difference in the adaptation of two plants to their environment, worked out above, p. 138. Every successful trial to generate a and not-a on the basis of the R of the problem alone, increases the difference between the probability of the result on the hypothesis that it is due to the known factors included in the R of the problem, whose certainty of existence is assumed [1], and the probability that the successive occurrences of a and not-a are due to independent causes, some of which must therefore fall outside the persistent conditions which make up R_2 and R_3.

If, on the other hand, we confine ourselves to the R of the problem in its most limited sense, viz. to R_3 analysed as β, γ, δ, then the assumption that we have in β, γ, δ an ultimate analysis of R can only be questioned on the ground of a further analysis suggested or presumed. The possibility of a *positive suggestion* needs no explanation; it would arise from conjunctive induction and pass through analogy in the ordinary way, having the form 'δ is probably complex, consisting of λ, μ, ν,' and would be tested by further experiment in the ordinary way, some part of such experiment probably coinciding with passing $\beta \gamma \delta$ through their possible variations. This experiment would however then be extended by taking account of the variations and zero values of $\lambda \mu \nu$ and including or excluding these, as the result might require, in the analysis of a and not-a. A *presumption* of further analysis very commonly arises when no positive suggestion is forthcoming. We have a strong presumption e.g. from the history of chemistry and from the nature of ordinary substances that we shall not constantly be lighting upon new elements; and therefore we do not assume an unfamiliar substance to be an element—

---

[1] Because if we fail to produce them all, we do not expect a, nor count the case as a trial.

i. e. we presume that further analysis is possible—even though we should fail to analyse it at the first attempt.

After using the above example, however, I must guard myself against the idea that 'analysis' is for this logical purpose to be understood in a sense borrowed from chemistry. Logical analysis is the understanding of any whole in reference to its constituent parts or factors, and chemical analysis is only the understanding of a chemical whole as chemical. It is a trite observation, but perhaps necessary to be repeated here, that the analysis *of* an organism, if it is not its analysis *as* an organism, may destroy rather than display its inmost nature. If δ is an organic element, and λ, μ, ν are its chemical constituents, then our first business in 'analysing' is to ascertain whether we want these constituents λ, μ, ν, which are, strictly speaking, constituents not of δ but of δ_1 (δ as a *merely* chemical substance), or whether we want other constituents o, π, τ, which if we can we may then further construe into forms of combined chemical action $\lambda \mu \nu (o), \lambda \mu \nu (\pi), \lambda \mu \nu (\tau)$. In speaking of *organic* characteristics as capable of analysis, I have in mind such questions as the precise degree, direction and mode of transmission in which irritability in plants sets up reflex action; or how far certain movements are reflex and how far purely mechanical—e.g. in the case of circumnutation[1]. The description of analysis needed in each particular case must of course be determined by the nature of a, and the consequent nature of parts or factors with reference to which it is to be understood.

5. A very simple and beautiful example of the progressive reciprocal definition by experiment of a—a and not-a—not-a is to be found in the well-known verification of the connection between rapidity of periodic vibrations and

Experiment with the Siren analysed.

---

[1] I have not the smallest desire to deny that the joint action of $\lambda \mu \nu$ as chemical agents may make up, and, for all I care, initiate the action of δ as organic. The question of abiogenesis is an open one for Logic. I am only pointing out that, combined as δ, the constituents λ, μ, ν acquire organic attributes o, π, τ, which are capable of having their nature precisely determined by experiment.

musical pitch, as given by help of Helmholtz's Siren. The reader would do well to study the account and figure of this instrument in Helmholtz's Popular Lectures [1]. In the light of the account which has just been given of the logical purpose of experiment we may roughly analyse this arrangement as follows :—

R_1, or the not-R of the problem, may be typified by the action of gravity, which pervades all matter, but the variations of which within their actual limits are indifferent to the phenomena now in question.

The R of the problem, consisting of R_2 and R_3, within which a—a and not-a—not-a are to be sought for, is in general terms the musical sound produced by the machine, and its conditions, including the machine. Of these we may take as R_2 (extending, as we knew it must, continuously into R_1) the air in the room, the hearing ear, and the machine itself, as operative in the production of a physical effect which together with a hearing ear results in musical sound. R_2 is relevant as the proximate basis of the phenomenon itself, and as such, regarded by contrast to R_1 or not R, is itself an a defined by a not-a and connected with an a. But *prima facie* and outside the experiment itself, R_2 does not demand much analysis. The air in the room or some conductor of sound must act as a medium between the machine and the ear—sound cannot pass through a vacuum ;—the ear must not be outrageously abnormal—this is included in a reasonable interpretation of 'hearing ear';—and of course there must be no other source of sound undistinguished from the machine itself. And as R_3, the unanalysed whole which *is* the phenomenon, we must take the action of the machine as already somewhat idealised by analysis, i.e. in respect of its quantitatively specified effect upon the air in generating aerial impulses with a measurable rapidity of succession restricted to certain limits, and in one series, or in two simultaneous series, at pleasure.

---

[1] Engl. Transl., published by Longmans & Co., Series I, p. 57 ff.

a, the musical sound[1], is most conveniently considered as included in R_3, but as also distinguished by anticipation and confronted with the gradually narrowing R's and their analyses as the problem to which they are all directed. Ultimately, however, a itself will of course be reacted upon by analysis, and will be found to include distinct elements both in kind and in degree.

If we omit, for the sake of brevity, to speak of the characteristics of quality and loudness in musical sound (and these are in fact not especially illustrated by the Siren), we find that R_3 is immediately reducible to a very simple relation, the relation of comparative rapidity of succession between series of puffs of air, which series differ in no other assignable respect. R_3 is, in other words, assumed *ad hoc* to be exhaustively analysed. Confining our attention, to begin with, to the case of a single series (and not two sounding at once) we become aware *first* of a constant relation between any given rapidity and the pitch of the note which is heard while that rapidity is maintained, and *secondly* of a relation of quasi-proportion, sufficiently explained above[2], according to which rapidity is to rapidity in a definite numerical ratio, while pitch is to pitch in a definite recognisable relation, measurable by intervals but not made by summation of intervals. First, then, every particular rapidity is to us as an a, deviations from which on either side are *to it* as not-a, corresponding to an a deviations from which on either side are *to it* as not-a. But as each and every deviation from a brings a 'proportional' deviation from a with it, every such not-a is to some corresponding not-a as an a to an a; and we have therefore the most perfect case of negative relation between positive contents. But, secondly, when the quasi-proportional character of the two series attracts attention (which it did from the earliest times, as a fact demanding

[1] '*What* musical sound?' the reader may ask. I reply, *in fact* some musical sound in particular, but as a problem musical sound in general. It is impossible to particularise the sound you have heard, except as a result of advancing analysis.

[2] See p. 70, above.

explanation, owing to the relation of the length of strings to the notes which they sound) it becomes an essential element in the relation which constitutes R_3, and presents itself as a further determination of the mere principle ' rapidity has a constant connection with pitch,' which forms the first simple *a—a*. We thus obtain the suggestion of a *law*, and the verification of this suggested law becomes the object of the experimental process. A law is treated just like any content *a*. The object is to show that *a* the realisation of the condition is attended by *a* the realisation of the consequent, and that not-*a*, any deviation from the consequent (ultimately perhaps a variation of the consequent), is preceded or attended by a deviation from or variation of the condition. Thus as always our goal is in the Hypothetical judgment, 'If *a*, then *a*,' with its reciprocal, 'If *a*, then *a*.'

It is further worth while to mention how the experiment in question obtains minute measurable variations of *a* and *a* at pleasure. If rapidity corresponds to pitch in a certain proportion, then two rapidities in the right proportion correspond to a definite harmony. Deviations from a harmony are recognisable by a trained ear with extreme minuteness. Helmholtz's Siren will sound two sets of impulses, of controllable rapidity, together; and in the first place by adjusting the two precisely to the proportion required by the law, it verifies the law *a—a* in a compound case. But then by a contrivance for very delicately, and measurably, altering the rapidity of one of the series, a slight or considerable discord can be produced at pleasure. If we were interpreting *a—a* as '1 : 2 gives note and octave,' this result reads as a confirmatory content, 'not *a—*not-*a*,' i. e. 'deviation from 1 : 2 gives deviation from note : octave.' But of course, as before, this not-*a* is a case of *a*, rapidity corresponding to pitch, though not to two notes, one an octave above the other, *because* the sets of impulses are not as 2 : 1 in rapidity.

But here, with the Siren alone, we are pretty much at an end of our analysis. That R_3 is not merely a law of rapidity in succession, but a complex theorem concerning shapes of vibrations and their decomposition into pure pendulum oscillations, related to the *quality* of a and to discordant beats in a (if a includes two notes sounding together), does not appear from the above experiment. It would perhaps not have been suspected but for the obvious fact that an air wave must have some shape, on the one hand, and that pitch is not the only element in sound, on the other.

The point of the above illustration consists especially in displaying the various senses of not-a, and the various stages of its adjustment to a. R_1 is not-a in one sense, R_2 in another, and in a relative and shifting manner portions of R_3 are not-a also. The same applies throughout to not-a. Induction consists in separating the R's and in establishing those variations of a which appear, against any fixed starting-point, as relative not-a's (and the same with a).

I may conclude this chapter by calling attention again to what I have insisted on in another work[1], as the claim of an experimental apparatus to be considered in the light of a reasoning machine. It must be granted that in any logical engine whatever we have to make the conclusion, i. e. to read it off as a conclusion, and if we are to do this we may read off the connection of imperfect ratio and false harmony from the Siren as distinctly as we can read a combination of letters from Jevons' logical machine. In the operations of nature, causes have their consequences; but the causes are not precisely known, and the consequences are therefore not consequents. In experimental instruments we find the attempt made to generate actual consequences which shall also be consequents, as arising from conditions precisely known in respect of the mode and degree of their combination. Any instrument which does this may be called a reasoning machine, whether it deals with combinations and eliminations of letters as logical symbols, or with the same relations of actual number, or of

[1] Knowledge and Reality, p. 327 ff. Cp. Jevons, Principles of Science, p. 282 ff.

any definite motions with their effects. The value of the connections thus demonstrated is of various degrees; but a complex experimental apparatus has the advantage in the synthetic variety of the contents which it exhibits as relevant to each other, if the logical machine has the advantage in the abstract generality of its formal conclusions.

CHAPTER V.

SCIENTIFIC INDUCTION (*continued*).

1. HYPOTHESIS is a name that may be applied to any conception by which the mind establishes relations between data of testimony, of perception, or of sense, so long as that conception is one among alternative possibilities, and is not referred to reality as a fact. *[Hypothesis and Postulate.]*

i. From Aristotle onward, indeed, logicians have been anxious to consider a hypothesis as the suggestion of a real agent—a thing or occurrence in a thing—related to the data as 'cause' to 'effect'; and to distinguish such a suggested 'agent' from a mere suggested 'reading' of the phenomena —a principle, law, or definition. Of course there is a primary difference between a material agent and an ideal law or principle, but the distinction is not ultimate in theory and appears to be, for this reason, incapable of being sustained in scientific practice. A 'working hypothesis'—and most of the great unifying conceptions of modern science are working hypotheses—is the suggestion of a real agent taken as equivalent to the suggestion of a mere law or principle. It is worth while for the sake of clearness to look at the distinction between law and real agent in a form recently given to it by Lotze, viz. as the distinction between Postulate and Hypothesis. *[Hypothesis falls outside Postulate.]*

In the account to which I refer[1] the name of *Postulate* is given to the conditions which are absolutely and essentially involved in a given set of appearances, and apart from which 'the content of the observation with which we are dealing

[1] Lotze, Logik, sect. 273.

would contradict the laws of our thought.' These conditions, it must be observed, need not be abstract, except in the sense of being definite and precise. They might therefore, I infer, exhaust or define the nature of a real agent, in so far as a real agent is capable of being determinately known. But it is plain that as a rule they will not suffice to do so. The concrete nature of a material thing will contain much that is indifferent to the conditions precisely involved in any determinate effect.

By *hypothesis*, therefore, in this same account, is meant a conjecture which specifies the natural agents taken to be at work in a phenomenon and to be the means of fulfilling the postulate involved in it, in the case under investigation. In other cases, it is implied, the same postulate might be satisfied by means of other agents. And, it should be added, by a *fiction* is meant the reference of an effect to a cause or principle which we know to be incapable of producing it, but from the real effects of which it only differs by an error which is capable of being determinately assigned. Omitting the case of a confessed fiction, and including a fiction, not confessed to be such, under the title of a hypothesis, we may throw the remainder of our discussion into the form of an enquiry into the distinction between Hypothesis and Postulate.

The Postulate sets an abstract problem which Hypothesis has to solve in the concrete. The distinction *prima facie* coincides with that upon which Mill lays stress in his treatment of hypothesis, between a quantitative law of action, and the thing which acts according to that law. But it would certainly seem that every hypothesis in order to be established must be passed over into the content of the postulate, in the sense that, without the matter suggested in the *hypothesis* also, 'the content of the observations with which we are dealing would contradict the laws of our thought.' For this is ultimately the ground on which we affirm of Reality everything that we do so affirm. When the postulate is shown to contain the hypothesis, by a concrete proof that the suggested thing or fact is necessary to prevent self-contradiction in our thought, then we have a hypothesis with a *vera causa* (see ii. below). When the hypothesis is moulded into the postulate, not or not exclusively by proof of the concrete supposition, but in a great degree by attenuating its content into a 'law of action,' then we have a 'working hypothesis,' i.e. materially an abstract postulate, but formally a supposition of a real agent. Such a hypothesis is a fiction which may or may not be a confessed fiction. In Mill's notes on Whewell[1] we see the process of attenuation at work, reducing hypotheses to fictions which are confessed by Mill and not confessed by Whewell. Modern science seems to the outsider more and more tending to substitute explanation by laws of action for causation by unknown real agents. But, in theory, a determinate agent may be involved in the postulate just as much as an abstract law, supposing that the agent is operative in the content in modes sufficiently many-sided to assign it a determinate nature. For logic, law and agent are alike conceptions by which thought constitutes the content into an organised whole; both may be 'within' the content, if we include in the content what is needed to constitute it rightly; neither can be within the content if we separate it, by an unreal and indeed impossible distinction, from the work of thought in determining it. Every object of perception is such a conception, by which data of sense are determined in a way necessary to make them intelligible.

The real distinction which Lotze should have drawn is not between the law of action and the concrete real agent, but between the concrete real agent as known to be necessary for the explanation of the observations, and such an agent

[1] Mill's Logic, i. p. 335, and ii. p. 24; e.g. 'Can an agency undulate? Can there be alternate motion backwards and forwards of the particles of an agency?' Mill is maintaining in effect that Whewell's view of the imponderable agents reduces them to laws of action. He is distinguishing an *agency* from an *agent* (the ether). And cf. Clifford on Causation, Lectures, &c., vol. i. p. 153.

as not so known, but arbitrarily imagined, or identified with something known from other sources. If we assume a thing thus arbitrarily, or on the ground of extraneous knowledge, then (considering the thing in the latter case apart from the extraneous knowledge on the ground of which it is assumed) we have the relation 'If a, then a,' but not the reciprocal 'If a, then a'; i.e. in other cases other agents than a might satisfy the same postulate, or minimum of conditions, involved in a. But this unnecessary element in a hypothesis cannot of course be acquiesced in. The supposed real agent must either be elevated into the content of a postulate, or depressed into that of a fiction. Obviously, however, before deciding that the latter course is the only one open to us, we must concentrate *all* available knowledge upon the supposed real agent in order to test its right to become a postulate. One science e.g. may need one aspect of it, and another another.

Hypothesis with *Vera Causa*.

ii. Thus to meet the difficulty that many characteristics of a *thing* assumed hypothetically to account for certain data are likely to fall outside what those data demand and justify, it is usual to require of a hypothesis that a the supposed agent shall be a *vera causa*. This can ultimately have but one meaning. It must come to this, that a, though containing elements which are superfluous for the explanation of *the data from which we happen to have started*, yet contains no elements which are not necessary to the explanation of *some data or other*. It is commonly said that a *vera causa* is one independently known to exist, or accessible to direct perception. Of course we do not restrict our conviction of reality to matters accessible to direct perception—the centre of the earth, the inside of a block of marble, the other side of the moon, are cases in point. And if we did attempt this restriction, what is direct perception? All perception is inferential, and proceeds by furnishing conceptions which bring data of sense into intelligible relation. And if we require that the cause shall be independently known to exist, this is a mere question of

the range of observations which it is to explain. A *vera* √
causa then is a thing, or occurrence in a thing, whose reality
we are thoroughly convinced of from the necessity of
reconciling observed data [1], and there is no reason in the
nature of things why a single science or a single range
of reality should not suffice to produce such conviction.
'*Direct* perception' is a mere popular phrase without logical
meaning. The question is simply whether our data are √
determinate enough to guide us to the nature of a real
thing as explaining them. What is *really* demanded in
the *vera causa* is probably *independent* evidence of the
thing's reality, with an eye to the doctrine of chances.
A single coherent set of errors may vitiate a whole coherent system of appearances, but the chances against
errors in *independent* sets of observations are the same as
the rapidly increasing chances against coincidences of independent events [2]. This is a parody (as the doctrine of
chances is always a formal parody of some material truth)
of the operation of multiform data in moulding a concrete
hypothesis, which will be illustrated directly.

Thus in a 'working hypothesis' we have postulate and
hypothesis tending to identification by attenuation [3] of the
hypothesis, in a hypothesis with *vera causa* we obtain
the same result by extension of the postulate to cover the
alleged cause and turn it into a *vera causa*.

2. In an ultimate sense, there is no knowledge without Phases of
Hypothesis. Hypo-
thesis.

i. 'All science may be rightly described as progressive

[1] The most thorough and simple way of classifying matters known from
testimony or history is to include them under the head of conceptions which
are necessary to determine observed data, the observed data being the books,
speech, etc. which bring the facts to our individual notice. As to ranking
agents under the head of conceptions, I may say that this is not reducing
agents to mere conceptions. As known and established to us, they *are* conceptions, though they may be more.

[2] If the chance of error in one set of data is $\frac{1}{2}$, the chance of independent error in
two sets (of the same but independent liability to error) is $\frac{1}{4}$, in three $\frac{1}{8}$, and so on.

[3] A working hypothesis often, and perhaps usually, partakes of the character
of a fiction, being in fact suggested as a *vera causa*, and subsequently attenuated
till it is clearly not a *vera causa*, though retaining its original claim to be so.

Rudimentary Hypothesis.

"colligation of facts" through superinduction of conceptions[1]' if it is understood that, though such conceptions are present in the real facts and are not mere additions out of our heads, yet in the progress of our knowledge such colligation does not operate upon the real facts themselves, but only on the facts as imperfectly understood by us. Thus the whole course of the present work has been an attempt to trace the progressive determination of feelings, or of facts imperfectly understood, by conceptions which may be regarded as hypotheses in course of development and proof. The continued identity of an individual, for example, which is the soul of the individual judgment, may be regarded as a conception or hypothesis which is superinduced (though without conscious reflection) upon the successive appearances which we observe, and 'colligates' these facts. And as we have seen in speaking of Induction, hypothesis in a genuine sense, as a conscious activity, begins to operate where the individual judgment begins to be employed in explaining the conjunction of attributes, in conjunctive or enumerative Induction. From this point, at which Hypothesis is represented by the content of a generic or specific name, we have watched its development through analogy and through scientific analysis, till in the experiment of the Siren we found ourselves testing by determinate perceptive comparison a relation which can only be completely explained by a complex mathematical theorem[2].

Mediate Hypothesis.
ii. Procedure by Hypothesis proper is mediate.

Hypothetical Nature of Induction.
a. It is clear from what has been said that we must assent in substance to the view of Jevons and Sigwart which is in the main that of Whewell[3] and De Morgan[4], so far as it asserts the essential identity of Induction with procedure by Hypothesis. And indeed Mill himself might almost be reckoned on this side. He shows[5] triumphantly that the

---
[1] Green, Philosophical Works, ii. p. 288.
[2] The theory of wave-propagation, which explains among other things the discordant beats produced by sonorous impulses which have not certain definite ratios of rapidity.
[3] See Mill's Logic, ii. 24.   [4] Budget of Paradoxes, p. 49.   [5] Logic, ii. 12.

Function of Hypothesis.

Method of Difference will test the premises of a Deduction, and the fact that the 'instances' on which it operates are in that case obtained by Deduction, he sets down as of no consequence, i.e. as not interfering with its Inductive character. But it is not so clear that this method, which unquestionably will test the consequences of a precise deduction and therefore the truth of its premises, will perform any other function that could be called Inductive. Mill's objection [1] against Whewell's hypothetical method, on the ground of insufficient provision for excluding unproved or unproveable elements of hypothesis, is an objection which arises from the impossible demand for *merely* negative and exhaustive determination. It is very probable that Whewell makes too little of the necessity for showing or for its being possible to show that *nothing but* a could produce *a*; but what Whewell seems to have rightly felt is that this is after all in its essence a material and positive question, depending on the degree and mode of connection between a and *a*, and being for logic the same as the question whether a *as such* produces *a*. The possibility of proof or disproof, which is claimed as essential to the 'legitimacy' of a hypothesis, must be a material or real possibility, and reduces itself to specific presumptions that proof may be had, which are in themselves grades of proof. But while accepting the general view to which I have alluded of the importance of hypothesis in Inductive Inference, I am unable to agree with some important results which have been held to follow upon such a view.

β. I shall begin by endeavouring to lay the true doctrine very briefly before the reader, in the sense in which I understand it and in which it seems to me to follow from our previous discussions. It will then be necessary to speak of the relation between Induction in the scientific sense and the work of generalisation which is popularly ascribed to it, and I shall conclude the present chapter with some observations on the above-mentioned misapprehensions,

Example of fusion between hypothesis and data.

[1] See Mill's Logic, ii. p. 24.

and on the true relation of Induction to Inference as such.

The purpose of the example which I propose to analyse is to exhibit the mediate identification of a hypothetical cause, at first sight somewhat remote, with a given effect. I intentionally select an instance in which the identification is not quite perfect, in order to display the full nature of the difficulty to be overcome.

As a datum to be explained, we will take the curious fact, long known to scholars, that the Greek god Apollo, especially the Apollo of the Troad, is associated with the mouse, both in his appellation Smintheus and in recorded usages—there were sacred mice and figures of mice in his temple, and so forth [1].

The conjunction of aspects which excites surprise in this fact is the association of an insignificant animal with the worship and the temples of a comparatively pure religion. A large choice of analogies lies open to us, any one of which might furnish some sort of mediation between these two extremes, and of these that which is at first sight the most remote may perhaps on a consideration of all the phenomena be considered the most hopeful.

It seems that in the Peruvian religion we find this same conjunction of aspects, the association of insignificant animals with the worship and the temples of a comparatively pure creed. And in that instance, it further appears, we have a definite and complete mediation or explanation of the two terms or 'extremes.' Before the establishment of Sun-worship by the Incas as the creed of the state, the Indians of the various tribes worshipped tribal animal gods, including all sorts of insignificant animals, the Indians of each tribe believing themselves to be descended from some one of these animals. 'After the establishment of the purer religion, the Incas had the good policy to collect all the

---

[1] My example and my arguments are all drawn from Mr. Lang's Custom and Myth, p. 103 ff. My purpose however only permits the most meagre reproduction of some points out of this interesting study.

tribal animal gods into their temples in and round Cuzco, in which the two leading gods were the Master of Life, and the Sun.' This toleration of an older and cruder in subordination to a purer faith is a very common phenomenon, as Mr. Lang truly observes, in religious evolution. And he cites an example of a festival described by Theocritus which still continues in a Catholic country.

Here then we have a content the whole of which is given (I assume) in perception or in the *proximate* interpretation of perception, viz. in history. Analogy or Induction would not commonly be held to apply within the limits of this content; but nevertheless in as far as within the single 'instance' or range of reality—which is really the life of a whole nation—a *principle* is detected by our thought, there is operative what constitutes the essence of inductive as of all other inference. But no details have to be referred to reality solely on the strength of the principle, because it happens that they are all warranted by testimony [1].

Now if the content which perplexed us in Greek religious history fell *bona fide* within the lines of the content thus warranted and interpreted in Peruvian religion, no inference would be necessary, or rather, the purely formal inference which recognised the identification would suffice to include the Greek problem under the same solution as that which supplies itself for the Peruvian problem. But the very slight and superficial abstraction which is all that we have thus far formulated of the Greek problem can warrant no such material identification—so far as we have yet stated the point, almost any hypothesis might explain it; the misunderstanding of a name, or the caprice of a priest or king. What we must now do is to look in the Greek problem for the facts and relations of which we have seen

---

[1] It is probable, and appears I think from Mr. Lang's account, that the interpretation even of the known succession in Peru into an intelligible evolution would involve, as almost every interpretation does, some remodelling and supplementation of details. So far we have inference in the popular sense.

the significance in the Peruvian problem. But as historical data such facts and relations are wanting; and here we have the essential difference between Induction by analysis of Perception, and Induction by mediate Hypothesis. Our hypothesis is *prima facie* a conjectural matter of fact falling wholly outside the content which has to be explained. The view which I wish to illustrate is that our proof of the hypothesis must ultimately depend upon the characteristic positive connection between the hypothesis and its consequences. This connection is as we have seen elucidated and purged of irrelevancy by the establishment of limiting negations, but is not otherwise dependent on the disproof of an indefinite number of alternative hypotheses, and is no more restricted to mere probability than is the determination of any perceived data by any conception which makes them intelligible[1].

We have before us, as a datum of fact, a surprising conjunction between Apollo and the mouse, especially in Apollo's temple. We have as a suggested fact which might explain this conjunction, a previous state of Greek or neighbouring tribes in which they worshipped animals such as the mouse, together with a religious evolution in which the earlier cult survived by the side of the later and purer worship. According to the ordinary process of Induction as inverse Deduction, we proceed to 'deduce the consequences which might be inferred from the hypothesis.'

In drawing consequences from a hypothetical state of facts we have to apply that state of facts to the reality on the basis of which it is supposed, and to examine in detail the results of the combination. This analysis of the content of the hypothesis is not a contrivance of demonstration, but an inevitable necessity of knowledge. In working

---

[1] Contrast with this the mechanical views of Jevons, Principles of Science, p. 152, and Sigwart, Logik, ii. p. 357. Jevons thinks that no proof by Imperfect Induction (Induction falling short of complete enumeration) can be more than probable. Sigwart thinks that a hypothesis is refuted by refuting its consequences, but not proved by establishing them, though it grows in probability as its consequences agree with the facts.

Results of Hypothesis.

out, for example, the hypothesis now before us, we must take into account the customs relating to marriage and to names which belong to that phase of savage life which we are conjecturally imputing to the Greek race in the past. Among savages named after tribal animals which they worship and bear as name or emblem, and from which they trace their descent, the members of one family do not intermarry with people bearing the same name or emblem, and the children of every marriage take the mother's name or emblem (totem). These names consequently tend to become scattered throughout a large region, and are associated with the well-known phenomenon, for which in very early society there are obvious grounds, of counting kinship through the mother and not through the father. On the the other hand, when this state of society passes away, as in European nations it has passed away, it is plain that a powerful family will crush out the names of the other families in a district, and form a local tribe called by an animal name. From this hypothesis thus analysed, if applied to 'mouse families,' there follow primarily four results, which briefly stated amount to this :—

(1) There would be places named from mice, and mice will be held sacred in those places. This was so in the Troad.

(2) The mouse-name would be given locally to the god who superseded the mouse. This was so in the places called after the mouse.

(3) The figure of the mouse would be associated with the god in his temple, and used as a badge or local mark in places where the mouse had been venerated. The former usage was found, and the latter was not uncommon, in Greece.

(4) Stories would be told in the district in question to explain the worship of the mouse. This was so in the Troad.

I do not say that these four points, thus baldly stated, carry us very far. But in so far as they support the hypothesis at all, they do so not merely as an arrangement of coincidences due more probably, in a calculable degree, to a single cause than to independent unknown causes; but, like an arrangement of results *which some person has the power and a strong motive to produce*, they support the conjectural cause by the material connection of the data with it, or a material extension of the data towards including it. One of the above points for example is the appearance of the figure of a mouse as a badge or city emblem in Greece. This, when referred to an actual race of men exceedingly conservative in its customs, is a point, though a trifling one, actually in common between hypothesis and data. The badge or crest of a city is not the same thing as the totem of a family, but the connection of parts of cities with local tribes is too well made out in Greece and elsewhere to give us pause. And the veneration of an animal by the people of a city in ways strikingly analogous to totem worship is made out in the case of Egyptian cities. Of course this point *may* be otherwise explained than by the suggested hypothesis, and so may all the others; but they all, as referred to the life of a race, demand some explanation, and the only difficulty is to model that explanation rightly. It is this idea, that of moulding a hypothesis, that should be substituted for the idea of gauging its probability as something attaching to its definite and irrevocable form. To meet paradox by paradox, rather than admit that a hypothesis can only be established by the refutation of infinite others [1] and the non-refutation of itself, I would maintain that *of every set of data some positive hypothesis* (viz. that 'something or other' conditions these data) *is within our knowledge demonstrably true*, and that the problem of induction by the inverse method or by hypothesis is merely to further determine

---

[1] This is the root of the idea that no results of hypothetical Induction can be certain. The idea is ridiculous when it is once seen that hypothetical Induction is identical in principle with common perception and with all Inference whatever.

this 'something or other.' In this work of definition, as we have abundantly seen, negation is all-important; but it must be motived and relevant negation, 'not *this*, because *that*, which has a determinate relation to this.'

I should weary the reader by further discussion of the mouse hypothesis, which moreover space forbids me to treat in its interesting details. But I must point out that by considering the peculiar marriage customs (e. g. maternal kinship), sacrificial and festival rites, and animistic beliefs, which are traceable throughout Greek life, and which are characteristic of the primitive phase that forms the content of our hypothesis, we can remodel hypothesis and data once more, and this time into a really intimate approximation to each other. Hypothesis and data approach amalgamation in the conception of a finely gifted race still bearing in its prime the traces of a natural though characteristic evolution out of a savage past. We might almost claim that a savage phase of life is a *vera causa, apart from the proof of our special hypothesis*[1], not only in the Peruvian but in the Greek race. Is not the conception of a past and natural evolution, in the case of *any* race of men which we may be considering, a conception 'apart from which the content of the observation with which we are dealing would contradict the laws of our thought'? But if so, then, according to the distinction accepted above, the conception, *although* that of a real agent or event, is a postulate and not a mere hypothesis, and therefore is the conception of a *vera causa*; and the work of induction is, as said above, to assign to the postulate in detail its actual content or law of action.

Other hypotheses, independent of that which the author advocates, are carefully dealt with in the chapter from which I have been quoting. And I think that any one who considers the matter in the light of this or any equally genuine piece of research must feel that just in so far as the adverse hypotheses are independent, their refutation, although a *sine*

---

[1] Every hypothesis *when proved* is a hypothesis with *vera causa*.

qua non of the establishment of the hypothesis advocated, can never genuinely contribute to that establishment. In other words, the refutation of other hypotheses is a genuine assistance to one hypothesis only when it elicits positive content which goes to model this latter hypothesis.

Before leaving this subject I must refer back to the discussion of Book I[1] on cause and ground, and must explain that the content of a hypothesis may correspond, according to the degree of its purity or relevance, to any member of the series there described; to cause, to effect, to antecedent, consequent, or ground. The reason for treating an example in which the popular sense of cause is dominant was simply that the equally popular sense of hypothesis, from which the theoretical difficulty of its use arises, corresponds to the popular sense of cause (or effect). The more scientific type of hypothesis approaches more nearly *prima facie* to the nature of a postulate or ground—of a principle included in the facts, or of a systematic reality which they constitute. And hypotheses which are, to begin with, of this type do not present the great apparent difficulty of passing by sheer inference from isolated data to actual things and facts not included in them. As we have seen, a hypothesis which to begin with is not of this type, necessarily tends, in course of demonstration, to approximate to it; just as, in the case which we tried to analyse, certain isolated data and isolated suggestions about the Greek race tended to coalesce into a systematic conception of that race as developing in a normal fashion under the natural influences and conditions which appear to be common to mankind.

Generalisation.

3. It is unquestionably the case, that a process or result which may be termed Generalisation is somehow connected with Induction. The only question is how to state the connection.

'From many to all' exploded.

i. I trust that the popular idea according to which Induction is a process from what happens often to what happens always, from particulars to the totality of particulars, has

[1] Chap. vi.

been set in its true light by the whole scheme of our account of Induction. The conception, to which unhappily Professor Jevons adhered, of Perfect and Imperfect Induction as corresponding to complete and incomplete enumeration is hopelessly fallacious. It cannot, I think, be necessary to pursue this error at the present stage.

ii. There is a sense in which all abstraction, i.e. all becoming conscious of the determination of sensuous data by explicit conceptions, operates as Generalisation. Such generalisation is embodied in the hypothetical judgment, which of course is not hypothetical *qua* judgment and is in no sense a hypothesis, but is an affirmation, based upon a reality illustrated by a hypothesis. The explicit conditions forming a determinate case which, as the antecedent in the hypothetical judgment, illustrate or qualify Reality, take the consequent with them wherever they go, and in this sense the judgment is general, absolute, or universal. Supposing the judgment to be absolutely true—and formally we can suppose nothing else of a judgment which we make, though of natural phenomena no judgments are absolutely true—it is absolutely universal. Varieties of detail may fall within it, but they do not affect it. Against such unessential variations, and against mere number of examples in time and space, the explicit antecedent appears as general, and in selecting and defining it a work of generalisation has practically been accomplished. There is no advance from known to unknown in the strict sense of the case we are now considering. There is no advance from known to unknown in saying that a pair of parallel straight lines which you may intend to draw to-morrow will never meet. If the 'intent and purpose' of the antecedent 'hath full relation' to the example to be adduced, there is *prima facie* no inference, no extension, no advance, in affirming the consequent true of that example.

A still stronger and a far more important case of such *generalisation by mere determination* is afforded by mediate or inverse induction through hypothesis. A hypothesis is

By mere determination.

a hypothesis because it is not to begin with present in the data, and has to be brought there by mediation. But to supply matter for modelling a conception which is not furnished by mere direct interpretation of sense, i.e. by perception or by testimony, a set of data must have wide range and be capable of a high degree of systematic inter-relation. Thus e.g. in an anthropological hypothesis about the past of the Hellenic race a considerable portion of the history of Europe is ultimately involved, and the data bearing on it are inter-related and elucidated.

In this sense a hypothesis or mediately obtained determination of observations by a conception superinduced upon them, is likely to involve as a result an elucidation and articulation of a wide range of reality. Sparta and Athens, Crete and the Troad, Sicily and Magna Graecia, all fall within the region of reality which through determination of our knowledge about it by the anthropological hypothesis in question would acquire for us a certain set of highly important common properties and relations. Here the generalisation results from the range of the explicit system, and not from the mere abstract precision of a hypothetical antecedent. What we are systematising is a reality, and the judgment which expresses our conclusion may indeed, like all precise judgments, be thrown into hypothetical form, but its content makes it really categorical. In it therefore we have two kinds of generalisation, one depending on the range of the system which we have constituted, the other on the hypothetical abstractness which makes even this concrete system a case, within the lines of which systems differing from it in other relations may conceivably fall.

Material or Analogical Generalisation. iii. The generalisation that falls within the limits of strictly scientific Induction is confined to what has just been described as Generalisation by mere determination. It is not generalisation in the sense of an advance from the known to the unknown. Obviously there can in no case be such an advance except in the sense that the unknown becomes known. And this advance is made in the determination itself; the case, when determined, is known, and is generalised in so far only as it is known. Water is composed of oxygen and hydrogen in certain proportions. There is no further generalisation in applying this to water such as we have analysed; and if there could be a doubt whether a certain liquid was in that sense 'water,' the judgment gained by previous analysis would not *prima facie* determine it. The hypothetical character of this judgment is an automatic apparatus for excluding material generalisation. In the extreme instance of such exclusion the antecedent 'water' is little more than a name, to which 'composed of oxygen' etc. supplies the content. Then if 'composed of oxygen' etc. is not true in a particular case, that case *ipso facto* falls outside the hypothetical judgment. Or in a less extreme instance, 'water' may indicate certain visible or other properties which are synthetically related in the judgment to the chemical composition. But here again the least variation in those index-properties may formally throw the case in which it occurs outside the hypothetical judgment.

This is all very well so long as we interpret the hypothetical judgment to be strictly hypothetical abstract or necessary. But the account given in Book I of the Universal Judgment in its sub-forms of Corporate and Generic Judgment reminds us that we have a Categorical element to deal with in the characteristic nature which binds things together into ideal or actual totalities, and we have to face the possibility that the nature of these totalities may conflict with the content of hypothetical judgments in which they are set down as antecedents. Every universal is an identity in difference, and the identification of the conditions by which inductive enquiry has determined a content is not, as we assumed just now, a purely formal activity, but is, like every judgment, a synthetic and material operation. Reliance on the accuracy of our analysis will lead us back to a Lockeian formalism, if we neglect the identification of the data analysed. 'Man is rational, because if a creature turns out not to be rational, it is not what we called a man,' is an argument which, unless specifically justified, has no more content than A is A because we called it A. If no distinct elements are fixed within the synthesis, the synthesis itself is destroyed. But on the other hand, if we affirm our analysis directly of a generic content which is categorically taken and includes a system of differences, it is clear that we are pledging ourselves to a material generalisation. Does 'water' for example, in the judgment above cited, include steam and ice? Apart from specific chemical knowledge, I do not see how we could predict that it would do so. And if we say 'water' for chemical science *is* matter of a certain composition, whether in a liquid, solid or vaporous state, then we have got back to the nominalist judgment criticised above; 'a is xy because what is not xy is not called a.'

I do not mean to say that the above considerations are of serious importance in precise scientific induction, in which the definition of the data as elements in a synthetic relation is always a primary problem. But *either* in popular applications of science—the most fertile of all sources of fallacy—*or* in provinces of knowledge which are largely dealt with by analogy, it is essential to bear in mind that the identification of the datum, which has been analysed or determined by a conception, with either the popular import or the analogical generic content of that datum, is always a matter involving a material synthesis and not a mere formal recognition. Where indeed the precise determinate conditions of a phenomenon are explicitly recognisable, there the identification of the phenomenon is a formal act, and the hypothetical judgment applies *ipso facto*. But where, as is constantly the case in practice, and, *owing to the nature of a universal, always in theory*, the conditions are not unambiguously recognisable, but only either a *part* of them, or a *case* of them, or an *index-mark* of them can be discovered, then we must form a synthetic judgment of identification or distinction, based on the general principles which we have seen to govern argument by analogy, viz.

on the reality of a system of recognisable types and purposes.

Apart from such a material assumption the truth of principles derived from Scientific Induction itself would be practically though not theoretically destroyed[1]. A system of unapparent deviations in the properties of natural objects, such as to defy classification, might be such as to destroy the applicability, while not interfering with the formal truth, of hypothetical judgments. In our earlier discussions on the hypothetical and categorical aspect of judgments, it was conceded that the *pure* hypothetical judgment does not allege the existence of the elements which it explicitly puts in relation. But it is also clear that no ordinary result of Induction ought to be taken *bonâ fide* as a judgment of this type. A judgment which cannot be denied but which has no range of real application has only abstract and not concrete truth. If all our knowledge were of this character, as *qua* mere determination it conceivably might be, it would have no hold upon reality.

So long indeed as the variations of natural objects observed a continuous and mutually coherent progression, we should only have a state of things not unlike the system of animated nature, which would be in some respects favourable to knowledge by the clearness with which it would mark the course of evolution, and might not be incompatible with human life. But it is easy of course to imagine varieties in fundamental properties of substances not indicated by external appearance, which though following strictly from natural antecedents, and not in any way miraculous, would yet be incompatible with such a degree of knowledge as is necessary to maintain human life on the surface of the globe. No analysis of water would help us, however true under the conditions under which it was made, if something which we could not distinguish from water except by renewed chemical analysis were liable to arise

---

[1] i. e. would be destroyed for concrete and real theory, but not for abstract and formal theory.

out of water by a concealed process of causation, and were endowed with the properties of sulphuric acid. No formal principle will meet this conceivable difficulty. Many distinctions all-important for human life *are* only learnt by degrees or are only drawn with imperfect success—e.g. between pure water or milk and the same liquids when contaminated with sewage-poison. We can only say that *if* we are to live on the surface of the globe the results of scientific induction must not only have formal or hypothetical truth, but must also have that degree and proportion of categorical application which is necessary to enable us to adapt ourselves to the environment. This degree of categorical application, of which mere determination, except in the case of an extended system of reality like the Hellenic race, or Europe, or the British Constitution, or the Solar System, can tell us nothing whatever, measures the work of recognition or of generalisation which is over and above the work of generalisation by mere determination. When I say 'Water is composed of Oxygen and Hydrogen,' I must mean by water, not necessarily all, but some large proportion of what I commonly take to be water. If not, my judgment, however true in the abstract, fails to grasp reality in the concrete.

The ideal of knowledge, no doubt, is not in this analogical generalisation, but in the second and larger kind of generalisation by mere determination, viz. in the progressive reduction of reality to a single system or to comprehensive single systems. It must be remembered, too, that the synthetic nature of every universal or identity is double-edged. If all sets of conditions have to be recognised and interpreted as universals, all sets of conditions should be fixed and determined in the inductive analysis as universals—i.e. with the full prevision that differences, variations, extreme cases, will arise within them. Nevertheless, it seldom happens even in geometry that a principle when first established is established in its full content and application. Inductive analysis can never make full provision for the application to fresh cases of a principle which it discovers, except in as far as it discloses the nature of a comprehensive *individual* system of Reality within which other individuals fall.

4. Our results as regards Induction are then as follows. i. Our view of Induction as an inverse process differs essentially from that of Jevons by its dependence on material and positive connections, which are only defined by negation. Inverse procedure by hypothesis is for him essentially a matter of probability, and depends on the exclusion of alternative hypothesis simply *qua* alternatives, i. e. ultimately on the statement of chances[1] or the number of cases out of all conceivable cases which are in favour of the result in question upon the hypothesis proposed. This view essentially depends upon the false conception of generalisation which has been frequently alluded to, and according to which the ideal of Induction is perfect Induction, i. e. the summation of an infinite series. As we have seen[2], the statement of chances admits of valuable and extended application where we are dealing with classes of unknown conditions, i. e. conditions known to us simply as furnishing such and such numbers of 'equal alternatives;' and in astronomical and other exact science it is justified by the splendid success of its results. I will venture however to point out, in respect of one example adduced by Jevons, that other considerations seem to have contributed to the inference beyond those which fairly arise out of the statement of chances. Kirchoff's proof of the presence of iron in the sun[3] depends upon the exclusion of the alternative that the 60 dark lines of the solar spectrum coincide *by chance* with the 60 bright lines of the incandescent vapour of iron. The probability of a chance coincidence being (from the distance between the lines on the spectrum) about $\frac{1}{2}$ for each line, the probability in favour of a chance coincidence for all 60 lines is about $(\frac{1}{2})^{60}$, i. e. less than one in a trillion. 'But on the other hypothesis,'

General view of Induction. Difference from Jevons.

---

[1] Sigwart seems to waver between this view, and the true view of proof by content. Logik, ii. pp. 384–5.
[2] p. 137, supra.   [3] Jevons, Principles of Science, p. 245.

Jevons continues, 'that iron exists in the Sun, it is highly probable that such coincidences would be observed.' Here the proof seems to appeal to some of the considerations which belong to the positive connection between given content and hypothesis, or to material generalisation, or to both. Why should '*the* other hypothesis' be 'that iron exists in the Sun'? The answer must be, I should suppose, either that the 60 bright lines have a connection with the nature of iron, as *a characteristic* or exclusive differentia, which would dispense with the proof by calculation—or that though there is no exclusive connection between the nature of iron and the production of 60 bright lines, yet *in fact* no known substance but iron produces such lines, *and* it is very improbable on general grounds that a substance unknown to us but sharing this property with iron is present in the Sun[1]. The former of these considerations would belong to the nature of true Inductive determination, the latter group to the postulates of material generalisation. The real function of number and ratio in Induction has been sufficiently illustrated above.

Ultimate nature of Induction.
ii. After the discussion on p. 118 above of the connection between Induction and other inference, I need only sum up the view which I have taken in a very few words. Induction is not a species of inference, as calculation, geometrical reasoning, analogy and subsumption, are species of inference. It has not, that is to say, for its differentia any peculiar nature in the universal which carries the conclusion. It is consequently, like Comparison or Recognition, like Observation or Experiment, a transient and external characteristic of inference. An Inductive proof, when completed, may be a geometrical construction or an arithmetical calculation, an articulate subsumption or a morphological analogy. Its

[1] The fraction $(\frac{1}{2})^{60}$ represents, I suppose, the chance of 60 coincident cases all produced by independent causes; but ought we not also to consider the probability not merely of one unknown cause producing all the cases, and that cause being iron, but that of all the possible alternatives in which 2, 3 and so on up to 58 inclusive, of the coincident cases, are produced by a single unknown cause, and the remainder in each alternative by accident?

Inductive character belongs exclusively to the process of discovery, and depends on the relation between the elements of the content and the qualification of reality from which the process of cognition starts. Inferential connection is one, and is necessary and invariable; but the points at which a single and coherent system may be in contact with the real world as known to an individual cognitive subject are infinitely various. From these points, whatever they may be, the cognitive subject has to build up the single and coherent system, which he then refers to reality. When these points are isolated perceptions, occurrences or qualities, then the task of building up the system which they necessitate is called Induction.

Inductive proof rests, like all Inference, on systematic and √ necessary connection of content. How many observations, what experiments, how many and how favourable conjunctions of phenomena, may be needed to disclose the connection to us, is, as Aristotle implied in the Posterior Analytics[1], theoretically indifferent. The observations do not give us the connection, but we judge the connection on the basis of the system demanded by the observations, and this systematic or reasoned judgment is the essence of the proof.

Is a principle then proved by the number and variety of its verified consequences? It gains nothing from any repetition of identical consequences once established to be fact; but variety of consequences may be said to prove it by displaying its nature as actual and modelling it into concrete identity with themselves. I incline to think that the truth upon this point is best stated through the paradox proposed above[2]. Every fact, every sense-perception, every datum of testimony, absolutely and irrevocably proves *something* and necessitates the assumption of *some* agent or principle. Repetition of the same datum, *qua* the same (i. e. assuming that it was completely and correctly observed

---

[1] Anal. post. p. 90, a. 24; cp. p. 87, b. 39; and see the author's Knowledge and Reality, p. 285.
[2] p. 166.

at first, which is *never true*), can add nothing to what it proves. But every further datum which can be connected with the first goes to develop the content of that agent or principle which both the data prove. If therefore we speak of the mere proof that *something or other beyond the datum* must be assumed, one datum is as good as a host to prove this, and the proof of it is absolute at first; and to allege variety and range of data as contributory to *this* proof is to fall once more into the fallacy of generalisation from number of instances. What is proved once does not need to be proved again. Every datum proves irrefragably the reality of the system to which it belongs, *whatever that may be*.

But this representation of the matter, though it leads up to the truth, is in itself a paradox without real import. A proof which proves the reality merely of something or other is a proof of nothing at all. But if we speak of the proof of a determinate agent or principle or real system, then both range and variety of data are essential to the proof, and the proof of the whole is not absolute at once, and therefore the proof of any part, *as a part in that whole*, is not absolute at once. For the proof depends upon the intelligibility with which the hypothesis—to use the terms explained above—is adjusted to or included in the postulate; that is to say, with which the alleged real system is identified with the real something demanded by all the data taken together. And from the nature of knowledge as a system the necessity of this synthetic connection can only be evident in an extended range of applications; and hence it is—not from number of consequences, but from the varied determinations which are indispensable to define any universal in its inter-connected differences, that range and variety of data are contributory to the proof of a hypothesis[1]. Thus we may say, if we like, that variety and

[1] I am omitting, to avoid confusion, the consideration of repeated observation as eliminating accidental errors, which depends on the principle of chances illustrated above. Accidental errors are errors arising from a variety of unknown causes. Repeated observation distinguishes series such as are likely to be due to a single cause, from series likely to be due to unknown causes.

range of data contribute nothing to the proof of a hypothesis, but only aid in its definition. But we must then bear in mind that the proof to which range does not contribute, and which each isolated datum effects absolutely and ultimately, is a proof of something in general, but of nothing in particular.

Induction, then, is the reference to reality of a system on the ground of particular differences within it by which reality is taken as qualified; and may involve, in the constitution of the system for knowledge and in its identification with those differences, any process known to Logic. It is essentially an advance from the Individual or concrete Generic judgment to the pure hypothetical, or to its higher form, the Disjunctive judgment. When we are able to start from a reality qualified to us by pure hypothetical or by disjunctive judgments, then we can go at once from the differences as in the universal to the relations of other differences, and we can refer these differences to reality on the basis of the universal itself which is accepted as real. We do not in this case employ species of inference unknown to Induction; but the process in which we employ them has not the peculiar relation to given Reality, e.g. the gradual emergence of negative determination, which constitutes Induction.

CHAPTER VI.

CONCRETE SYSTEMATIC INFERENCE.

A PURE hypothetical judgment, the outcome of scientific Induction or the embodiment of abstract relations in combination, expresses a synthetic connection based upon an underlying real system. Analogical inference, from which scientific Induction was a divergence, depended rather upon an estimate, usually inadequate, of such real systems in their concrete import. Now if, as a result of a highly exhaustive Scientific Induction taken together with an Analogical reasoning, we are able to recombine the abstract relations which the former has disclosed one by one, into a single totality which has an obvious significance, then this totality or system is the real determinate ground of each separate relational judgment that enters into our conception of it, and belongs, at the same time, to the concrete or categorical type of knowledge. For the ground which warrants a hypothetical judgment is in the last resort always a real system, and moreover the content of every judgment is understood[1] to have such Reality as it is capable of.

Philosophical Subsumption.
1. Therefore, in dealing with totalities which are thus thoroughly concrete and thoroughly rational, we are able to advance from the figure of analogy 'A and C are B, therefore A is probably C,' to the first figure of the Aristotelian syllogism, 'A is B, B is C, therefore A is C.'

In spite of all that has been written about and against the syllogism, I can find no more simple and natural expression than this for the reasoned judgment which embodies

[1] See Bk. I. chap. ii, on Categorical and Hypothetical Judgment.

An individual System.   181

a *real necessity*. Thus applied, the syllogism is subsumptive in so far as it appeals to unity of relations within a concrete subject, but has abandoned the differentia of subsumption proper, in so far as the definite form taken by the result of the appeal depénds on intelligible coherence and not on mysterious conjunction. It is essential to such arguments that the teleological or quasi-teleological unity of the subject, which in analogy was conjectural and obscure, should be absolute and explicit. It is only this absoluteness that can warrant the position of the middle term as subject in one premise, i.e. as a qualification which prescribes the precise content affirmed of it in the predication. It is only this explicitness that can justify by a specific[1] necessity the determinate relations which the unity of the subject imposes on the two extremes. The conditions thus demanded can only be fulfilled in subjects the nature of which is known as a definitely organised system. We saw indeed, in the earlier discussions of Book I[2], that such a system cannot avoid presenting quantitative relations between its parts, in as far as its pervading unity contains within itself differences of a common quality. But in a true concrete individuality such quantitative relations are secondary, resulting from the nature of the system but not exhausting it, and therefore the system, although definitely intelligible, cannot be 'constructed' by geometrical or numerical combination. Such combinations may however enter into it in various degrees. Judgments which deal with these concrete individualities are at once individual and universal, and have been analysed in Book I as a combination of these characters[3].

Fluid though the distinctions between types of inference necessarily are, it will be convenient to distinguish the important class of inferences now before us by an unmistake-

[1] See Bk. II. chap. i, on specific necessity of Judgments.
[2] See Bk. I. chap. iii.
[3] See on the Corporate Judgment and the Individual Generic Judgment, above, Bk. I. chap. v.

able differentia, at the risk of unduly limiting their province. This differentia is the ascription of *real teleology* to the content analysed. And by real teleology I mean the embodiment or operation of a conscious purpose entertained by a human intelligence. All other teleological inferences, such as those depending upon the *de facto* teleology (quasi-teleology) of the organic world are most conveniently relegated to the category of analogy.

The lowest case of real teleology is closely akin to that which was the highest case of analogy. A tool, instrument, or machine, of which we know the use intended by the maker, furnishes this lowest case of real teleology, while any object of the same class the use of which we could only conjecture, furnished the highest case of quasi-teleology or analogy. It was in part from the example of an instrument contrived by human intelligence that Plato introduced the conception of function or final cause into philosophy [1]; and the ultimate meaning of 'organism' is a system of tools or instruments. The term 'mechanical' in its modern philosophical acceptation abstracts from one-half of the import of 'machine'; for though we are accustomed to think of *mechanical* determination as a resultant of any *de facto* combination of forces, yet we are not accustomed to think of a *machine* except as a combination of forces for a purpose consciously entertained.

At first sight, then, we have in the tool, instrument or machine with known purpose, an adequate example of the type of knowledge before us. 'A screw that is meant to turn one way only must have its head cut so as to give the screw-driver no purchase when turning the other way; a coffin-screw is a screw meant to turn one way only; therefore a coffin-screw is one which has its head cut,' &c., &c. Or

---

[1] Republic, end of Bk. I; δρεπάνῳ τῷ ἐπὶ τοῦτο ἐργασθέντι. The examples alleged by Plato in this important passage are of very different values, and are well worth careful attention. The well-known description of the function of a thing as ὃ ἂν ἢ μόνῳ ἐκείνῳ ποιῇ τις ἢ ἄριστα leans to *de facto* teleology, and would not of course protect an object from a function alien to its nature but relative to human purpose. *Such* a function could justify no analogy.

CHAP. VI.] *Purpose in Mechanical Form.* 183

again: 'A locomotive engine meant to drag a weight a at a velocity b must have boiler-space x and cylinder-stroke between the limits z and z_1; a locomotive which is to work in the Newcastle coal traffic must drag a weight a, &c., &c.; therefore a locomotive which is to work this traffic must be constructed as above determined.'

It will strike the reader however on looking at such examples as these that the premises are very closely allied to hypothetical judgments, and are much more 'constructive' than 'subsumptive.' It is true that in the analysis of a machine the inference does rest on the *system* of the mechanical combination, and that this system with all the details dependent on it can, *in a machine that works well*, be deduced from the intellectual purpose which the constructor proposed to himself to realise in that mechanical combination. So far, as reading the significance of the parts in the coherent whole without which they would lose it, the inference is subsumptive. On the other hand, all tools or machines are liable to initial or acquired maladaptation. Their *de facto* function or actual result may diverge from their intended function. And when this comes to pass, their existence as mechanical combinations is not thereby terminated. A clock that has a hopelessly variable rate may not, philosophically speaking, be rightly called a clock (being absolutely useless to indicate time), but it remains a real mechanical combination in which cooperating parts produce a necessary result. In other words, though a machine embodies a purpose, yet it only embodies it in a mechanical form, dependent, that is, on the right adjustment of a mechanical combination, and therefore on the continuance of that right adjustment. Therefore in every such inference there might be substituted for the statement of purpose a statement of the mechanical system in which the purpose is supposed to be realised; and as the purpose is only present in the actual system of adjustment, and not as an intellectual idea, such an analysis would be in one sense adequate to the nature of the object analysed.

Such inference might fairly be treated as employing merely hypothetical judgment and constructive combination, taking no account of any significant unity in the content of inference, or of any special relation between it and the real world. The system would, by such a transformation, have forfeited its individuality and have become a mere necessary sequence of relations upon relations in the abstract world of force and mass, instead of an actual whole in the unique structure which we call reality. It must be noted however that the limitation or abstraction which is needed to make such an account intelligible, has by the change supposed become merely arbitrary. *Qua* mechanical result, every cinder that dropped from the fire-box and every cloud of vapour blown from the funnel would have as good a right to be described and deduced from the mechanical combination which makes up the locomotive, as would the capacity of the engine in the way of traction.

'But the purpose may be hypothetically inserted into the inference, as indeed was done above.' We may state a purpose or any other content hypothetically, if we indicate that by intentional abstraction we are doing so. I only say that, apart from any mark of forcible abstraction from reality, a judgment or inference that deals with a system having unity in a purpose presupposes the reality of that system because its content is adequate to reality, while a judgment which merely draws the necessary consequences of a determinate combination of forces, without reference to any purpose to which that combination is directed, is essentially hypothetical, for the particular combination has no pre-eminent individuality or *raison d'être*; and essentially imperfect, because in the absence of a *raison d'être* there is nothing to guide the selection of aspects or of consequences. In *this sense* the hypothetical, the arbitrary, and the merely mechanical coincide.

In the distinction between a machine which serves a purpose, and a machine which does not, we have in a nutshell the question of categories. Both are actual mechanical combinations producing results, and neither has in it one whit more life or intellect than the other. But it is perfectly clear that our understanding of the useful one is incomplete if by preserving our ignorance of its purpose we remain on the same level of apprehension with reference to it which is the highest we can possibly attain with reference to the other. And it is absurd to say that the category so implied is an accidental aspect and does not represent a fact. It is true however that this category of purpose does not exist within a mechanical system in its proper or intellectual form, and that therefore the system can be regarded by a natural abstraction as on a level with a purposeless combination, and may by internal or external changes at any moment become such. This hypothetical aspect of a combination of forces, in virtue of which it produces its resultant according to fixed necessities and in complete indifference to any purpose, is the purely 'mechanical' relation of a machine, and if exclusively pressed home destroys as we saw all possibility of regarding it as an individual thing having its unity in a function.

Beginning with the mechanical contrivances of which we have been speaking, there extend upwards in a series which forms the content of philosophy the phases and embodiments of man's intelligence and conscious will. All of these, the individual will with its complement in the moral order of society, the product of fine art, and the religious or philosophical system, are totalities which combine an explicit intellectual unity with determinate interdependence of parts. The statement of the general character of these embodiments of mind may serve as an example of the argument we are considering. 'The mind is a unity of reciprocally determinate but not reciprocally exclusive parts. A feeling is an element in the mind; therefore a feeling enters into a unity of reciprocally determinate but not reciprocally exclusive parts.' Or again: 'The British Constitution is in its main features determined by the thoroughgoing application of ordinary law; the position of the prime minister is a function of the British Constitution; therefore the position of the prime minister is in its main features determined by the thoroughgoing application of the ordinary law.' Or, finally: 'The general will is expressed in the moral order of society; the individual will finds its freedom in the general will; therefore the individual will finds its freedom in the moral order of society.'

When we consider the logical nature of such arguments as these, we notice two obvious characteristics of the content, and one, resulting from them, of the form.

<small>Logical Content. Real System.</small>

i. In respect of their logical content they are at once categorical and hypothetical. *a.* The systems which form the content of such reasoned judgments as these are naturally taken as real systems in virtue of their individuality. It is of course not impossible to construct a political or religious system on paper the consequences of which are laid down in hypothetical judgments and inferences from them, which in form might be identical with such judgments as are here employed. The content of such judgments has an indeterminate place in reality so far as it has a meaning or objective reference, and depends on determinate reality so far as it proceeds to affirm actual consequences. But the content of a judgment which deals with an individual system is taken as real in our world unless the contrary is indicated; and even in hypothetical judgments that depend on the nature of the human mind, the real ground which would have to be made explicit in order ultimately to justify the consequences drawn is the intelligible and concrete system of that mind itself. *Primâ facie*, therefore, we are dealing in these arguments with categorical judgments about reality, which explicitly postulate the real grounds that in the hypothetical judgment were latent.

<small>Apodeictic Sequence.</small>

β. The nexus of the inferences in question is not, as in Analogical Reasoning and in Enumerative Induction, devoid of strict apodeictic sequence. The systems of which we have been speaking, although they need not be capable of mechanical, numerical or geometrical construction,—which however, as in the case of a machine, may play their part in the analysis of the concrete whole,—are nevertheless invested with hypothetical or apodeictic necessity in two forms; in the relation of their parts one to another within the systems themselves as wholes, and in their own *ultimate* relation as parts to the unique system of reality as a whole.

Of these the former is for our logical purpose the more important. Within such a whole as the moral order of civilised society, regarded as the expression of the general will, it is obvious that there are parts united by necessary relations dependent on the nature of that whole and capable of being expressed in hypothetical judgments if we abstract from the explicit assumption of the whole itself. We may say, for example, 'If a right, then a duty.' The justification of this statement would be given by the affirmation, as a real ground, of the moral purpose involved in the moral order, which purpose exhibits itself as right or duty according to the attitude which the individual will may assume towards it. Such an inference as this does not cease to be necessary when its ground, in this case the moral purpose and moral order, is affirmed to be real. . The basis of the synthetic transition is here as everywhere the nature of an identity or universal, and that the universal is affirmed to be fact makes no difference to its apodeictic force. What in particular that apodeictic force may be, how it should come to pass that one thing can necessitate another, depends, as I have said before, on the ultimate fact of the nature of knowledge. What we have more particularly to observe at this point is the coarseness of the illusion that systematic necessity can only exist in spatial and numerical perception. Given the relation of man's intelligent will to an actual moral order, the relation of right and duty is as plain a consequence as, given the nature of space, the equality of vertical angles. And apart from a given reality, there is in either case nothing, from which nothing can follow.

Hence we arrive at the second aspect in which individual

188   *Concrete Systematic Inference.*   [BOOK II.

systems, though real, are nevertheless hypothetical. They are each and all of them, for us, hypothetical upon the *whole* given reality within which they exist. When we speak of a thing as real, we imply that it is complete and self-existent; for if it is not, its reality includes a condition beyond the content which we have included in the thing, and *it* therefore, *as we have formulated it*, not including the conditions essential to its own reality, is falsely asserted to be real.

Here we have the aspect of relativity which prevails throughout our knowledge, which is increasingly overcome by the work of intelligence in as far as it connects the actual and intellectual world into an organised whole, but is never thoroughly done away.

Logical Form.
Syllogism in fig. 1.

ii. As regards the form of these inferences, it follows from what has been said that the only value of the syllogistic arrangement is to exhibit the structure of the reasoned judgment, which itself contains or displays the articulated universal. No question arises as to which premise we know first, and so which supports the other. The prior or previous phase of the inference is not the proof of detached premises, but the entire thought in a less precisely articulated form. If we are urged to say whether we know the major, the minor or the conclusion first, the only true answer is that, in their full import, we know them all simultaneously. As detached fragments of experience we may know any one of them first. And as each element of the universal when rightly understood involves the others in their full determinateness, there can be no real difference in kind of import between major and minor premises, and no reason for preferring one order of the terms to another. The order will in fact be subjective, depending upon the qualification of reality which we take as starting-point, whether in time—if our inference has the accidental aspect of a progress in time—or because of its individual nature. The real purpose is the dominant essence of the universal, but the real purpose may be taken as conveyed by the general idea of the system in question as a whole, represented by its *name*, or as involved in the analytic scheme of its parts, or as concentrated into some special application by which some one part does the work of the whole. And thus any one of these elements of the universal may stand as the middle term in reasoning, i.e. as the ground or universal *par excellence*. Hence there is no use in considering the syllogistic rules at the point we have now reached. They belong to collective and in some degree to analogical argument; but the postulate on which they rest, of the absence of reciprocal determination between the elements of inference, does not hold good of a coherent system when thoroughly known. We have thus arrived at a goal analogous to that attained by the theories of Quantification and of Equation in judgment, at a perfect reciprocal identity between the elements of the reasoned judgment, so that any one of the terms may occupy any place in the argument. But we have attained it, as we hope, without sacrificing difference to identity, and thereby destroying the identity itself. The equational form, though it symbolises correctly certain results of the reasoned judgment (the conjunctions which this judgment in fact involves), yet crushes into shapelessness its true living texture, and, as a simple sign of the deformation, forbids all growth and reconstruction within the inference itself, which reconstruction nevertheless, as we have seen and shall further see, cannot be avoided.

As a particular case of the inapplicability of the syllogistic rules to the inferences now before us, it may be mentioned that we have here nothing to do with inference from negative premises. We must take the negative form to have done its work and obtained positive significance, in the process which we have watched of constituting such a system as that which we are now considering. We are now considering these systems as real grounds, and so with reference to what falls within them, and not with reference to what falls outside them. For to what falls outside the system itself, unless with reference to a further system including that 'outside,' the system can *ex hypothesi* only be related in the way of bare negation that has no import and is no judgment. In analysing the completion of a type of knowledge it is vain to raise a question which would take us back to the beginning of the course we have traversed. But as a determining agency *within* a real system, and as invested by that function with positive import, negation reappears in disjunctive reasoning.

Disjunction and Disjunctive Reasoning.
2. The nature of disjunction and its imperfect forms have been discussed under the head of the disjunctive judgment, and it only remains here to recapitulate the inferential nature of this the most complete and explicit form of the universal.

Inference under a disjunction is usually represented thus: 'A is either B or C, A is not B ∴ A is C;' or, 'A is B ∴ A is not C.' Yet such an inference has no meaning except in the case of a disjunction of ignorance or a disjunction referred to a point of time. The categorical minor premise adds nothing whatever in the way of content to the disjunctive major premise. It only has meaning as resolving a doubt or as affirming one member of an alternative to be true in a given point of time. This defect could not be removed by specifying in the minor the ground on which that one member of the alternative is affirmed, for this ground cannot really fall outside the content of the disjunction and its specification can only throw a doubt on the categorical nature (in the narrower sense) of the minor premise itself. 'The signal is either danger or safety; it is red and so danger ∴ not safety.' Obviously here, if we can conclude from 'red' to 'danger' in the minor premise, this relation must fall within the knowledge which constitutes the major; and moreover, by introducing a specific ground of assertion it exposes the minor to a charge of being hypothetical.

We saw in treating of the disjunctive judgment that the disjunction of ignorance and the disjunction referred to time are not cases fundamentally distinct from the true disjunction of knowledge, being justified, in as far as they are justified, by the same type of knowledge which forms the basis and content of disjunction proper. Only, being limited by an accidental condition (the speaker's knowledge, or an arbitrary point of time), they lend themselves to an appearance of progressive inference through supplementation by a perceptive or narrative judgment, which applies them under a limiting condition without expressing that condition. In the true disjunction, which expresses the organisation of a system as such, the reference to an arbitrary condition falls away, and although the judgment is capable of inferential application under specified conditions, whether of time or of other kinds, yet this application is not essential to its import, and is not demanded by its form.

We are thus driven to the paradoxical conclusion that the essence of disjunctive argument is included within the disjunctive 'major premise'; in other words, that this judgment is in fact not a mere premise but at once a categorical judgment and a complete systematic inference, in which the content of a real system, thoroughly understood, is developed in its reciprocal positive and negative bearings. The universal, or pervading identity, is developed in it as a system of a's and '*just* not a's[1],' such that in virtue of every 'not a' the system is positively determined to a certain definite a, and in virtue of every a the system is negatively determined to a certain definite not-a (which is b). Our ideal of inferential knowledge does not go beyond an individual system of this kind, of which every part is mediated in its turn by all the other parts and assigned by them its appropriate place in the whole, whose pervading nature is present in every part and prescribes the arrangement and content of all. Such a system contains its own applications, for the material conditions under which it develops its nature are given within it. The mere realisation of one alternative member as fact or as a point in time, e.g. in present perception, has in relation to such disjunctive knowledge the aspect of a case brought under it by an un-

---

[1] See account of Scientific Induction, chap. iv, above.

known condition, and so implies a defect in the disjunctive knowledge itself. For if there is no such defect, then perception or testimony can add nothing to the *necessary reality* embodied in the disjunction. A watch is either going or not going; and I do not need observation or testimony to tell me that at any time when the mainspring is broken it is not going. 'But your disjunctive knowledge will not tell you beforehand or apart from observation whether the mainspring *is* broken.' I reply, 'Oh yes it will, *up to the limits to which it extends*.' It will tell me the signs of breaking, the risks of breaking, the limit of breaking-strain; and therefore, supposing my knowledge of the world were disjunctively complete, it would tell me exactly when and how often the mainspring has been or will be broken. That it does not practically tell me this is not owing to the defectiveness of disjunctive knowledge but to my not possessing it. Therefore, as in all the affairs of life, I have to supplement scientific knowledge from testimony and unorganised observation, i.e. observation of what occurs under conditions not precisely known. But this observation, *qua* unorganised, adds nothing to knowledge, though in fact every content that is distinctly observed has necessarily *some* organisation, and leaves the disjunctive judgment a little richer than before. But as mere abstract position or affirmation of a case fully known before, it adds in theory no element whatever to our disjunctive knowledge of a real system.

Therefore the disjunctive judgment must be taken to correspond not to the major premise of the syllogism, but to the whole syllogism. The syllogism must tell us, for instance, that the human will, being an activity of the human intelligence, sets its purposes before it in the form of definite ideas. The disjunction would in this case perhaps tell us that the human animal asserts himself practically either through the intelligence as will or through the sensuous instincts as appetite; or again, that he asserts himself through the intelligence either practically as will or theoretically as knowledge. Here we obviously have the whole content of the syllogistic 'reasoned judgment' but in a more elaborate and more thoroughly articulate form. It is clear that the whole conclusion, in so far as it is a conclusion that grasps scientific truth as the definition of a real system, falls within this disjunctive judgment. The application of it in a special historical case can be of no importance, unless the new example suggests new matter for the definition of the term involved; in which case the content of the example must be taken up into the disjunctive judgment.

I need hardly remark that it need not be an objection against a disjunction of this class that the determinations of the system do not exclude one another in time. The essential point is to know how the system in question, e.g. the mind, is organised into parts which as such exclude one another. I am not prepared or concerned to deny that will and appetite may coexist in a mixed state of mind, or even that appetite may be included in will; but in as far as the mind merely has appetite, it does not will, and in as far as the mind distinctly wills, it has not mere appetite. The disjunction would only be false if appetite and will were essentially identical parts of the mental system, and not, *so far as the mind enters wholly into either*, reciprocally exclusive [1].

'Then mere differents are disjunctively opposed?' Yes, *if the conditions are precisely assigned under which the real subject becomes capable of the one and incapable of the other.* A 'conjunction' or conjunctive judgment about a single subject differs from a disjunction merely by the non-assignment of the precise relations under which the various determinations attach. Thus it is, as Plato showed, that knowledge can solve the apparent contradictions of the perceptive judgment. 'A is both great and small.' Know-

[1] Appetite, when it enters into will, must surrender its character as mere appetite, not merely by the addition of something else, but by taking on a new character in itself.

VOL. II. O

ledge distinguishes cases and explains, 'A is compared either with x and then is great or with y and then is small [1].'

The inferential principle of Disjunction is nothing more than the principle of all inference in its most explicit form. Every matter capable of being known consists in a common nature including within it and constituted by parts or differences, which are related to one another at first sight negatively *qua* excluding one another, but further, through this very negation, are related positively because by their negative relation they positively determine one another. Every such matter when explicitly stated in articulate form, is known as a disjunctive judgment. And this is the nature of the ultimate judgment by which the individual consciousness sustains its real world. The simplest cases of these reasoned judgments are to be found in the spatial perception, in which the determining differences take the shape of parts external to each other and so negatively related, but nevertheless by their position determining one another, and so through their negative relation positively related. But the most perfect cases are those intellectual creations that are the objects of philosophical science, in which the whole system not merely appears by its common nature in parts which remain external to each other, but tends to throw itself in its entirety into each of these differences, passing by an organic necessity from one difference to another. Here, in short, the differences are not merely parts which remain outside one another, not merely phases which succeed one another, but moments which succeed one another so that the earlier are retained in the later through a progressive development, and yet the distinctive character of each moment is not weakened. Such, for example, is the relation of the conceptions which by their development constitute the history of philosophy.

It is usual to treat of classification as one special form,

[1] See Plato, Republic, p. 524.

among others, of logical thought. I am unable to regard it in this light. It appears to me to be merely an external consequence, reappearing in every kind of universal, of the relation between universal and differences. The nearest approach to pure classification is therefore to be found in superficial arrangements destined merely to facilitate reference, in the dictionary, the index, the Linnæan system. After this come the natural or morphological systems of botany and zoology, in which the universal appears though not explicitly, yet effectively, through analogy. While in mathematical conceptions as in the true systematic disjunction we have classification relegated to its proper place, as a corollary of the comprehensive application of explanatory theory.

3. By introducing into logic the real or conscious teleology of the human intelligence, we have rendered unavoidable some consideration of the judgment of value, which rests upon the correspondence of a real system and the purpose for which it exists. This judgment obviously presupposes two conditions; i. our knowledge of the purpose for which a system exists, and ii. our knowledge of the degree in which the system fulfils that purpose. *The judgment of Value.*

i. The former condition demands a real teleology; that is, a conscious purpose for which the system is intentionally recognised or maintained by the human will. We cannot here enter upon the questions, belonging to ethical science, which arise with reference to the objective justification of man's recognition of a purpose in the non-intellectual world. Indeed we cannot avoid extending such questions in some degree to the world of man's own volition by admitting that e. g. the systems of law and government which appear *prima facie* to be made and maintained by man with a view to a purpose which he consciously sets before him, have nevertheless an element of growth or development which goes beyond the knowledge or intention of any single individuals at any time concerned in framing them. The works of mind, in short, are something more, as the works *Real Teleology.*

of nature are something less, than the intentional achievements of any individual will, and therefore our estimate of their value is in many respects analogous to that recognition of a purpose which we apply so fallibly to natural objects. We may however—for we must—assume on the whole that the persistent purposes of mankind are represented within our own intelligence, and that therefore in our estimate of law and morality, of art and religion, of political and social institutions, there is at any rate some firm foundation of real teleology.

Mediation.   ii. The second condition demands *mediation*. We have to ascertain whether a whole fulfils its purpose by comparing the operation of its mechanism with the idea which is intended to be its essence. This mediation was involved in the philosophical syllogism, in so far as the purpose of the whole was taken to be its essence or unity. But after analysing, in the disjunction, the matter of the universal into a system of reciprocally determined parts and moments, we have forced upon us the question whether the totality of these parts or moments corresponds in detail to the purpose with which we credit it. Such correspondence is what we understand by goodness or value. We may say for instance of a given social system that under it the people are either aristocrats who are not the best and do not rule, or a proletariate who pay no honour to those above them and who cannot be ruled. And this contradiction between the effect of the system as realised in its parts, and its recognised purpose, entitles us to say that it is a bad system; in the form 'a being either ξ not x or ζ not z is not A.'

Extra-logical as this judgment of value may seem to be, it is really implied in the constitution of knowledge from the point at which quasi-teleology begins, and with it the conception of 'a thing' takes its rise. I shall have to return to this subject in the last chapter when I come to speak of the ultimate nature of dialectical or logical necessity to which the term æsthetic has sometimes been applied.

CHAP. VI.] *No schedules of reasoning.* 197

4. Inference was first defined on p. 1 as the 'mediate reference of an ideal content to Reality,' and further explained on p. 4 as 'the indirect reference to reality of differences within a universal, by means of the exhibition of this universal in differences directly referred to reality.' And we have gone throughout on the principle that the species of inference are determined by the species of universal which occur in the realm of knowledge. Having attempted to analyse these species, and to point out their affinities and their distinctions, we have not much more to say about the nature of inference.

The main features of Inference.

But it may be useful by way of recapitulation to read off from the somewhat tedious treatment to which we have subjected the phases of inference a few answers to the vexed questions which concern it.

i. Is the syllogism a complete antecedent scheme, prescribing the shape and outcome of every possible inference?
ii. Is there any fundamental set of conditions to which all Inference must conform, and further, iii. what relation does the syllogism bear to such a set of conditions?

i. There is no such thing as an antecedent scheme prescribing, so to speak, a set of schedules in one or other of which every argument can be written out merely by filling up the blanks. The form of knowledge is an active and constructive principle, to the workings of which no abstract type antecedently prescribed can be adequate. Not merely is Logic incapable of passing judgment on actual truth, but it is incapable of prescribing beforehand the type of relations which an inferential totality may impose upon its parts. Granting that where we are dealing with imperfect subsumption, with the relations of attributes conjoined in individual subjects according to unknown grounds, the syllogism is able to anticipate the very indefinite form of combination that can result, yet we should not dream of claiming for it this capacity of prediction in the region of calculation, of mechanical or geometrical construction, or of philosophical subsumption. It is true that as regards the

No antecedent scheme of Inference.

last-named process we found a type of reasoning which appeared to represent it adequately in the syllogism in Barbara. But the reader must have observed in the examples which were given, if judged by the standard of formal logic, that irritating inaccuracy of form which is known to teachers in the first attempts of pupils to construct a precise syllogism. In our examples and in their efforts this inaccuracy is due to the same cause; to the difficulty of moulding the vital and constructive action of thought into shapes prescribed by an artificial scheme, which does not precisely correspond to any single type of intellectual action. The violent transformations by which formal logic attains this end are not perhaps an undesirable scholastic exercise; for they unquestionably drag into light, though only as a meagre and skeleton framework, a certain ultimate community of type in all inferential operations. In so far as the difficulties of pupils arise from inability to transform or translate their intellectual operations *at all*, any exercise which demands such transformation is perhaps better than none. But in the analysis of operations that constitute highly determinate individual totalities the difficulty of conforming absolutely to the scheme of the traditional syllogism rises into something like impossibility, because the parts within such a totality do not lie side by side like units in a 'class,' but have peculiar and distinct relations, imposed, each upon each, by their individual place within the whole.

Thus we cannot preserve, or can only by a *tour de force* succeed in preserving, the identical correlations of terms demanded by the rules of formal logic. In our example 'the mind is a unity of determinate and not exclusive parts;' we could not go on to affirm 'a feeling *is* the mind,' according to the good old type 'Socrates *is* a man,' and so we could not conclude that 'a feeling is a unity,' etc. But we were obliged to say either that a feeling is a reaction of the mind, or that a feeling is an element in and is a part of the mind, and could only conclude that a feeling is a factor or element in such a unity. And the other examples given in the same context, which preserve more appearance of correct formulation, are in reality no less charged with individual and diverse relations. The mere fact that the syllogism naturally leads on to the complete disjunctive judgment is the most striking proof of this. I may say at this point that to treat [1] the disjunctive judgment in systematic Logic as a form of thought needing completion by Induction, Analogy and Subsumptive Syllogism, seems to me to be a hopelessly erratic selection of phases out of the progress of the individual mind. This progress includes no doubt even in very early stages those imperfect shapes of disjunction which I have called the disjunctions of ignorance; and *these* disjunctions are expanded into systematic knowledge by the progress of determining thought in its various forms. But to make the complete disjunction prior to the imperfect forms of syllogism involves a retrogression from complete systematic knowledge of a real ground to the knowledge of the operation of this ground in individual cases and in a latent form.

ii. If we ask the more reasonable question, *not* whether a form can be laid down beforehand for every possible inference such that the inference can be drawn by merely putting terms into the blank spaces of one or another of certain prescribed schedules, *but* whether in the common nature of thought a system of conditions can be discovered which in one way or another is conformed to by every act of inference, on this head I think that an affirmative answer may be gathered from our previous discussions. *Condition of Inference.*

(*a*) *Inference must have three terms and no more.*

The explanations given in chap. i of the present Book appear to me to justify this assertion. They consist in a sharp distinction between *terms* and *data*—the number of data being accidental, while the number of terms or moments depends on the essential nature of the universal; *and* in the restriction of Inference proper to mediate Inference.

[1] As Lotze does, Logik, sect. 97 ff.

200 *Concrete Systematic Inference.* [BOOK II.

We *admit* however that the function of thought from elementary reproduction upwards is essentially one, and we more especially *contend* that every judgment, in so far as it is explicitly synthetic, that is to say in so far as it affirms one definite content to be a consequence of another definite content, is an activity only separated from Inference by the degree of distinctness with which its parts are analysed. Every such judgment, and therefore ultimately every judgment, can by further reflection be expressed as a three-term inference, and this is especially the case with what we called the true Immediate Inferences, Comparison, Abstraction, and the rest.

(*b*) *An explicit Inference is a conclusion from two premises and no more, which assert relations between differences qua belonging to a single universal.* Assuming therefore that the *propositions* which express the premises are not to be disguised purposely or through negligence, but are *bonâ fide* to express the judgments employed in reasoning, the two premises must have an identical term in common. And

(*c*) that *this identical term must be universal* follows necessarily from the theory of inference which has been developed, and follows also from the fact that this one term is able to stand in both premises. For a universal is that which without prejudice to its identity persists through or contains in itself different relations. The simplest example may be found in what we termed the 'Inductive' Syllogism, in which, if we take the middle term as the meaning of a proper name, we argue that Socrates is both good and a Greek, therefore a Greek may be good. Here Socrates, although *ex hypothesi* an individual, is universal *at least* in virtue of the double relation to good and Greek—i.e. of the synthesis, in the 'middle term,' of these differences. The universal or identity, however, need not, as in this case, be a 'subject,' although it will be found ultimately to imply a subject. The identical point in space, in which two lines meet in a spatial construction, is the synthesis of two relations in space, but *is* not, only *implies*, space itself as a whole containing these relations.

And (*d*) I do not see how we can escape from saying that *not only one premise, but both premises must be universal*. The only apparent exception would be the case in which one premise is negative; about which it might be urged that the common term does not stand in two relations, but in one and none, i.e. in one only. If this were so, however, the negative premise would be a bare denial, would be no judgment, and could give rise to no conclusion. I do not see how a conclusion can arise without a synthesis of two positive relations.

If then (*e*) negation means bare denial, it results that there can be *no negative premise*. But as bare denial is not a case of genuine judgment we must interpret negation to mean significant denial only, and in this sense we must lay it down that *both premises may be negative*[1].

iii. If now, in order to define our attitude towards the controverted questions which centre in the doctrine of syllogism, we enquire; In what relation does syllogism stand to the type of inference determined by the conditions just enumerated? we shall obtain the following results. *Relation of Syllogism to these conditions.*

We must distinguish the traditional syllogism with its apparatus of rules and its distinctions of quality and quantity from the syllogism as treated in the present work.

α. The traditional syllogism is a hybrid between what we have called analogical inference and what we have called inference or induction by complete enumeration. It would therefore (*a*) *exclude many forms of inference which perfectly conform to the above conditions, and also some which have been included in our account of the syllogism*. Not only would it exclude 'calculation' and what has been called 'construction' in the mechanical or geometrical sense; but it would find no place for Induction or Analogy or even for philosophical subsumption as above described. Induction would be excluded by the conjunctive premise consisting in a *The traditional Syllogism.*

[1] See chap. iv above.

number of individual judgments; Analogy by the material weight and stress thrown upon the definition of the predicate, which the ordinary half-numerical syllogism has no power of indicating; and philosophical subsumption by the genesis within it of new relations, not prescribed by any major premise. The traditional syllogism, in short, fails to recognise the synthetic activity of thought.

(*b*) *The form of universality relied on by the traditional syllogism is vicious*, except for purposes of calculation, which it does not attempt. It is true that its express form of totality 'All A are B' does not really cover what we understand to be its import; but its rules and transformations are derived from this express form, and exclude such vital and genuine processes as for example modal conversion. The fact that we interpret the numerical totality into true synthetic connection only shows that the inadequacy of this form of universal is actually recognised.

(*c*) There is *no justification for the traditional pre-eminence assigned to one premise as the 'major'*; a pre-eminence which depends on the vicious quantitative form of the universal, and carries with it the *petitio principii* which has been irresistibly demonstrated to be present in the traditional syllogism.

(*d*) *There is no justification for the distinction between universal and particular premises*, except in as far as by a reservation depending on unknown conditions one premise may become merely *probable*.

(*e*) *The true 'reduction' or transformation of arguments in figs. 2 and 3 into fig. 1 can only be effected by a material transformation of their content into the content demanded by fig. 1 through the processes of analogy and scientific induction.* Reduction without transformation of content is a grammatical *tour de force* which illustrates no principle except that a simple inference can be awkwardly expressed.

The syllogism as reasoned judgment.

β. When we come however to make the comparison between our general conditions of inference and the syllogism as described in the present work, our results are somewhat different. Syllogism as we have described it is a subsumptive reasoned judgment depending upon the unity of differences within an individual subject, and making the intelligible ground of this unity explicit in various degrees, according to which the unity displays itself as a conjunction or as a coherence.

The syllogism as thus understood is (*a*) *co-extensive with subsumption, and exclusive only of calculation and construction*. The differences between the syllogistic figures in the sense in which we have retained them depend on the degree in which the Reality that stands as subject to the reasoned judgment is already qualified by antecedent judgment as a concrete unity or individual system. In the Inductive Syllogism the Subject is as nearly as possible a particular, a mere name or designative reference; in the Analogical Syllogism it is a particular as known under a universal characteristic, an individual; in the Syllogism of Philosophical Subsumption it is an individual thoroughly known as a universal in its particular differences, and so a concrete system.

(*b*) The *difference between the syllogism thus understood*, and *the abstract combinations of arithmetical or geometrical reasoning*, lies merely in the correlative imperfections of the two processes. The syllogism begins with the perception of unanalysed individual unity, which it is unable to bring to bear as a determinate relation upon the attributes conjoined within it, and thus rests in the mere fact of their conjunction. Calculation and construction begin with the perception of a specific determinate unity by which relations affect and generate each other, without making clear at the outset within what concrete system, and subject to what ultimate conditions, these determinate combinations (e. g. in space) are effected. The two sets of Inferences ultimately involve the same elements.

And therefore (*c*) *if the determinate ground is made clear within a subsumption*, or *the individual subject is made clear which includes a combination of relations, the two types of inference fall theoretically together*, and either may be classed as the perfect form of the other. But, as we have seen, this identification would remain formal and not wholly *bonâ fide*, because of the comparatively indifferent and unconstraining character of the abstract totalities within which geometrical or arithmetical reasoning is carried on. It is true, on the other hand, that the syllogism as we have treated it has no repugnance to the genesis of constructive relations within the unity that is expressed in the inference.

Here we see the true interdependence of the classificatory ideal of knowledge with the ideal which takes the shape of explanatory theory. The former is teleological, categorical, and concrete; the latter is mechanical, hypothetical, and abstract. It is only by a combination of the two—which are not ultimately separable—that a real and coherent world can sustain itself in the judgment which is knowledge.

CHAPTER VII.

THE RELATION OF KNOWLEDGE TO ITS POSTULATES.

1. IT is usual to devote some discussion in a logical treatise to the principles or axioms on which the possibility of knowledge is supposed to rest. Adhering as I do to the conviction that 'The truth is the whole,' I cannot be expected to attempt a justification of any abstract principles as points of attachment antecedently furnished upon which the truth of knowledge could be supposed to depend. But as postulates, as general characteristics of known Reality, which it is convenient to state in an abstract form in any systematic treatment of knowledge, because they are inwoven in the whole texture of the real world, some of these axioms call for comment both on their actual import and on their alleged necessity. *The formal postulates of knowledge.*

It is convenient to distinguish the abstract principles or postulates which are thus found to be involved in the nature of knowledge, as 1. Formal, 2. Material Postulates. This distinction must not be understood to mean that some are drawn from the nature of intelligence exclusively, while others are merely drawn from the content furnished by perceptive experience. It would be more correct to say that those which we call formal are drawn from the character of experience merely as experience, existing no doubt solely for intelligence, but for that very reason not separable in its source or nature from any other source or nature which could be described as intelligence pure and simple. Whereas those which we call material are drawn from the actual significance which we ascribe to the content of experience as developed in a concrete system, and being ultimately coincident with the conclusions of philosophy and of science must necessarily vary with the progress of these constructions. And it is obvious that the formal principles are in fact continuous with and grow into the material principles, the two kinds of axioms bearing at bottom the same relation to one another that exists between the judgment that there is a system, and the judgment that the system is of such and such a nature. The former, of course, implies the rudiments of the latter, as the latter includes the import of the former. Accordingly the distinction between the two classes of principles will correspond to the distinction between abstract and concrete science[1]; between explanatory theory and classification; between the law of sufficient reason and the conception of a teleological whole.

I call these principles by the name of Postulates, because when presented to us as abstract reflective ideas they operate as guides to knowledge[2] which lead to their own subsequent substantiation in a concrete form. As reflective conceptions, then, they are postulates, i. e. principles which we use because we need them. But they only come to be reflective ideas because on analysis of experience they are found to be active factors in it from the first, factors which acquire their content *pari passu* with experience itself, of which they merely express the animating principle of growth. They cannot therefore be taken in a definite form as hypotheses or axioms antecedent to experience. Experience may be said to begin with the certainty that 'there is somewhat;' and the postulates of knowledge do but express in abstract form the progressive definition of this 'somewhat.'

Among formal postulates of knowledge it will be sufficient very briefly to examine the four most notable; the Law of Identity, the Law of Contradiction, the Law of Excluded Middle, and the Law of Sufficient Reason. As a sub-form

[1] This is in strictness almost equivalent to the distinction between physical science and philosophy. But of course evolutionary science with the conceptions of 'higher' and 'lower' does not fall within physical science as thus defined.

[2] See the account of reflective ideas as guides to knowledge in comparison, etc., Bk. II. chap. i.

of the latter the Law of Causation demands no separate treatment.

Each of these laws may be interpreted in more ways than one, according to the degree in which we may acquiesce in its mere abstract form, or attempt to penetrate its further meaning. But at any rate with a view to anything like a separation between intelligence and experience, as such a separation is purely fictitious, there is nothing to be gained by cutting down the content of these principles to a minimum, in the hope of restricting their reference to thought as opposed to things.

i. The Law of Identity must be taken to signify *at least* that it is possible to make judgments that have a meaning and are true. The Law of Identity.

a. In the bare form 'A is A,' however, a form which is not drawn directly from Aristotle or from Plato, the law does not *prima facie* possess this significance, and therefore indeed not any. If it means that A is A and no more, or is *mere* A, then it is aggressively untrue, for it denies the synthesis of differences which alone can make a judgment. If, again, the law is taken as a mere symbol of the pervading unity of the logical subject, and not as intended to exclude all differences from entering into it, then it is an inadequate symbol, erring by omission though not by exclusion. In an absolute tautology which excludes or omits difference, identity itself disappears and the judgment vanishes with it[1]. Tautology.

Therefore, β. we can only assign a meaning to the law 'A is A' if we take the repeated A to be not a specification of the identical content, but an abstract symbol of its identity. The law will then mean that, in spite of or in virtue of the differences expressed in a judgment, the Symbol of Concrete Identity.

---

[1] It is desirable to remark upon this peculiarity of the formal 'Laws of Thought' as represented in symbolic letters, because the error to which it tends is characteristic of false doctrines of identity and difference. Locke defines Identity by saying, 'When the ideas—vary not at all,' and the notion of negation in formal logic is also that of 'mere' or 'bare' negation. Cf. Euler's circles.

208 *Relation of Knowledge to its Postulates.* [BOOK II.

content of judgment is a real identity, that is to say, has a pervading unity. It says that there is such a thing as identity in difference, or in other words, there is such a thing as genuine affirmation—synthesis of differences referred to reality—which yet is true, that is to say, does not interfere with (but in fact is indispensable to) identity.

Unity of Reality.
And, γ. we are only expanding what is implied in the allegation of real identity if we say that the law 'A is A' ultimately asserts the thorough-going unity of Reality. A significant judgment, symbolised by 'A is A,' lays down for itself no reservation beyond that which its own content may dictate, and claims therefore to be true without any reserve. Its simple affirmation leaves no room for any discontinuity in the real world, such that on one side of it the judgment may be true, and on the other false. If there were such a discontinuity, the judgment, such is the claim of the categorical affirmation—and all affirmation *qua* affirmation is at least categorical—would have taken note of it within its content, and would in that respect affirm under a reservation. But once true, always true. All reservations necessary to truth are included in the content. Reality, therefore, is one throughout. Relation to time, for example, is not involved in the fact of affirmation, but only, if at all, in conditions belonging to the content affirmed which depend upon facts in time[1]. Affirmation as such is unconditional, that is to say, is not limited by conditions outside its own content, and so if true, is true without reserve. There is not one Reality of which it is true and another of which it is false. Reality is what it is, and if it turns out not to be what we thought, then we thought amiss, i.e. judged falsely.

Law of Contradiction.
ii. The Law of Contradiction is but the complement of the Law of Identity. It supplies something without which the Law of Identity is not logically complete nor *distinctly* intelligible. But yet, by the fact of conferring distinctness, it is an addition.

[1] See Bk. I. chap. v, on Time in the singular judgment.

CHAP. VII.] *Contradiction and Excluded Middle.* 209

This Law also, a. in its barest statement 'A is not both A and not-A,' if understood to deny that A can be B, is either unmeaning or aggressively false. Considered as the principle of the negative infinite judgment A is not *mere* B, it *corresponds* as the form of bare negation, to A is mere A as the form of bare affirmation. In this form it is simply inadequate or unmeaning, and *equivalent to* 'A is at least A.' But taken as the exaggerated abstraction of negative judgment in the sense ' No A can be any not-A,' i.e. 'No A can be B at all,' it *corresponds to* the more open interpretation of the Law of Identity as 'A is at least A,' and is *equivalent to* the more aggressive interpretation of that law as 'A is mere A.'[1] For it then denies that *any* B (not only that *mere* B) can be united in a judgment with A. This is simply a reiteration in negative form that A is mere A and no more.

Truism or false.

But if, β. we take the Law of Contradiction in the obvious sense that a statement and its denial cannot both be true, it bears witness to the fact that a judgment *may* be truly denied, i.e. that a judgment may be false, and therefore that there may be truth in a negation[2]. It has been observed above[3] that, apart from the traditional distinction of quantity, the difference between the Logical contrary and the Logical

A genuine law of thought.

---

[1] The *corresponding* meanings of the Law of Identity and the Law of Contradiction, judged by the latitude employed in interpretation, are not their *equivalent* meanings. The more exaggerated denial is *equivalent* to the more tautological assertion, and the more pregnant or significant assertion to the denial of mere identity. Thus

'A is mere A' *corresponds to* 'A is not mere B.'

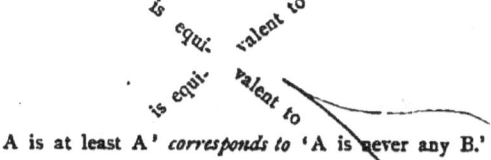

'A is at least A' *corresponds to* 'A is never any B.'

[2] According to the traditional rule, a statement may be so denied that both judgment and denial are false. But obviously in such a case some denial is true, though the one made is not. To say that a judgment is false is to say that it is truly denied.

[3] See above, on negation, p. 312 ff.

VOL. II.   P

contradictory, i.e. between the principle of contradiction and the principle of excluded middle, disappears. But because they retain a meaning for vital thought although not for formal logic, even in the absence of quantitative distinctions, we will distinguish the two aspects of negation treated of by these two principles, and will speak first only of falsehood established by truth, and not of truth established by falsehood. Though really, if our instance of contrariety[1] is 'A is B' and 'A is not B,' we have before us both falsehood established by truth, and truth established by falsehood.

A law of Reality. γ. If we do not press hard on the implications of the Law of Identity, it may be said that the significance of the Law of Contradiction carries us one step further. But it is doubtful if truth can exist apart from the conception of falsehood, and therefore it is better to say that the Law of Contradiction simply confirms and reiterates that assumption of the unity of reality which the Law of Identity involved. Reality, the Law of Contradiction asserts, is a *consistent* unity; which is merely to say over again that it is a unity. You cannot, that is to say, play fast and loose with reality. What is true at all, as the Law of Identity said, is true throughout Reality; but more than that, every such truth is double-edged, and carries with it throughout Reality consequences by which it affects and limits matters that are *primâ facie* outside itself. To infer from 'A is B' that 'A is not not-B' means at bottom that A is determined by B in respect of C or D.

Law of Excluded Middle. iii. The law of excluded middle, expressed by Aristotle as 'Between the assertions of a logical contradiction there is no middle,' i.e. no third alternative, applies of course to all strict denial, for all strict denial is a logical contradiction of the judgment denied.

A Truism. *a.* In its symbolic form 'A is either B or not-B' it lays down the ultimate formal *schema* of negation as the absolute

---

[1] I have pointed out before the inconvenient accident that the Law of Contradiction applies to Contraries only, while Contradictories or Logical Contradiction come under the Law of Excluded Middle.

alternative. Literally interpreted according to this symbolic form it has corresponding defects to those of the previous laws when interpreted in the same way. That is to say, all that it absolutely lays down is the form of bare negation which is *per se* not enough to constitute a judgment, because it involves the truth of the infinite judgment; but which in relation to anything further, for example to the intelligible antithesis 'A is either B or C,' is only the affirmation of a possibility, and the hypothetical definition of a relation. To invest a positive contrary C with the logical character of a contradictory not-B, is the work of determinate knowledge.

β. Interpreted in the plain sense, e. g. as by Aristotle, the law of Excluded Middle means that the *significant* negation of any judgment is an absolute alternative to it, viz. that not only the judgment and its negative cannot both be true, but one or other must be true, and if true, we may fairly add, must be significant. This means that falsehood can establish truth, or that negation can involve affirmative consequences. In this sense the postulate in question is the essential principle of disjunction, which is an absolute alternative *between two or more positive and significant members*. Therefore genuine disjunction has not the form 'A is either B or not-B,' but has the form 'A is either B or C,' which invests the positive assertion, in virtue of which C is taken to deny B as its contrary, with the absolute exclusiveness that only belongs of right to the bare form of denial, which has for its essence to express the contradictory. In other words, the old account of the *contrary*, that it denies, and also asserts something more beyond the denial, must also be true of any *significant* contradictory.

A law of Thought.

γ. The principle of Excluded Middle, then, ultimately affirms that Reality is not merely one and self-consistent, but is a system of reciprocally determinate parts. In affirming that a significant or genuine judgment is possible, such that within it a negation [1] shall carry a determinate

A law of Reality.

---
[1] According to the *bare* scheme of Excluded Middle, the significant negation

and explicit positive consequence—not merely, as the law of contradiction affirms, that a truth may carry with it definite negative consequences—the law of Excluded Middle fixes upon that reality which is constructed and maintained by judgment the character of a self-determining whole. For a nothing can only be invested with the character of a something by being a precisely limited nothing that implies a positive nature in the limiting and sustaining something, such that in affirming the nothing we are not affirming an absolute nothingness, but are covertly alleging a positive something which is or is involved in *the* nothingness of something in particular. From the mere and entire non-existence of mechanical cohesion, i.e. of any such thing as mechanically coherent substances, nothing strictly speaking could be inferred. The idea would be the content of a bare denial, and unintelligible. But from the failure of mechanical cohesion in the axle of a locomotive running at sixty miles an hour under precisely known conditions, all other substances retaining their mechanical properties, the most precise and detailed results could be predicted and must follow. This is a simple instance of the difference between the negation which has meaning and consequences, and that which has none.

Law of Sufficient Reason and of Causation.

iv. The law of Sufficient Reason, with its sub-form the law of Causation, is a corollary from that aspect of reality which the negative laws of thought have brought to our notice. Reality being a system of reciprocally determining parts, every part or feature of reality may be regarded as a consequent to which some other part or parts, or ultimately the whole, stands as ground. Every consequent, so this law tells us, has a ground from which it necessarily follows. Necessity indeed means nothing but the

must be a negation of the negation; for though the falsehood of the affirmation involves the truth of the negation, yet in the phase to which such a scheme belongs we are hardly warranted in affirming that a negation as such has positive significance. This use of double negation is a factor in identifying contrary with contradictory opposition.

inevitableness of the consequent when the ground is given[1].

In plain English, the Law of Sufficient Reason represents the demand of intelligence for the explanation of everything by something else. And it is plain that in the case of anything but the absolute whole this demand must go on to infinity, for outside any given content there is always something which can be regarded relatively to that content as something else. We have sufficiently criticised the operation of this law, the law of natural science as such, in the construction of the would-be totalities of abstract time and space, and it is not necessary to repeat the proof that this aspect of experience, taken *per se*, generates and must generate the infinite series. For it rests on the relations of parts in abstraction from the whole, or in other words, without the element of totality.

One point must be noticed here. Schopenhauer rightly maintains that *absolute necessity* is a *contradictio in adjecto*, because all necessity is *ex hypothesi* conditional. We have therefore not spoken of an absolute necessity but only of a real necessity, namely a necessity rooted in a ground which is a fact. We ought not to feel as if in this substitution the world had lost something of its rational coherence. Absolute necessity was a false ideal, and produced a fallacious preference of necessity to reality. For a *part*, necessity is a higher point of view than mere *perceptive reality*, because necessity involves relation to the whole, whereas perceptive reality, being isolated, is only formal[2] or potential reality. But for the whole, reality is a higher point of view than necessity, for reality is its self-dependence as a whole, while necessity would at once depress it into a part.

[1] See the admirable section 49 in Schopenhauer's treatise on the 'Satz vom Grunde.' His attempt, however, to show (sect. 50) that the law of ground and consequent in cognition does not entail an infinite series, although in causality or in space this is entailed, cannot be called successful. It depends on his distinction between Causality and Sufficient Reason.

[2] i.e. it has the contact with feeling which is the form of all contact with reality, but it falls short in content and is a mere fragment which has *something*, we do not yet know *what in particular*, of reality in it.

The above are the principal 'Laws of Thought.' We class them *not* as principles of intelligence apart from experience, but as principles of science or of rational experience as such, discoverable by analysis in every minutest portion of its texture, and capable of being regarded by a very easy abstraction as essential to its *existence* as contrasted with its special *significance*. They may therefore be ranked together as the formal postulates of knowledge, or as the formal aspect of the principle of Uniformity, in contrast with those which are not *prima facie* necessary to the existence of experience, or involved, at all events equally, in all reality as such; and which may therefore be considered under the head of material postulates of knowledge. The reciprocal implication of the formal and material postulates in one another, of a teleological significance in a self-consistent system, is plainly a matter of degree, and our task is to analyse the mode in which it does exist, not to predict how it must exist.

2. To emphasise the transition from the formal to the material postulates of experience, I make use of the following sentence from a distinguished writer [1]:—

'It is conceivable that man and his works and all the higher forms of animal life should be utterly destroyed; that mountain-regions should be converted into ocean depths; the floors of oceans raised into mountains; and the earth become a scene of horror which even the lurid fancy of the writer of the Apocalypse would fail to portray. And yet, to the eye of science, there would be no more disorder here than in the sabbatical peace of a summer sea.'

Translated into simpler language, this sentence means

[1] I quote and comment upon this passage purely because it is a striking illustration of my point. I have not the least intention of imputing to its eminent author (Professor Huxley in Contemp. Review for February, 1887) that he in fact undervalues those activities, the annihilation of which, according to this passage, would make no breach in the order of science. I cannot but think, on the other hand, that any logical theory with which such a statement were compatible would be gravely defective.

CHAP. VII.] *Laws of Nature.* 215

that if all these things happened, they would happen without a miracle; or in logical phrase, they would be capable of explanation according to the law of sufficient reason. And this is undoubtedly a truth that we must lay to heart. Our choice, being what we are, lies between the experience intelligible according to the formal laws, or none at all. A 'suspension of the laws of nature,' a 'supernatural interposition' or 'interference,' is perhaps the one and only matter that if alleged as a fact can be denied on the sole evidence of the abstract 'laws of thought.' Against any phenomenon, any occurrence, however extraordinary, these laws, apart from more concrete experience, have no foothold and no purchase. But the allegation that something is known and yet not knowable, nay more known *as* not knowable and in respect of the peculiar essence which makes it not knowable—this, if we would retain our sanity, we must refuse to entertain as conceivable. And if supernatural means anything but this, any causation handled by superior knowledge and power within the unity of Reality, then *for logic* it is *natural* and we must treat it as we treat all natural phenomena. We deny no occurrence on the strength of formal laws; we only deny a theory about the occurrence. Formal laws do not care how extraordinary a phenomenon may be; anything *may* have happened or may happen; the only question is whether it *did*, or *will*.

Much unclear thinking and much false sentiment might have been avoided if the mechanical aspect of nature had been recognised[1] long since as Professor Huxley states it. Nature, as a mechanical system, is not teleological. Disease and deformity are as natural, as orderly, as much according to law, as health and beauty. It is idle verbiage to enlarge upon a contrast between law and lawlessness in the natural world, considered as a natural or formally knowable system. The only lawlessness is in the supposed supernatural within the natural. Nothing that happens can escape from the

[1] e.g. by Charles Kingsley and teachers of his school who preach concurrence with and conformity to the ' laws of nature.'

principle of sufficient reason, and therefore nothing that happens is without an aspect of law.

But these considerations, though true, are not the whole truth. We unquestionably expect something more of the world than a capability of being known according to the law of sufficient reason. It is the nature and the warrant of these expectations that I now desire briefly to examine.

The maintenance of Life.   i. I do not think that it can be doubted that we expect an indefinitely prolonged—not necessarily everlasting—continuance of such conditions of the earth's surface as are compatible with human life. It would not be justifiable to derive this expectation from the formal postulate considered above on any such ground as the necessity of a human intelligence to the existence—as we understand existence—of the actual world. This merely logical necessity might at worst be satisfied by an appeal to our ignorance; for how can we know that the human intelligence is the only intelligence, in the system of things? But in any case we are now compelled to accept as fact a state of the globe prior to the existence of the human race, or even of organic life, and if we find no insuperable difficulty of form in this view of the past, why should there be any in a corresponding belief as regards the future?

It may be said, again, that our whole state of knowledge, and the absence of urgent warning from our scientific lookout men, justifies a disbelief in any imminent disaster or transformation of the earth's surface. Now it is my contention in the present chapter that the postulates of which we are speaking simply sum up the pith and essence of our knowledge, and I have no reason to doubt that the actual state of scientific prediction is a large element in the practical certainty with which we regard the future of our globe. Unmotived possibilities rightly go for nothing, and it is the case, I suppose, that there are not at present above the scientific horizon any seriously motived possibilities of a speedy end to man's existence.

CHAP. VII.] *Eschatology.* 217

But I cannot think that this exhausts the question. It appears to me that the real root of our conviction is ethical, and ultimately depends upon our confidence in the relation of our purposes to the scheme of the universe. Such an ethical conviction is not a ποῦ στῶ outside our knowledge, but is the very core of almost all that knowledge on which our distinctively human life essentially depends. The purposes of the civilised world form the real teleology on which our organised knowledge of society and of all human achievement is based, and it is on the conviction, inwoven in this knowledge, of the reality of these purposes in their essential content, that our faith in the future seems to me to be founded, and under present conditions of knowledge to be rightly founded.

It may be said, with an appeal to eschatology, that such a faith is not even a '*quod semper, quod ubique,*' etc. and that a speedy end to man's existence on earth has in fact frequently been expected by large bodies of human beings. On this suggestion two observations are to be made. In the first place, it would be interesting, both logically and psychologically, to know the exact effect of such a belief on the practical postulates of civilised life in those who hold it—to know, in short, the degree of reality with which, as a working belief, it has ever been held. To some extent the doctrine has been specially directed to meet the dangers which it tended to cause, by inculcation of the duty of diligence in business and of orderly conduct as the best preparation for the end. And then in the second place, as this adaptation of the doctrine shows, the conception of an ethical continuity of purpose is satisfied by the idea in question, although not necessarily under the form of a continued terrestrial existence [1].

---

[1] Under this head, of a satisfaction for our ethical demand otherwise than in the form of our continued existence, may be classed in great part the curious psychological fact of the slight practical effect produced by prospective death even on men whose lives are by any cause gravely imperilled. I ascribe this, though in part only, to our prospective satisfaction in the maintenance of our essential activities and purposes by others after our death; and I do not think

If the question were pushed home, and we were asked to translate our ethical postulate into terms of time and degree, we could only, I think, fall back on conceptions akin to the βίος τέλειος of Aristotle, i. e. on the conception of a duration and environment of life adequate to the accomplishment of some worthy purpose. And what catastrophes befalling the human race are compatible with the purposes of the world we cannot presume to guess[1]. It would be hard to believe, for example, in the likelihood of a catastrophe which should overwhelm a progressive civilisation like that of modern Europe and its colonies, so that the history of the world would have to be begun anew, without any influence at any time arising, by rediscovery of remains, from the prior civilisation.

'But we may be mistaken in our postulate.' Certainly we may be mistaken, as in our present knowledge, so in the sum and substance of our present knowledge. But unmotived possibilities of error must go for nothing; and in departing from the positive import of the knowledge which at present we possess, we abandon concrete reality for more or less abstract imagination. In this first material interpretation which we have been putting upon the law of the Uniformity of Nature, we have simply been analysing a condition which is essential to the maintenance of human life as reality now presents it to us, viz. the prospect of continuance. If the constancy of content which this prospect demands were ever to become doubtful with good reason, the doubt would *ex*

that this satisfaction would exist in view of a prospective extinction of the race. Again, the truth that a belief in *some* continuance is necessary to *any* action, and that *some* action is necessary to *any* continuance, is merely the minimum grade of the postulate we are discussing.

[1] The writer is aware of a strong prejudice in his own mind that a disastrous earthquake in London is an exceedingly improbable occurrence. Not, of course, that volcanic agencies can act otherwise than they must, but that such a degree of inconstancy as to tempt an enormous heavily built city to be erected, and then to turn and rend it, would seem malicious on the part of Nature. The prejudice is only mentioned as a psychological curiosity, and is not defended for a moment. The writer believes it to be a blundering application of an ultimately genuine principle.

hypothesi show itself in our knowledge on positive grounds; but till then we must accept this constancy not indeed as an ultimate certainty, but as a leading characteristic of our actual world.

ii. But the uniformity of nature as materially understood goes at least one step further than to postulate the maintenance of human life on the earth's surface. It also postulates the reality of those purposes and achievements which make man what he is. *The reality of human purposes.*

It is possible to fancy not merely a state of the earth in which the life of the human animal should be physically impossible, but a state in which though life were possible and actual, yet the apparent caprices of nature, however *formally* rational, should prohibit all advance in knowledge and civilisation. What degree of ambiguity in the appearance of natural bodies, in spite of an actual constancy of their properties, might make knowledge impossible, is a question which there is no sense in asking, as we have no measure by which to estimate the answer. Many ambiguities have been resolved by knowledge; but the operations of the intellect unquestionably demand not only the theoretical constancy of properties, but *some* degree of limitation in their variety. Exhaustiveness is, in short, though not theoretically deducible from the law of Sufficient Reason, a largely and increasingly essential element of knowledge. What would it help us that the specific gravity of gold is constant, if elements undistinguishable from gold by other ordinary tests, but differing in specific gravity, were continually to present themselves in our operations upon Nature? And although infinitesimal variation is a predominant law of the organic world, yet knowledge is at least greatly facilitated by the existence of marked points of transition between species and species [1], and it is plain that a succession of animals differing by variations of minute and equal value would not be compatible with our present modes of natural knowledge, although in geometrical

---

[1] Owing, no doubt, to the extinction of intermediate forms.

matter the intelligence has displayed the power of theoretically grasping an absolutely continuous evolution.

It might be said indeed that we were alleging above that 'If there is to be human life there must be human life,' and are alleging now 'If there is to be knowledge there must be knowledge,' truisms which amount to nothing. So far as content goes, this may, by abstraction, be true. A mere analysis of content is *eo ipso* hypothetical. But the content which we are analysing is, moreover, affirmed of our real world as an integral element of the significance of that world, which significance is primarily ethical.

And this significance for which I am contending is not an *a priori* postulate or axiom, from which any specific knowledge could be derived apart from experience. If I am asked 'What is the material uniformity? How do you limit it? What does it imply?' I can only answer by pointing to the progressive content of knowledge itself. The postulate of Uniformity is ultimately that there is such uniformity as our knowledge in detail reveals to us. Do I believe that mass and energy are constant, that gravity operates in the region of the fixed stars, that any of the heavenly bodies have animated inhabitants, or that the elements are ultimately reducible to a single form of matter? None of these, I should have to reply, are questions of an ultimate logical postulate. Our convictions upon all of them must be determined by the state of our knowledge and by our estimate of its tendencies. From an ethical postulate we can deduce nothing but the empty form of a logical principle, the form that 'what is involved in ethical reality is real;' the material details must come from science only.

Three interpretations of Uniformity of Nature.

The three degrees then which may conveniently be distinguished in the interpretation of the Law of Uniformity of Nature or of the Unity of Reality, considered as the postulate of knowledge, may be assigned as follows.

Reality is mechanical.

1. Reality is a mechanical system through and through. This postulate is expressed in the so-called 'laws of thought'

which find their most explicit form in the 'Law of Sufficient Reason,' or principle of Relativity.

2. Reality as a mechanical system is adapted to the evolution and maintenance of life, i.e. is at least quasi-teleological. This is a first approximation to what is practically assumed as the material Uniformity of Nature. *Reality is quasi-teleological.*

3. Reality as a mechanical system is further adapted to, or includes as elements within its unity, the substantive purposes of human intelligence, i.e. is really teleological. *Reality is really teleological.*

It is possible, by intellectual abstraction, to dissociate the first of these aspects from the others, as the import of 'mechanical' can be dissociated[1] from the import of 'machine.' It is not possible to dissociate either quasi-teleology or real teleology from a mechanically-conditioned system. The nature of a system can only be real in as far as the parts or differences that enter into it have a real mode of activity. Miracle destroys teleology, for it destroys the relation of part to whole. And activity or variation of activity, that has no ground in the one Reality, is miracle.

3. It seems desirable to conclude the present work by bringing to a point the views that have been implied throughout it upon the ultimate nature of intellectual necessity, and upon the sense in which such necessity can be predicated of any elements within knowledge. *The ultimate nature of Necessity.*

i. It would be a tedious task to analyse at length the components of Mill's discussions[2] relating to the basis of necessary truth. But nothing could, in my judgment, be more conducive to a thorough mastery of the question than a careful study of the chapters referred to in Mill's Logic in the light of some plain distinctions, which, in default of a better guide, I will here endeavour to lay down. By Mill himself, together with the writers whom he quotes, nearly every position of importance in the *A priori necessity and mediation.*

---

[1] This concession must be read subject to the reservations of p. 97. This dissociation is not possible in an ultimate sense. But of course dissociation from any particular teleological scheme is abundantly possible, and that is the point of material importance.

[2] Mill's Logic, Bk. II. chaps. v. and vi.

controversy is assumed in its turn, and the argument is a strange mixture of penetrating sagacity with unphilosophical confusion.

Mediate nature of necessity forgotten.

a. Necessity, as we have abundantly convinced ourselves[1], involves mediation or inference. No isolated judgment *qua* isolated can have necessity. Every necessary truth must, in so far as it is necessary, present itself as the conclusion from an antecedent. In the idle controversy whether axioms are known *a priori* or 'from experience' this aspect of necessity is forgotten on both sides.

'From something prior.'

(1) If *a priori* necessity is taken as inherent within the four corners of the axiom itself, the very nature of necessity is contradicted, and the only meaning which I presume the phrase *a priori* can ever have had is stubbornly denied to it[2]. '*A priori*' (ἐκ προτέρων) says in so many words that the knowledge to which this term applies is '*from* something prior to it,' i.e. is derivative, inferred and mediate. The metaphor involved in 'prior' no doubt created for Aristotle a problem about the series of premises, which, it would seem, must come to an end somewhere in an ultimate premise; a problem which could only be solved, as Aristotle, I imagine, was really quite aware, by making the series ultimately return into itself, and lose its successive character by transformation into an organised system. But this difficulty about the ultimate premise of a series, even if unsolved, does not justify the neglect of the plain logical differentia imposed by the term *a priori* upon all that claims to be known *a priori*[3], viz. that it shall be inferred from knowledge, whatever this may be, other than itself.

---

[1] Cp. especially above, i. 144.

[2] I am quite unable, for the reasons assigned in the text, to subscribe to the views as to *a priori* knowledge which are stated in sections 355-6 of Lotze's Logik. In placing the test of 'self-evidence' in an immediate recognition without any process of proof, he appears to me to surrender altogether the rational character of knowledge. His subsequent explanation, sect. 358, seems to me exactly parallel to Whewell's practical retractation respecting the law of atomic weights. See below, p. 225.

[3] Prantl, Geschichte der Logik, vol. iv. p. 78, quotes from Albertus de

(2) If, on the other hand, by those who object to the '*a* Indis-*priori*' origin of knowledge, supposed to be alleged as not sociation. experiential, an appeal is made to any form of indissoluble association, originating no doubt in constant experiential conjunction, but operating finally through a sheer psychological inability to disjoin the parts which insist on presenting themselves together in the mental picture, here if anywhere we have the *vicious* doctrine of *a priori* knowledge in its most outrageous form. For, it must be remembered, the past is past; the psychological history of our conviction cannot come into court when we wish to demonstrate the conviction to be true or false. It is of no use to say, 'I have seen it so often that I cannot help believing it true.' One might almost as well say, 'I have said it so often that I cannot help believing it true.' The question is not how often you have seen it, but what you now know that you saw, and under what precise conditions. If nothing in the content of the experience, as it now is in the mind, goes to exclude error or to carry conviction[1], then *we believe it simply because we find it in the mind*, which is just the description of vicious or intuitional *a priori* belief[2].

Saxonia, A. D. 1390, as the oldest authority for the dualistic use of '*a priori*': 'Demonstratio quaedam est procedens ex causis ad effectum, et vocatur demonstratio *a priori* et demonstratio propter quid et potissima; .... alia est demonstratio procedens ab effectibus ad causas, et talis vocatur demonstratio *a posteriori* et demonstratio quia (that) et demonstratio non potissima.' Nothing could be more sharply opposed to 'immediate' knowledge.

[1] The distinct relations to the percipient, which make us sure that our recollection is not a fancy, are what perform this office in an act of 'simple' memory. In fact, no act of memory is absolutely simple, as indeed no intellectual act of any kind is. The truth of our recollection is inferred from content, not accepted because of mere psychical indissolubility.

[2] In the discussion alluded to in the text, Mill is on the whole the champion of organised knowledge and inferential necessity against unreasoned conviction and mere indissoluble association. But he wavers in his position, (1) by refusing to maintain against Whewell that a justifiable *necessity can* be generated by experience, and confining himself to the contention that an illusory show of necessity can be so generated—this means that the experience of which he is thinking is the mere repetition of sense-perception and not a determinate system of science; and (2) by the constant appeal to the profusion of experimental evidence in favour of geometrical axioms, and in particular to the mental

Organised and unorganised experience. β. The distinction on which the relation of necessity to Experience really turns is the distinction between organised and unorganised experience. The former can give necessity; the latter cannot give knowledge. To maintain with Whewell that there is a necessity which does not depend on experience is to concede Mill's contention that necessity is a psychological illusion. If there is no organisation of experience into a system, the latter view is obviously the truth; but with the necessity which Mill rejects there must in that case also be thrown overboard the knowledge which he maintains. If there is organisation of experience, then the necessity which attends complete conception, although nothing irrational, supernatural, or immutable, is more than a psychological illusion. It simply means that given this and that, being the conditions imposed by our knowledge of the matter in hand, then the other must follow because of the relation between them.

This distinction may be, I think, pretty thoroughly elucidated with reference to Whewell's treatment [1] of the principle, in his time quite a recent discovery, that chemical combination takes place between elements in certain constant definite proportions only. Whewell was able to persuade himself that this law, when once understood by a mind with adequate scientific resources, could not but be accepted as a law whose falsity was inconceivable. Of course such an assertion, made by a writer suspected of a belief in intuitional or something like innate and unreasoned convictions of necessity, about a principle 'the discoverer of which was still living,' was open to the ridicule with which

picture of parallel straight lines as the instrument, by a constant repetition of experiment, of generating the certainty that they are incapable of meeting. Here we lose sight of the principle which owes so much to Mill's advocacy, that one good experiment will establish a law. Sir J. Herschel as quoted by Mill wavers in precisely the same way, appealing now to iteration of experience, and now to systematic knowledge. Spencer seems to hold the view characterised in the text, not interpreting his test by conception into logical proof and therefore leaving us to suppose that it consists in psychical conjunction.

[1] Fully adduced and discussed in Mill's chapters above referred to.

Mill assailed it. But the interest lies in the explanations which Whewell subsequently offered, and which make the course of his mind in the matter tolerably clear. In order to perceive necessity in such a case, you must, he says in effect, understand the terms, you must conceive all the elements of the problem *distinctly*, and you must be furnished with a degree of scientific knowledge which not every man of science possesses. The 'intuition' of the truth, he says, 'may be a rare and difficult attainment.'

There can hardly be two opinions as to what all this means. Conception as thus understood is simply systematic knowledge, and the reason why you cannot conceive the law false is that you have attained a thoroughly *mediate* insight that the system of science requires it to be true; i.e. that if it were taken not to be true your system of reality would be shattered and overthrown. This necessity is read into the terms of the principle in question, the interpretation of which has been insensibly enlarged, and without careful analysis there is great likelihood that the principle will seem to possess a necessity involving no relation to anything outside itself. In the particular case in question it may be—though the suggestion is hazardous—that a confusion was operative in Whewell's mind between a very abstract principle which is involved in the place held by quantity in the real world, and the peculiar law discovered by Dalton as the law of atomic weights. All quantity is definite, and every combination is a combination of definite quantities. Nor can there be any doubt that every mixture has different properties according to the relative quantities of the things mixed together. Wine and water will mix in any quantities, but the mixtures will not all be the same. I venture to write down these platitudes, as Mill, in maintaining that the occurrence which Whewell called inconceivable really represents the general rule, almost seems to forget that every mixture is a mixture of definite quantities, and that a change in the proportion will make a difference in the mixture. No doubt this comparatively formal principle is a long way from the law which Dalton discovered, viz. that the peculiar combination known as chemical combination would not take place at all except between definite proportions of the elements. But yet, assuming the *constancy* of the resultant combinations, e. g. that there is only one kind of water and not two or more kinds, and also the *limitation of their number*, i.e. that there is not in nature a series of compounds containing the same elements as water but in slightly different proportions—and I should have imagined that the truth or untruth of these two suggestions must have been notorious to chemists before Dalton's time —then presupposing all this it does seem to an outsider as if the law of combination in definite and constant proportions [1] was pretty much rendered necessary by the mere nature of quantity. At all events, without being so rash as to infer from the operations of my own mind to those of Whewell's, I may suggest that some such process as the above, which is obviously a mediate inference from matters of fact combined with a formal principle about quantity, constantly follows upon the discovery of a law. We are apt then tacitly to presuppose the matters of fact, and to identify the new law with the formal principle which it interprets. This, I venture to think, is the key to the general character of the process which Whewell's mind must have passed through in the case before us, with the result of his mistaking mediate for immediate necessity [2]. In any case, his reason for believing Dalton's law plainly was, as he says in so many words, that he thought he saw

---

[1] The theory of atoms goes further than this in form. But I understand Mill and Whewell to be speaking of the law only in as far as it refers to definite proportions.

[2] It is said that men always begin by denying a new truth, and then say that they knew it before. This is simply that the material interpretation or development of an accepted abstract principle is at first strange to them and they resist it; but when they have understood it, they pass it over into the old formal principle, identify the two, and become unconscious that they have made any advance.

CHAP. VII.] *Conception and Imagination.*   227

the whole order of nature to be involved in it. If the intuition of an *a priori* necessity excludes mediation or inference, then this logical process was not the intuition of an *a priori* necessity.

In as far then as Conception means this complete insight, its necessity is clearly the sole test of truth, being simply identical with the necessity of knowledge. Mill's polemic against the test by mere Conception is largely justified by the ignorant use that was made of this test, as if it were immediate and operated by mere inspection. In this polemic Mill shows himself alive to the true source of experiential necessity, although he rejects the term necessity except in reference to mathematical reasoning. Thus, strangely enough, Mill reintroduces into knowledge the distinction between necessary and not-necessary truth, which the experiential school might be expected to deny. And his account of the distinction is on the whole sound, referring it simply to the difference between the complete knowledge of the conditions, which is possible in mathematics[1], and the partial knowledge of the conditions which alone is possible in ordinary physical investigation. It would be better, however, either to abolish the term necessary altogether, or to extend it to all scientific knowledge as such.

Mere *imagination*, on the other hand, as Mill rightly contends, though inclined to extend the contention erroneously to *conception*, has nothing to do with truth or knowledge either way. Allegations are not more likely to be true because we can imagine their content, nor less likely because we cannot.

It follows from the above considerations—

(1) That every judgment is *necessary*[2] and *mediate in as far as it is known*; and that no judgment has necessity or precision (which depends on the explicitness of the me-

[1] The view of mathematical conceptions as hypothetical does not concern us here. See Bk. I. chap. iv.
[2] See also chap. i. of this book, on the specific necessity of judgment.

Q 2

diating conditions) if taken apart from the totality of knowledge;

and (2) That the content of every judgment, as well as its truth or necessity, is correlative to the one ultimate judgment, i.e. to the whole system of knowledge; and that therefore while we do well to maintain that the body of knowledge has certain indispensable functions, we nevertheless commit an error of principle if we deny that the identity of these functions is like other identities compatible with variation.

Thus for instance knowledge, or reality as known, must have such a function of relativity as that which we express by the law of causation. But to suppose that the shape in which that function happens to be familiar to us, involving perhaps homogeneity of cause and effect, is necessarily an ultimate shape, is one of the most mischievous results of the fallacy of an isolated necessity. I do not think that there can be any doubt that even the conceptions of the straight line or of three-dimensional space are modified in their content by the explicit distinctions needed to save them from being confounded with arcs of great circles on a sphere surface or with space of more or less than three dimensions. Unquestionably the new conceptions, however unreal, make themselves felt as restricting the absoluteness of the old ones. Every judgment is relative to the whole of knowledge, and no judgment entirely escapes modification as this whole is modified.

Rehabilitation of formal distinctions.
ii. In order to illustrate the true import and value of such conceptions as that of *a priori* truth or of necessary knowledge, I will venture to give a brief sketch of the process, tending to repeat itself in history, by which such distinctions are most thoroughly apprehended, and which, if only in the individual mind, is perhaps necessary to their apprehension.

When, in an epoch of genuine enquiry, a student first opens his eyes, so to speak, in the philosophical world, he finds himself confronted by a multitude of traditional distinctions, some of which claim to be fundamental lines of demarcation. Impressed with the ruling idea of all great epochs or earnest intelligences, that of the unity of reality, he assumes a protestant attitude towards these distinctions, which appear to him incompatible with the demands of his genius or of his time. His iconoclastic zeal is inflamed by the justification which it finds in the obviously meaningless and mechanical rigidity of the tradition which it attacks, a tradition that has come to be in many respects a real offence against the primary postulates of intelligence. And turning from his contemporaries to the great masters of thought whom they profess to interpret, he finds in them also the phrases and ideas which he has learnt to regard as the symbols of an unmeaning superstition. And therefore, finding no help in man, such a protestant reformer in philosophy will proceed to reconstruct his world on the basis of that aspect of it in which its unity has been revealed to him ; that is to say, in the case of logic, probably on the basis of sensation, of observation, of particulars, of inductive experience.

But when with labour and pains some progress has been made in this reconstruction, then for the reformer or for his successors there arises a further stage. The duty now falls upon them of maintaining the essential distinctions of thought, between perceptive comparison and geometrical demonstration, between empirical laws and laws of nature, between induction by simple enumeration and the constructive processes of methodic science. When these antitheses are fully developed, then the time has come for a rediscovery of the meaning of Plato and Aristotle. The language which science is compelled to hold reveals itself as coincident with that of the teacher who first explained in what science consists. The distinction between the province of self-contradictory opinion[1] and the province of

[1] De Morgan's Budget of Paradoxes is little else than the self-defence of science against opinion. The failure to distinguish relations, which in the world of opinion makes difference into contradiction, is well illustrated by one

coherent knowledge recovers for science the meaning which it had all but lost for scholarship. When it becomes unavoidable to erect, within the whole of 'experience,' which has been passionately proclaimed to be coextensive with knowledge, the included wholes of 'empirical' observation and mere fact, as opposed to deductive certainty and mathematical necessity, then it is understood how such distinctions as these when originally made were distinctions within the knowable world, and were not incompatible with the unity of experience. No geometrician, I imagine, would accept the statement that the ratio of the diameter to the circumference of a circle, so far as ascertained, is ascertained by observation, because this would mean that it was found by direct measurement. But, in denying this 'empirical' origin of the cognition in question, he would not suppose that he was alleging its independence of our acquired knowledge concerning space and spatial relations. He would explain, I suppose, that no doubt the calculation in question was based upon spatial relations that could only come into the human intelligence through its being aware of a spatial world (however this its spatial perception is attained), but that nevertheless the conclusion is reached by a process of reasoning or calculation, and is not an observation in the sense in which it is an observation that there are ten volumes in the shelf at my right hand. And by extending the same reasonable interpretation to Plato and Aristotle which we extend to ourselves, remembering, that is, that all contentions are relative to certain purposes and proceed on certain assumptions, it becomes possible to recover something like their natural meaning.

The development of Logic in England from Bacon to Mill and Jevons is a good illustration of the process which I have attempted to describe. And on a still larger scale, extending to every side of life, I make no doubt that the

of De Morgan's cases, an argument against the rotation of the earth which asks 'How can a man go 200 yards to any place if the moving superficies of the earth do carry it from him?' p. 78.

Renaissance itself, and also the new Renaissance of Winckelmann, Schiller and Goethe, were examples of a similar phenomenon. Ancient systems of thought or of religion can in fact only be interpreted in as far as their interpreters feel the necessities which were pressing upon their authors. And thus the individual mind, in as far as its ideas develope from a root of genuine interest in reality, tends to pursue an analogous course. If a great master of thought could come on earth again after some centuries, he would seldom find his true followers among those who have never deviated from the straitest sect of his exponents.

Thus a cynic might say that the history of philosophy is a process in which the meaning of Plato and Aristotle is periodically forgotten by their disciples and rediscovered by their antagonists; who then, perhaps, become their disciples and so the cycle recommences. And the observation would be just except in so far as it implies that in each rediscovery no advance is made on the meaning as understood before. The cycles of philosophy repeat themselves, but not with identical content. The Encyclopaedia Britannica is a very different thing from the Encyclopaedia of existing knowledge as sketched in Plato's Republic.

iii. It has been suggested by a great writer [1]—and the suggestion falls in with many current ideas about philosophy—that the necessity or propriety on the strength of which synthetic connections are derived from or combined into an including unity, ultimately the unity of the world, may be rightly described as 'aesthetic.' This conception contains elements of very unequal value, and I suspect that the element for the sake of which it is recommended is one for the sake of which it ought to be rejected. 'Aesthetic necessity.'

It does not matter, or ought not to matter, whether we speak of self-evidence, propriety, or necessity. They all attempt to express the same fact, that in knowledge, that

[1] Lotze, Logik, sects. 364-5.

is in judgment, we are not free, but are under a constraint exercised upon us by the content of knowledge itself, such that some judgments have to be accepted and others to be rejected. But if we express this fact by the term necessity, then in virtue of the explanations which have been given above we exclude, and rightly exclude, an interpretation which the terms self-evidence and propriety admit if they do not compel, that is to say, an intuitional interpretation.

'Aesthetic necessity,' then, would either mean something which we might accept as a fact, though we should pronounce its appellation unduly limited, or else would be a contradiction in terms. I will consider the latter alternative first.

<small>In one sense, a contradiction.</small> *a.* An aesthetic judgment, like a moral judgment, is in everyday life, at any rate, not explicitly mediated. It is the peculiarity of the aesthetic product, or of the aesthetic aspect of any object, that although coherent and rational, having passed through the medium of mind, yet nevertheless, *qua* aesthetically operative, it is not discursively analysed. Although in aesthetic judgment discursive analysis must play its part, yet such analysis is not the essence of aesthetic appreciation, but is on the contrary that which aesthetic appreciation has in common with scientific understanding, and is the mere organon of careful perception, by which the aesthetic product is constructed and brought to notice in the mind. A work of art, or any object regarded as beautiful, makes an appeal to feeling; which, as such an appeal, must be immediate, although the feeling to which it appeals is moralised or spiritualised, and consequently there is on both sides, in the work of art and in the spectator, a rational content. This, though it appeals to feeling in an immediate form, is of course capable of being analysed in mediate form. But yet, as the work of art is the outcome of a spiritual mood of feeling in the artist, so it appeals to such a mood in the spectator. It was not constructed by combination of abstract relations, and though its fabric must be coherent and charged with intelligence,

yet no mere intellectual reconstruction of such a fabric can reproduce the spiritual mood which is the essence of the work of art. This, if expressed in an abstract or inferential form, may retain a value for philosophy, but loses the differentia of fine art. Therefore, as necessity involves explicit mediation, and aesthetic judgment in the strictest sense excludes explicit mediation, to speak of aesthetic necessity is a *contradictio in adjecto*. It is this immediate or intuitional self-evidence, this appreciation by *feeling*, which, as I suspect, the suggestion before us intended to identify with logical coherence or necessity. If recommended in this sense, the suggestion must I think be absolutely rejected. Necessity only attaches to a judgment in as far as that judgment involves the whole of knowledge. Unreasoned necessity is irrational belief.

β. If, on the other hand, aesthetic necessity merely meant that synthetic coherence of parts which every aesthetic whole shares with all universals whatever, then though we should admit the description to be true, and in one respect striking, yet we should have to add that it really did no more than refer us to one instance, and that an imperfect one, of the general relation to be described. An aesthetic whole is, so to speak, a universal made easy. In it the individual unity which belongs to everything real is not left to be toilsomely unravelled by reflection, but is presented in a shape capable of at once appealing as a unity to sense-perception or to imagination. Hence the discursive analysis which is instrumental in the apprehension of a work of art, however subtle in its ultimate refinements, is *ex hypothesi* in great part evident and unavoidable. In this sense and to this extent the rational coherence in which all knowledge consists is strikingly illustrated, not by the aesthetic judgment itself, but by the analysis which accompanies the apprehension of a work of art in so far as this apprehension is of the same nature with the apprehension of *any perceived object or complex of relations whatsoever*. For this reason it is not uncommon to take a work of art as an example of

[margin: In another sense, a type of logical necessity.]

the compulsion by which the nature of a whole controls its parts, simply because this control, which is the essence of individuality, lends itself readily to analysis in a work that is pervaded by an especially harmonious unity [1]. But precisely the same is the case with geometrical conceptions, and for precisely the same reason geometrical necessity, which is not only rational but also essentially mediate, is often taken as the type of logical necessity.

Of these two classes of examples the geometrical conception is the more perfect in one respect and the aesthetic in another. The aesthetic object is an imperfect type of necessity because its nature is not exhaustible by reasoned judgment, but consists in being such as to produce a certain spiritual mood. As this mood involves and is accompanied by some degree of reflective apprehension directed to the coherence of parts in the artistic whole, which coherence is necessary, there is apt to be a confusion between the feeling and its concomitant insight which leads to an erroneous notion of *immediate necessity*. And it may be added that in trained artistic perception there is an immediate reaction of repugnance or acceptance, analogous to the every-day moral judgment, which is right and accountable in its place, but is the worst possible elucidation of logical necessity, with which the form of feeling is wholly incompatible. The geometrical object is not open to this censure. Its nature is to be capable of systematic construction through and through. And the pervading nature in virtue of which the universal determines its differences, the root of logical

---

[1] The famous simile of the statue in the beginning of the fourth book of Plato's Republic will occur to every one. This simile, occurring at a critical point in an important work, is perhaps responsible for a current idea that the Logic and Ethics of Plato and Aristotle were 'aesthetic' or 'artistic.' But the fact is that Plato and Aristotle dealt almost exclusively with the general principles which underlie all individuality and function, and illustrated these from fine art, from industrial art, and from science, almost indifferently. They possessed indeed no specific term for fine art, and though they gave a just weight to the idea of beauty, yet nothing in their theories was aesthetic if that means sentimental or unreasoned. If anything, they were too systematic and intellectual.

necessity, is nowhere more explicitly formulated and applied than in geometry.

As to individuality, however, the matter is reversed. A √ work of art, though not an embodiment of real teleology,—for it has not a purpose conceived as a definite reflective idea,—has nevertheless the content or nature of real teleology, being thoroughly penetrated with reason [1] in the form of feeling. It is therefore individual in a special sense, as an outward and visible form thoroughly identified with an idea that pervades it, so that the work of art is distinctly relative to human intelligence, though it has no separable purpose embodied in abstract human thought. Thus a work of art is an exceptionally effective instance of an individual whole. In geometrical objects the pervading unity is of the most various kinds, and sometimes, taking the imperfect form of a progression to infinity, appears to be incapable of constituting a whole complete in itself. Even space seems powerless to limit itself, and therefore its parts seem rather to lie indifferently behind one another than to constitute a totality in which each has its peculiar place and function. In this sense no doubt the *peculiar* and *specific* necessity imposed upon parts by the whole which they constitute is better illustrated by the aesthetic than by the geometrical whole.

Yet the wholes of real teleology, the moral order, for example, as exhibited in a moral person filling his place in a community, illustrate the nature of rational necessity better than either the aesthetic or the geometrical system. The identification of necessity with the idea of an intuitional or isolated self-evidence is the rock to be avoided.

Necessity, then, is a character attaching to parts or differences interrelated within wholes, universals, or identities. If there were any totality such that it could not be set over against something else as a part or difference within a further system, such a totality could not be known

[1] Mr. Matthew Arnold's phrase 'criticism of life,' applied to poetry, explains what is meant by saying that art contains reason. That the reason must be in the form of feeling this term 'criticism' appears to ignore.

under an aspect of necessity. The universe, however we may conceive of it as including subordinate systems, must ultimately be incapable, *ex hypothesi*, of entering as an element into a system including more than it. Strictly speaking, therefore, its relation to knowledge must be one of reality, not of necessity. But also, strictly speaking, it is a reality which we have no power to question or to explain, because all our questioning or explanation falls within it. There can be no meaning in talking about what might be the case if the universe were other than it is, or about what has been the case to make the universe what it is.

But except in the case of this unique and imaginary reference of that which is assumed to be the absolute whole to something outside itself, every judgment is the synthesis of differences, in a whole or identity expressed or understood, and is therefore at the same time the analysis of that identity. It makes no difference to the ultimate or actual import of a judgment whether as a process in time it took its rise from the synthesis of two data, or from the analysis of one. In every judgment there are differences within an identity. In every judgment therefore there is affirmed a necessity based on a reality. The necessity itself may have for its content a further reality, or may remain an abstraction which can only be set down as descriptive or illustrative of reality. The latter is the case with the more extreme forms of the hypothetical judgment.

The various forms of universal which are the source of necessity and constitute the content of judgments, the comparative value of these forms for knowledge, and the affinities between them, are the object-matter of Logical Science. And because our intelligence creates and sustains our real world by a continuous judgment which embraces these forms, in their concrete connection, within the unity of its system, it is further true that Logical Science is the analysis, not indeed of individual real objects, but of the intellectual structure of reality as a whole.

INDEX.

Absolute Necessity, a contradiction, ii. 213.
Abstract Number, i. 167.
Abstraction, i. 65; ii. 21 ff.
Abstraction and Necessity, i. 43 ff.
Added Determinants, ii. 61.
Addition and Multiplication, ii. 52.
Addition and Multiplication of Indices, ii. 53 ff.
'Aesthetic necessity' criticised, ii. 231 ff.
Affirmation and Negation, i. 294 ff.
Albertus de Saxoniâ, on '*a priori*' and '*a posteriori*,' ii. 222 note.
All, meaning of in Judgment, i. 163.
Allness and Necessity, i. 224.
Alternative Classifications, i. 63.
Analogical Judgment, i. 226 ff.
Analogy, True and false basis of, ii. 98 ff.
Analytic, i. 97.
Annual rings in trees, i. 234.
ἀπόφασις, dist. στέρησις, i. 332.
A priori, ii. 222.
Aristotle, i. 9, 12, 15 note, 25, 80, 224, 271, 298, 332; ii. 177, 218, 222, 234 note.
Arnold, Mr. Matthew, ii. 235 note.
Association of ideas, ii. 15, 223.
Atomic weights, theory of, ii. 224.
Axioms, ii. 205.

Bare Denial, i. 299.
Bee Ophrys, ii. 125.
Bradley, 'Principles of Logic,' i. 14, 30, 49 note, 59, 79 note, 107, 252, 279 ff., 285, 296-7, 323, 332, 342, 378, 382; ii. 40, 61, 112.
Brown, Dr. Thomas, ii. 60.
'Budget of Paradoxes,' De Morgan, i. 389; ii. 120.

Calculation, ii. 31.

Categorical and Hypothetical, i. 93 ff., 285.
Categories of Sense, i. 199.
Causation, law of, ii. 212.
Cause, i. 264 ff.
Chances, statement of, i. 352.
Change and Difference, i. 141.
Characteristic Ratio, i. 133.
Characters, 'important,' ii. 91.
Chronological indications, i. 211.
Classifications, alternative, i. 63.
Clifford, on Causation, ii. 157 note.
Collective names, i. 57.
Colligation of facts, ii. 160.
Colour-match, i. 206.
Comparative Judgment, i. 116.
Comparison proper, ii. 20.
Complete Enumeration, ii. 49.
Complex Enumeration, ii. 52 ff.
Conception, test of truth, ii. 225 ff.
Concepts, i. 39.
Condition and Conditioned, i. 262.
Conjunction and Disjunction, i. 349.
Consciousness and Energy, ii. 74.
Constitutive Equation, ii. 65.
Construction, ii. 36.
Continuous magnitude, i. 159.
Contradiction, law of, ii. 208.
Contraposition, i. 331.
Contrariety and Contradiction, i. 309-10.
Conversion, i. 324.
Copula, i. 80.
Corporate Judgment, i. 212.
Counting analysed, i. 156.
Counting mediate, i. 170.
'Criticism of life,' ii. 235.
Cross-fertilisation, ii. 126.

Dalton, ii. 226.
Darwin, Origin of Species, i. 1; Fertilisation of Orchids, ii. 101 ff.
Day cause of Night? i. 275.

Index.

De Morgan, 'Budget of Paradoxes,' i. 389; ii. 120, 160, 229.
Determination, Generalisation by, ii. 169.
Dicey, 'Law of the Constitution,' ii. 19.
Difference and Change, i. 140.
Difference needs a standard, i. 126.
Discovery, ii. 8.
Discrete Magnitude, i. 159.
Discrimination, ii. 26.
Disjunction and Conjunction, i. 349.
Disjunctive Judgment, i. 341.
Distinction, i. 22.
Double Negation, i. 320.

Ehrenberg, i. 315.
Elements (formative), i. 20.
Enumerative Judgment, i. 160.
Enumerative Induction, ii. 43.
Equation, ii. 31.
Equation, Constitutive, ii. 65.
Equation and Judgment, i. 202.
Equational logic, ii. 33.
Exception, i. 384.
Excluded Middle, law of, ii. 210.
Exhaustive Judgment, i. 168, 225.
Existence of geometrical figures, i. 191.
Existential meaning in Generic Judgment, i. 237.
Experiment, ii. 143.
Extension, i. 46 ff., 55, 59.
External Proportion, i. 137.

Figures of Syllogism, 1st, ii. 180; 2nd, ii. 88; 3rd, ii. 44, 115.
Final Cause, in Plato, ii. 182 note.
Formative elements, i. 20.

Generalisation, kinds of, ii. 168 ff.
Generic Judgment, i. 222.
Green, Prof. T. H., ii. 160.
Ground, i. 259 ff.

Hegel, i. 1, 79, 378, 380, 397; ii. 47, 61, 70, 81.
Helmholtz, Popular lectures, ii. 150.
Herbart, i. 151.
Herschel, Sir J., in Mill, ii. 224.
History and Science, i. 276–7.

Huxley, Prof., ii. 106 note, 214 note.
Hypnotism, degrees of, i. 395.
Hypothesis, dist. Postulate, ii. 155.
Hypothetical, i. 93 ff., 250 ff., 285.

Idea, i. 46.
Ideas, Locke on, i. 73.
Identification, i. 27; ii. 26.
Identity, i. 14, 28; Locke on, ii. 207; Law of, ii. 207.
Imagination and Conception, ii. 227.
Imperative, i. 107 note.
Impersonal Proposition, i. 108.
Indices, ii. 53 ff.
Individuality and Proportion, i. 135.
Individuality and Reality, i. 147.
Induction, Essence of Perceptive, ii. 135; not a species of Inference, ii. 176.
Inductive Syllogism, ii. 13, 46.
Inference, Nature of, ii. 1, 3; Ultimate Conditions of, ii. 199 ff.; Conditions of, compared with Syllogism, ii. 201 ff.
Infinite Judgment, i. 298.
Infinite Series, i. 173.
Intension, i. 46 ff., 59.
Interjection, i. 107.
Internal Proportion, i. 137.
Instance, i. 384.
Intensive Equation, ii. 34.

Jevons, Principles of Science, i. 59, 371; ii. 34, 112, 153, 160, 175; on Natural Experiment, quoted, ii. 144.
Judgment, i. 34, 72 ff.; and Equation, i. 202.

Kant, i. 99, 377, 380; ii. 81.
Kind and Quality, i. 125.
Kirchoff, on Iron in the Sun, ii. 173.

Lang, Custom and Myth, ii. 162 ff.
Laws, 'Formal' laws of Thought, ii. 207 ff.
Liberty, Equality, and Fraternity, Sir James F. Stephens quoted, i. 203.
Limitation, conversion by, i. 326.
Linnaean classification, i. 10; ii. 124.
Locke, i. 73, 97 note, 180 note; ii. 207 note.

Lotze, Logic, i. 14, 19 note, 31 ff., 59, 68 note, 83, 151, 378-9; ii. 13, 46, 56, 68, 80, 81, 103, 112, 122, 155; Microcosmus, i. 232.

Machinery, double import of in Logic, i. 223: ii. 182.
Major Premise, ii. 46, 60.
Material truth, ii. 173.
Measurement, i. 128.
Mechanism, i. 200 ff.
Mediate enumeration, i. 186; ii. 77.
Mill, i. 9, 14, 78, 266-7, 280, 398; ii. 17, 29, 44, 60, 71, 85, 93, 98, 122, 157 note, 160, 221, 227.
Mill and Lotze, i. 151.
Miracle, ii. 221.
Mommsen, i. 11 note.
Morphology, i. 1; as weakened Teleology, ii. 92.
Mortality, i. 388.
'Mouse' families, hypothesis regarding, ii. 165.

Naming, i. 8, 22.
Necessity, a real, ii. 187.
Necessity and Abstraction, i. 143 ff.
Necessity and Allness, i. 224.
Necessity: see 'Absolute,' 'Aesthetic.'
Negation, i. 293 ff.
Negative Instance, ii. 115 ff.
Night cause of Day? i. 275.
Number (see counting), i. 159.

Omission, how related to Abstraction, i. 67.
Ophrys Apifera, ii. 125.
Opposition of Judgments, i. 310.
Organon (Aristotle), i. 271, 332.

Particulars to Particulars, ii. 29, 44.
Parts and whole, i. 103.
Personal era, i. 216.
Physical Alternatives, i. 357.
Physiology, i. 1.
Plato, i. 9 ff., 91; ii. 182, 194, 234 note.
Plurality of Causes, in Mill, i. 268.
Possibility, i. 384.
Posterior Analytics, i. 271 note; ii. 177 note.
Postulate, dist. Hypothesis, ii. 155.

Predicate, i. 80; (in Aristotle), i. 20.
Predication, i. 81.
Premises of Inductive Syllogism, ii. 13.
Privation, i. 322.
Proper Name, i. 50; dist. Generic Name, i. 234.
Proportion as Inference, ii. 68 ff.; as Individuality, i. 135.
Proposition, dist. Judgment, i. 79.
Pure Case, i. 260.

Quality and kind, i. 125; meaning of, i. 105.
Quantity, category of, i. 205.
Question, i. 35, 380.

Ratio, i. 161.
Real world and *my* world, i. 82.
Reality and Individuality, i. 147; in Judgment, i. 76.
Recognition, ii. 24 ff.
Reduction, in the true sense, ii. 202.
Relative, i. 25.
Republic, Plato's, ii. 182 note, 194.
ῥῆμα, i. 20.
ῥῆμα ἀόριστον, i. 298.

Scheme of Arguments, ii. 42; of Judgments, i. 92.
Schopenhauer on Euclid, i. 252; on Necessity, ii. 213; on Causa Essendi and Fiendi, i. 267.
Science and History, i. 276-7.
Self-fertilisation, ii. 125.
Sigwart, i. 35 note, 59, 63, 151, 294, 321, 332, 378; ii. 16, 21, 160, 175.
Singular Judgment, i. 208.
Στέρησις, dist. ἀπόφασις, i. 332.
Structure and Individuality, i. 138.
Subject, i. 80.
Subjectivity of Space and Time, i. 197.
Substitutive Inference, ii. 57.
Subsumption, ii. 30.
Sufficient Reason, law of, ii. 212.
Syllogism, fig. 1. ii. 180; fig. 2, ii. 88; fig. 3, ii. 44; traditional, ii. 201; as reasoned judgment, ii. 203.
Symbolic Ideas, i. 73.
Synthetic, i. 97.

Tense, i. 112, 216.
'Thermometer of Probability,' i. 389.
Thing, what is a, i. 138.
Three Terms, ii. 13.
Time, Constancy of, i. 179; Judgment in, i. 85; *in* Predication, i. 215; *of* Predication, i. 215; Reality of, i. 273.
τὸ καθ' ἕκαστον, in Inductive Syllogism, ii. 13.
Totems, hypothesis of, in Greece, ii. 165.

Understanding, the, ii. 81.
Universal Judgment, i. 220 ff.

Venn, Logic of Chance, i. 363 ff.

Whateley, on Privative and Negative Terms, i. 332.
Whewell, i. 398; ii. 17, 160–1, 223-4.
Whole and parts, i. 103.
Word, no Greek term for a, i. 12.
Wundt, i. 59, 68, 82, 151; on Constancy of Energy, ii. 75.

THE END.

CLARENDON PRESS, OXFORD.
SELECT LIST OF STANDARD WORKS.

DICTIONARIES	page 1
LAW	,, 2
HISTORY, BIOGRAPHY, ETC. . . .	,, 4
PHILOSOPHY, LOGIC, ETC. . . .	,, 6
PHYSICAL SCIENCE, ETC.	,, 7

1. DICTIONARIES.
A NEW ENGLISH DICTIONARY
ON HISTORICAL PRINCIPLES,

Founded mainly on the materials collected by the Philological Society.

Imperial 4to.

EDITED BY DR. MURRAY.

PRESENT STATE OF THE WORK.

				£	s.	d.
Vol. I.	A, B	By Dr. MURRAY	Half-morocco	2	12	6
Vol. II.	C	By Dr. MURRAY	Half-morocco	2	12	6
Vol. III.	D, E	By Dr. MURRAY and Dr. BRADLEY	Half-morocco	2	12	6
Vol. IV.	F, G	By Dr. BRADLEY	Half-morocco	2	12	6
Vol. V.	H—K	By Dr. MURRAY	Half-morocco	2	12	6
			L—Lap	0	2	6
			Lap–Leisurely . . .	0	5	0
			Leisureness–Lief . .	0	2	6
Vol. VI.	L—N	By Dr. BRADLEY . .	Lief–Lock	0	5	0
			Lock–Lyyn	0	5	0
			M–Mandragon . . .	0	5	0
			Mandragora–Matter .	0	5	0
			O–Onomastic . . .	0	5	0
			Onomastical–Outing .	0	5	0
Vol. VII.	O, P	By Dr. MURRAY . .	Outjet–Ozyat . . .	0	2	6
			P–Pargeted	0	5	0
			Pargeter–Pennached .	0	5	0
			Pennage–Pf	0	5	0
			Q	0	2	6
Vol. VIII.	Q—S	By Mr. CRAIGIE . .	R–Reactive	0	5	0
			Reactively–Ree . .	0	5	0
			Ree–Reign	0	2	6

The remainder of the work is in active preparation.

Vols. IX, X will contain S–Z with some supplemental matter.

Orders can be given through any bookseller for the delivery of the remainder of the work in complete *Volumes* or in *Half-volumes* or in *Sections* or in *Parts*.

HALF-VOLUMES. The price of half-volumes, bound, with straight-grained persian leather back, cloth sides, gilt top, is £1 7s. 6d. each, or £13 15s. for the eleven now ready, namely, A, B, C–Comm., Comm.–Czech, D, E, F, G, H, I–K, L–Matter.

SECTIONS. A single Section of 64 pages at 2s. 6d. or a double Section of 128 pages at 5s. is issued quarterly.

PARTS. A Part (which is generally the equivalent of five single Sections and is priced at 12s. 6d.) is issued whenever ready.

Nearly all the Parts and Sections in which Volumes I–V were first issued are still obtainable in the original covers.

FORTHCOMING ISSUE, 1905. A portion continuing R, by Mr. CRAIGIE.

Oxford: Clarendon Press. London: HENRY FROWDE, Amen Corner, E.C.

ENGLISH AND ROMAN LAW.

A Hebrew and English Lexicon of the Old Testament, with an Appendix containing the Biblical Aramaic, based on the Thesaurus and Lexicon of Gesenius, by Francis Brown, D.D., S. R. Driver, D.D., and C. A. Briggs, D.D. Parts I–XI. Small 4to, 2s. 6d. each.

Thesaurus Syriacus: collegerunt Quatremère, Bernstein, Lorsbach, Arnoldi, Agrell, Field, Roediger: edidit R. Payne Smith, S.T.P. Vol. I (Fasc. I–V), sm. fol., 5l. 5s. Vol. II, completion (Fasc. VI–X), 8l. 8s.

A Compendious Syriac Dictionary, founded upon the above. Edited by Mrs. Margoliouth. Small 4to, complete, 63s. net. Part IV, 15s. net. Parts I–III can no longer be supplied.

A Dictionary of the Dialects of Vernacular Syriac as spoken by the Eastern Syrians of Kurdistan, North-West Persia, and the Plain of Moṣul. By A. J. Maclean, M.A., F.R.G.S. Small 4to, 15s.

An English-Swahili Dictionary. By A. C. Madan, M.A. Second Edition, Revised. Extra fcap. 8vo, 7s. 6d. net.

Swahili-English Dictionary. By A. C. Madan, M.A. Extra fcap. 8vo. 7s. 6d. net.

A Sanskrit-English Dictionary. Etymologically and Philologically arranged, with special reference to cognate Indo-European Languages. By Sir M. Monier-Williams, M.A., K.C.I.E. New Edition. Cloth, bevelled edges, 3l. 13s. 6d.; half-morocco, 4l. 4s.

A Greek-English Lexicon. By H. G. Liddell, D.D., and Robert Scott, D.D. Eighth Edition, Revised. 4to. 1l. 16s.

An Etymological Dictionary of the English Language, arranged on an Historical Basis. By W. W. Skeat, Litt.D. Third Edition. 4to. 2l. 4s.

A Middle-English Dictionary. By F. H. Stratmann. A new edition, by H. Bradley, M.A., Ph.D. 4to, half-morocco. 1l. 11s. 6d.

The Student's Dictionary of Anglo-Saxon. By H. Sweet, M.A., Ph.D., LL.D. Small 4to. 8s. 6d. net.

An Anglo-Saxon Dictionary, based on the MS. collections of the late Joseph Bosworth, D.D. Edited and enlarged by Prof. T. N. Toller, M.A. Parts I–III. A–SÁR. 4to, stiff covers, 15s. each. Part IV, § 1, SÁR–SWÍDRIAN. Stiff covers, 8s. 6d. Part IV, § 2, SWÍP-SNEL-ÝTMEST, 18s. 6d.

An Icelandic-English Dictionary, based on the MS. collections of the late Richard Cleasby. Enlarged and completed by G. Vigfússon, M.A. 4to. 3l. 7s.

2. LAW.

Anson. *Principles of the English Law of Contract, and of Agency in its Relation to Contract.* By Sir W. R. Anson, D.C.L. Tenth Edition. 8vo. 10s. 6d.

Anson. *Law and Custom of the Constitution.* 2 vols. 8vo. Part I. Parliament. Third Edition. 12s. 6d. Part II. The Crown. Second Ed. 14s.

Bryce. *Studies in History and Jurisprudence.* 2 Vols. 8vo. By the Right Hon. J. Bryce, M.P. 25s. net.

Goudy. *Von Jhering's Law in Daily Life.* Translated by H. Goudy, D.C.L. Crown 8vo. 3s. 6d. net.

Digby. *An Introduction to the History of the Law of Real Property.*

Oxford: Clarendon Press.

By Sir Kenelm E. Digby, M.A. *Fifth Edition.* 8vo. 12s. 6d.

Grueber. *Lex Aquilia.* By Erwin Grueber. 8vo. 10s. 6d.

Hall. *International Law.* By W. E. Hall, M.A. *Fifth Edit.* Revised by J. B. Atlay, M.A. 8vo. 21s. net.

—— *A Treatise on the Foreign Powers and Jurisdiction of the British Crown.* 8vo. 10s. 6d.

Holland. *Elements of Jurisprudence.* By T. E. Holland, D.C.L. *Ninth Edition.* 8vo. 10s. 6d.

—— *Studies in International Law.* 8vo. 10s. 6d.

—— *Gentilis, Alberici, De Iure Belli Libri Tres.* Small 4to, half-morocco. 21s.

—— *The Institutes of Justinian.* Second Edition. Extra fcap. 8vo. 5s.

—— *The European Concert in the Eastern Question,* a collection of treaties and other public acts. 8vo. 12s. 6d.

Holland and Shadwell. *Select Titles from the Digest of Justinian.* By T. E. Holland, D.C.L., and C. L. Shadwell, D.C.L. 8vo. 14s. Also in Parts, paper covers—I. Introductory Titles. 2s. 6d. II. Family Law. 1s. III. Property Law. 2s.6d. IV. Law of Obligations (No. 1), 3s. 6d. (No. 2), 4s. 6d.

Ilbert. *The Government of India.* Being a Digest of the Statute Law relating thereto. By Sir Courtenay Ilbert, K.C.S.I. 8vo, half-roan. 21s.

—— *Legislative Forms and Methods.* 8vo, half-roan. 16s.

Jenks. *Modern Land Law.* By Edward Jenks, M.A. 8vo. 15s.

Jenkyns. *British Rule and Jurisdiction beyond the Seas.* By the late Sir Henry Jenkyns, K.C.B. 8vo, half-roan. 16s. net.

Markby. *Elements of Law* considered with reference to Principles of General Jurisprudence. By Sir William Markby. *Sixth Edition.* 8vo. 12s. 6d.

Moyle. *Imperatoris Iustiniani Institutionum Libri Quattuor,* with Introductions, Commentary, Excursus and Translation. By J. B. Moyle, D.C.L. *Fourth Edition.* 2 vols. 8vo. Vol. I. 16s. Vol. II. 6s.

—— *Contract of Sale in the Civil Law.* 8vo. 10s. 6d.

Pollock and Wright. *An Essay on Possession in the Common Law.* By Sir F. Pollock, Bart., M.A., and Sir R. S. Wright, B.C.L. 8vo. 8s. 6d.

Poste. *Gaii Institutionum Juris Civilis Commentarii Quattuor;* or, Elements of Roman Law by Gaius. With a Translation and Commentary by Edward Poste, M.A. *Fourth Edition,* revised and enlarged. 8vo. 16s. net.

Radcliffe and Miles. *Cases Illustrating the Principles of the Law of Torts.* By F. R. Y. Radcliffe, K.C., and J. C. Miles, M.A. 8vo. 12s. 6d. net.

Sohm. *The Institutes.* A Text-book of the History and System of Roman Private Law. By Rudolph Sohm. Translated by J. C. Ledlie, B.C.L. *Second Edition, revised and enlarged.* 8vo. 18s.

Stokes. *The Anglo-Indian Codes.* By Whitley Stokes, LL.D. Vol. I. Substantive Law. 8vo. 30s. Vol. II. Adjective Law. 8vo. 35s. First and Second Supplements to the above, 1887–1891. 8vo. 6s. 6d. Separately, No. 1, 2s. 6d.; No. 2, 4s. 6d.

Young. *Corps de Droit Ottoman Recueil des Codes, Lois, Règlements, Ordonnances et Actes les plus importants du Droit intérieur, et D'Études sur le Droit coutumier de l'Empire Ottoman.* Par George Young. Part I (Vols. I–III), cloth, 2l. 17s. 6d. net; paper covers, 2l. 12s. 6d. net. Part II (Vols. IV–VII), cloth, 1l. 17s. net; paper covers, 1l. 11s. 6d. The complete Parts I and II separately, will cost 2l. 12s. 6d. net in paper covers, or 2l. 17s. 6d. net in cloth each.

3. HISTORY, BIOGRAPHY, ETC.

Asser. *Life of King Alfred,* together with the Annals of St. Neots, erroneously ascribed to Asser. Edited with Introduction and Commentary by W. H. Stevenson, M.A. 2 vols. Crown 8vo. 12s. net.

Aubrey. '*Brief Lives,*' *chiefly of Contemporaries, set down by John Aubrey, between the Years* 1669 *and* 1696. Edited from the Author's MSS., by Andrew Clark, M.A., LL.D. With Facsimiles. 2 vols. 8vo. 25s.

Ballard. *The Domesday Boroughs.* By Adolphus Ballard, B.A., LL.B. 8vo. With four Plans. 6s. 6d. net.

Barnard. *Companion to English History (Middle Ages).* With 97 Illustrations. By F. P. Barnard, M.A. Crown 8vo. 8s. 6d. net.

Boswell's *Life of Samuel Johnson, LL.D.* Edited by G. Birkbeck Hill, D.C.L. In six volumes, medium 8vo. With Portraits and Facsimiles. Half-bound. 3l. 3s.

Bright. *Chapters of Early English Church History.* By W. Bright, D.D. *Third Edition. Revised and Enlarged.* With a Map. 8vo. 12s.

Bryce. *Studies in History and Jurisprudence.* By J. Bryce, M.P. 2 vols. 8vo. 25s. net.

Butler. *The Arab Conquest of Egypt and the last thirty years of the Roman Dominion.* By A. J. Butler, D.Litt., F.S.A. With Maps and Plans. 8vo. 16s. net.

Chambers. *The Mediaeval Stage.* By E. K. Chambers. With two illustrations. 2 vols. 8vo. 25s. net.

Clarendon's *History of the Rebellion and Civil Wars in England.* Re-edited by W. Dunn Macray, M.A., F.S.A. 6 vols. Crown 8vo. 2l. 5s.

Earle and Plummer. *Two of the Saxon Chronicles, Parallel, with Supplementary Extracts from the others.* A Revised Text, edited, with Introduction, Notes, Appendices, and Glossary, by C. Plummer, M.A., on the basis of an edition by J. Earle, M.A. 2 vols. Cr. 8vo, half-roan.
Vol. I. Text, Appendices, and Glossary. 10s. 6d.
Vol. II. Introduction, Notes, and Index. 12s. 6d.

Fisher. *Studies in Napoleonic Statesmanship.—Germany.* By H. A. L. Fisher, M.A. With four Maps. 8vo. 12s. 6d. net.

Freeman. *The History of Sicily from the Earliest Times.*
Vols. I and II. 8vo, cloth. 2l. 2s.
Vol. III. The Athenian and Carthaginian Invasions. 24s.
Vol. IV. From the Tyranny of Dionysios to the Death of Agathoklês. Edited by Arthur J. Evans, M.A. 21s.

Freeman. *The Reign of William Rufus and the Accession of Henry the First.* By E. A. Freeman, D.C.L. 2 vols. 8vo. 1l. 16s.

Gardiner. *The Constitutional Documents of the Puritan Revolution,* 1628–1660. By S. R. Gardiner, D.C.L. *Second Edition.* Crown 8vo. 10s. 6d.

Gross. *The Gild Merchant;* a Contribution to British Municipal History. By Charles Gross, Ph.D. 2 vols. 8vo. 24s.

Hill. *Sources for Greek History between the Persian and Peloponnesian Wars.* Collected and arranged by G. F. Hill, M.A. 8vo. 10s. 6d.

Hodgkin. *Italy and her Invaders.* With Plates & Maps. 8 vols. 8vo. By T. Hodgkin, D.C.L.
Vols. I-II. *Second Edition.* 42s.
Vols. III-IV. *Second Edition.* 36s.
Vols. V-VI. 36s.
Vols. VII-VIII (*completing the work*). 24s.

Johnson. *Letters of Samuel Johnson, LL.D.* Collected and Edited by G. Birkbeck Hill, D.C.L. 2 vols. half-roan. 28s.

——— *Johnsonian Miscellanies.* 2 vols. Medium 8vo, half-roan. 28s.

Oxford: Clarendon Press.

HISTORY, BIOGRAPHY, ETC.

Kitchin. *A History of France.* By G. W. Kitchin, D.D. In three Volumes. Crown 8vo, each 10s. 6d. Vol. I. to 1453. Vol. II. 1453-1624. Vol. III. 1624-1793.

Kyd. *The Works of Thomas Kyd.* Edited from the original Texts, with Introduction, Notes, and Facsimiles, by F. S. Boas, M.A. 8vo. 15s. net.

Lewis (*Sir G. Cornewall*). *An Essay on the Government of Dependencies.* Edited by C. P. Lucas, B.A. 8vo, half-roan. 14s.

Lucas. *Historical Geography of the British Colonies.* By C. P. Lucas, B.A. With Maps. Cr. 8vo.

The Origin and Growth of the English Colonies and of their System of Government (an Introduction to Mr. C. P. Lucas's Historical Geography of the Colonies). By H. E. Egerton. 2s. 6d. Also in binding uniform with the Series. 3s. 6d.

Vol. I. The Mediterranean and Eastern Colonies (exclusive of India). 5s.
Vol. II. The West Indian Colonies. Second edition, revised to 1905, by C. Atchley. 7s. 6d.
Vol. III. West Africa. *Second Edition, revised to the end of 1899, by H. E. Egerton.* 7s. 6d.
Vol. IV. South and East Africa. Historical and Geographical. 9s. 6d.
Also Vol. IV in two Parts—
Part I. Historical, 6s. 6d.
Part II. Geographical, 3s. 6d.
Vol. V. The History of Canada (Part I, New France). 6s.

Ludlow. *The Memoirs of Edmund Ludlow, Lieutenant-General of the Horse in the Army of the Commonwealth of England, 1625-1672.* Edited by C. H. Firth, M.A. 2 vols. 36s.

Lyly. *The Works of John Lyly.* Collected and edited, with facsimiles, by R. W. Bond, M.A. In 3 vols. 8vo, uniform with *Kyd.* 42s. net.

Machiavelli. *Il Principe.* Edited by L. Arthur Burd, M.A. With an Introduction by Lord Acton. 8vo. 14s.

Merriman. *Life and Letters of Thomas Cromwell.* With a Portrait and Facsimile. By R. B. Merriman, B.Litt. 2 vols. 8vo. 18s. net.

Morris. *The Welsh Wars of Edward I.* With a Map. By J. E. Morris, M.A. 8vo. 9s. 6d. net.

Oman. *A History of the Peninsular War.* 6 vols. 8vo. With Maps, Plans, and Portraits. By C. Oman, M.A. Vol. I, 1807-1809. 14s. net. Vol. II, Jan.-Sept., 1809 (from the Battle of Corunna to the end of the Talavera Campaign). 14s. net.

Payne. *History of the New World called America.* By E. J. Payne, M.A. 8vo.
Vol. I, containing *The Discovery and Aboriginal America*, 18s.
Vol. II, *Aboriginal America* (concluded), 14s.

Plummer. *The Life and Times of Alfred the Great.* By Charles Plummer, M.A. Crown 8vo. 5s. net.

Poole. *Historical Atlas of Modern Europe from the decline of the Roman Empire.* Edited by R. L. Poole, M.A. 5l. 15s. 6d. net. Each Map can now be bought separately for 1s. 6d. net.

Prothero. *Select Statutes and other Constitutional Documents, illustrative of the Reigns of Elizabeth and James I.* Edited by G. W. Prothero, M.A. Cr. 8vo. Edition 2. 10s. 6d.

Ramsay (Sir J. H.). *Lancaster and York* (A.D. 1399-1485). 2 vols. 8vo. With Index. 37s. 6d.

Ramsay (W. M.). *The Cities and Bishoprics of Phrygia.*
Vol. I. Part I. The Lycos Valley and South-Western Phrygia. Royal 8vo. 18s. net.
Vol. I. Part II. West and West-Central Phrygia. 21s. net.

PHILOSOPHY, LOGIC, ETC.

Ranke. *A History of England, principally in the Seventeenth Century.* By L. von Ranke. Translated under the superintendence of G. W. Kitchin, D.D., and C. W. Boase, M.A. 6 vols. 8vo. 63s. Revised Index, separately, 1s.

Rashdall. *The Universities of Europe in the Middle Ages.* By Hastings Rashdall, M.A. 2 vols. (in 3 Parts) 8vo. With Maps. 2l. 5s. net.

Rhŷs. *Studies in the Arthurian Legend.* By John Rhŷs, M.A. 8vo. 12s. 6d.

—— *Celtic Folklore:* Welsh and Manx. By the same. 2 vols. 8vo. 21s.

Rogers. *History of Agriculture and Prices in England,* A.D. 1259–1793. By J. E. T. Rogers, M.A. 8vo. Vols. I, II (1259–1400), 42s. Vols. III, IV (1401–1582), 50s. Vols. V, VI (1583–1702), 50s. Vol. VII, 2 Parts (1703–1793), 50s.

Sanday. *Sacred Sites of the Gospels.* By W. Sanday, D.D. With many illustrations, including drawings of the Temple by Paul Waterhouse. 8vo. 13s. 6d. net.

Scaccario. *De Necessariis Observantiis Scaccarii Dialogus.* Commonly called Dialogus de Scaccario. Edited by A. Hughes, C. G. Crump, and C. Johnson. 8vo. 12s. 6d. net.

Smith's *Lectures on Justice, Police, Revenue and Arms.* Edited, with Introduction and Notes, by Edwin Cannan. 8vo. 10s. 6d. net.

—— *Wealth of Nations.* With Notes, by J. E. Thorold Rogers, M.A. 2 vols. 8vo. 21s.

Smith (V. A.). *The Early History of India, from 600 B.C. to the Muhammadan Conquest, including the Invasion of Alexander the Great.* By Vincent A. Smith, M.A. 8vo, with Maps and other Illustrations. 14s.net.

Stubbs. *Select Charters and other Illustrations of English Constitutional History, from the Earliest Times to the Reign of Edward I.* Arranged and edited by W. Stubbs, D.D. Eighth Edition. Crown 8vo. 8s. 6d.

—— *The Constitutional History of England, in its Origin and Development. Library Edition.* 3 vols. Demy 8vo. 2l. 8s.

Also in 3 vols. crown 8vo. 12s. each.

—— *Seventeen Lectures on the Study of Mediaeval and Modern History and kindred subjects.* Crown 8vo. *Third Edition.* 8s. 6d.

—— *Registrum Sacrum Anglicanum.* Sm. 4to. Ed. 2. 10s. 6d.

Vinogradoff. *Villainage in England.* Essays in English Mediaeval History. By Paul Vinogradoff. 8vo, half-bound. 16s.

4. PHILOSOPHY, LOGIC, ETC.

Bacon. *Novum Organum.* Edited, with Introduction, Notes, &c., by T. Fowler, D.D. *Second Edition.* 8vo. 15s.

Berkeley. *The Works of George Berkeley, D.D., formerly Bishop of Cloyne;* including many of his writings hitherto unpublished. With Prefaces, Annotations, Appendices, and an Account of his Life, by A. Campbell Fraser, Hon. D.C.L., LL.D. New Edition in 4 vols., cr. 8vo. 24s.

—— *The Life and Letters,* with an account of his Philosophy. By A. Campbell Fraser. 8vo. 16s.

Bosanquet. *Logic; or, the Morphology of Knowledge.* By B. Bosanquet, M.A. 8vo. 21s.

Butler. *The Works of Joseph Butler, D.C.L.,* sometime Lord Bishop of Durham. Edited by the Right Hon. W. E. Gladstone. 2 vols. Medium 8vo. 14s. each.

Campagnac. *The Cambridge Platonists:* being Selections from the writings of Benjamin Whichcote, John Smith, and Nathanael Culverwel, with Introduction by E. T. Campagnac, M.A. Cr. 8vo. 6s. 6d.net.

Oxford: Clarendon Press.

Fowler. *Logic;* Deductive and Inductive, combined in a single volume. Extra fcap. 8vo. 7s. 6d.

Fowler and Wilson. *The Principles of Morals.* By T. Fowler, D.D., and J. M. Wilson, B.D. 8vo, cloth. 14s.

Green. *Prolegomena to Ethics.* By T. H. Green, M.A. Edited by A. C. Bradley, M.A. *Fourth Edition.* Crown 8vo. 7s. 6d.

Hegel. *The Logic of Hegel.* Translated from the Encyclopaedia of the Philosophical Sciences. With Prolegomena to the Study of Hegel's Logic and Philosophy. By W. Wallace, M.A. *Second Edition, Revised and Augmented.* 2 vols. Crown 8vo. 10s. 6d. each.

Hegel's *Philosophy of Mind.* Translated from the Encyclopaedia of the Philosophical Sciences. With Five Introductory Essays. By William Wallace, M.A., LL.D. Crown 8vo. 10s. 6d.

Hume's *Treatise of Human Nature.* Edited, with Analytical Index, by L. A. Selby-Bigge, M.A. *Second Edition.* Crown 8vo. 6s. net.

—— *Enquiry concerning the Human Understanding.* Edited by L. A. Selby-Bigge, M.A. *Second Edition.* Crown 8vo. 6s. net.

Leibniz. *The Monadology and other Philosophical Writings.* Translated, with Introduction and Notes,

by Robert Latta, M.A., D.Phil. Crown 8vo. 8s. 6d.

Locke. *An Essay Concerning Human Understanding.* By John Locke. Collated and Annotated by A. Campbell Fraser, Hon. D.C.L., LL.D. 2 vols. 8vo. 1l. 12s.

Lotze's *Logic,* in Three Books —of Thought, of Investigation, and of Knowledge. English Translation; edited by B. Bosanquet, M.A. *Second Edition.* 2 vols. Cr. 8vo. 12s.

—— *Metaphysic,* in Three Books—Ontology, Cosmology, and Psychology. English Translation; edited by B. Bosanquet, M.A. *Second Edition.* 2 vols. Cr. 8vo. 12s.

Martineau. *Types of Ethical Theory.* By James Martineau, D.D. *Third Edition.* 2 vols. Cr. 8vo. 15s.

—— *A Study of Religion :* its Sources and Contents. *Second Edition.* 2 vols. Cr. 8vo. 15s.

Selby-Bigge. *British Moralists.* Selections from Writers principally of the Eighteenth Century. Edited by L. A. Selby-Bigge, M.A. 2 vols. Crown 8vo. 12s. net.

Spinoza. *A Study in the Ethics of Spinoza.* By Harold H. Joachim. 8vo. 10s. 6d. net.

Wallace. *Lectures and Essays on Natural Theology and Ethics.* By William Wallace, M.A., LL.D. Edited, with a Biographical Introduction, by Edward Caird, M.A. 8vo, with a Portrait. 12s. 6d.

5. PHYSICAL SCIENCE, ETC.

Chambers. *A Handbook of Descriptive and Practical Astronomy.* By G. F. Chambers, F.R.A.S. *Fourth Edition,* in 3 vols. Demy 8vo.
Vol. I. The Sun, Planets, and Comets. 21s.
Vol. II. Instruments and Practical Astronomy. 21s.
Vol. III. The Starry Heavens. 14s.

De Bary. *Comparative Ana-*

tomy of the Vegetative Organs of the Phanerogams and Ferns. By Dr. A. de Bary. Translated by F. O. Bower, M.A., and D. H. Scott, M.A. Royal 8vo, half-morocco, 24s. net; cloth, 21s. net.

De Bary. *Comparative Morphology and Biology of Fungi, Mycetozoa and Bacteria.* By Dr. A. de Bary. Translated by H. E. F. Garnsey, M.A. Revised by Isaac Bayley Bal-

PHYSICAL SCIENCE, ETC.

four, M.A., M.D., F.R.S. Royal 8vo, half-morocco, 24s. net; cloth, 21s. net.

De Bary. *Lectures on Bacteria.* By Dr. A. de Bary. Second Improved Edition. Translated and revised by Isaac Bayley Balfour, M.A., M.D., F.R.S. Crown 8vo. 5s. net.

Ewart. *On the Physics and Physiology of Protoplasmic Streaming in Plants.* By A. J. Ewart, D.Sc., Ph.D., F.L.S. With seventeen illustrations. Royal 8vo. 8s. 6d. net.

Fischer. *The Structure and Functions of Bacteria.* By Alfred Fischer. Translated into English by A. C. Jones. Royal 8vo. With Twenty-nine Woodcuts. 7s. 6d. net.

Goebel. *Outlines of Classification and Special Morphology of Plants.* By Dr. K. Goebel. Translated by H. E. F. Garnsey, M.A. Revised by I. B. Balfour, M.A., M.D., F.R.S. Royal 8vo, half-morocco, 22s. 6d. net; cloth, 20s. net.

—— *Organography of Plants,* especially of the Archegoniatae and Spermophyta. By Dr. K. Goebel. Authorized English Edition, by I. B. Balfour, M.A., M.D., F.R.S. Part I, General Organography. Royal 8vo, half-morocco, 12s. net; cloth, 10s. net. Pt. II, half-morocco, 24s. net; cloth, 21s. net.

Miall and Hammond. *The Structure and Life-History of the Harlequin Fly (Chironomus).* By L. C. Miall, F.R.S., and A. R. Hammond, F.L.S. 8vo. With 130 Illustrations. 7s. 6d.

Pfeffer. *The Physiology of Plants. A Treatise upon the Metabolism and Sources of Energy in Plants.* By Prof. Dr. W. Pfeffer. Second fully Revised Edition, translated and edited by A. J. Ewart, D.Sc., Ph.D., F.L.S. Royal 8vo. Vol. I, half-morocco, 26s. net; cloth, 23s. net. Vol. II, 16s. net; cloth, 14s. net.

Prestwich. *Geology—Chemical, Physical, and Stratigraphical.* By Sir Joseph Prestwich, M.A., F.R.S. In two Volumes. Royal 8vo. 61s.

Sachs. *A History of Botany.* Translated by H. E. F. Garnsey, M.A. Revised by I. B. Balfour, M.A., M.D., F.R.S. Cr. 8vo. 10s. net.

Schimper. *Plant Geography upon a Physiological Basis.* By Dr. A. F. W. Schimper. The Authorized English Translation. Royal 8vo. With a photogravure portrait of Dr. Schimper, five collotypes, four maps, and four hundred and ninety-seven other illustrations. Half-morocco, 42s. net.

Solms-Laubach. *Fossil Botany. Being an Introduction to Palaeophytology from the Standpoint of the Botanist.* By H. Graf zu Solms-Laubach. Translated and revised by the same. Royal 8vo, half-morocco, 17s. net; cloth, 15s. net.

OXFORD HISTORY OF MUSIC.

8vo. Edited by W. H. Hadow, M.A. Price 15s. net each volume; but upon issue Vols. II and VI will be sold together for 15s. net, and the temporary price of the whole set of six volumes will be £3 15s. net.

I. *The Polyphonic Period.* Part I (Method of Musical Art, 330–1330). By H. E. Wooldridge, M.A.

III. *The Seventeenth Century.* By Sir C. H. H. Parry, M.A., D.Mus.

IV. *The Age of Bach and Handel.* By J. A. Fuller Maitland, M.A.

V. *The Viennese School.* By W. H. Hadow, M.A.

IMMEDIATELY.

II. *The Polyphonic Period.* Part II. By H. E. Wooldridge, M.A.

VI. *The Romantic Period.* By E. Dannreuther, M.A.

OXFORD
AT THE CLARENDON PRESS
LONDON, EDINBURGH, NEW YORK, AND TORONTO
HENRY FROWDE

www.ingramcontent.com/pod-product-compliance
Lightning Source LLC
Chambersburg PA
CBHW021407230426
43666CB00006B/665